Israel's Security Men

ALSO BY THOMAS G. MITCHELL

Israel/Palestine and the Politics of a Two-State Solution (McFarland, 2013)

When Peace Fails: Lessons from Belfast for the Middle East (McFarland, 2010)

Israel's Security Men

*The Arab-Fighting Political Careers
of Moshe Dayan, Yitzhak Rabin,
Ariel Sharon and Ehud Barak*

THOMAS G. MITCHELL

McFarland & Company, Inc., Publishers
Jefferson, North Carolina

All maps by George Colbert

LIBRARY OF CONGRESS CATALOGUING-IN-PUBLICATION DATA

Mitchell, Thomas G., 1957– author.
  Israel's security men : the Arab-fighting political careers of Moshe Dayan, Yitzhak Rabin, Ariel Sharon and Ehud Barak / Thomas G. Mitchell.
    p.   cm.
  Includes bibliographical references and index.

  ISBN 978-0-7864-9626-6 (softcover : acid free paper) ∞
  ISBN 978-1-4766-1759-6 (ebook)

  1. Dayan, Moshe, 1915–1981. 2. Rabin, Yitzhak.
3. Sharon, Ariel. 4. Barak, Ehud, 1942– 5. Generals—Israel—Biography. 6. Statesmen—Israel—Biography.
7. Arab-Israeli conflict. I. Title.
  DS126.6.A2.M57 2015
  956.9405'40922—dc23   2014040977

BRITISH LIBRARY CATALOGUING DATA ARE AVAILABLE

© 2015 Thomas G. Mitchell. All rights reserved

No part of this book may be reproduced or transmitted in any form or by any means, electronic or mechanical, including photocopying or recording, or by any information storage and retrieval system, without permission in writing from the publisher.

On the cover: Minister of Defense Moshe Dayan (center, with eyepatch) touring the southern front with Ariel Sharon (far left rear) in September 1967 (photograph by Ilan Bruner, National Photo Collection, State of Israel)

Printed in the United States of America

McFarland & Company, Inc., Publishers
  Box 611, Jefferson, North Carolina 28640
  www.mcfarlandpub.com

Table of Contents

Acknowledgments	vii
Preface	1

Part I: Moshe Dayan, 1915–1981

One • Israel's Military Politicians	13
Two • General Dayan	18
Three • Defense Minister Dayan	34
Four • Dayan as Negotiator	49

Part II: Yitzhak Rabin, 1922–1995

Five • General Rabin	67
Six • Rabin: Prime Minister to Defense Minister	86
Seven • From Defense Minister to Martyr	105

Part III: Ariel "Arik" Sharon, 1928–2014

Eight • General Sharon	121
Nine • Sharon Charges into Politics	135
Ten • Prime Minister Sharon	150

Part IV: Ehud Barak, 1942–?

Eleven • Barak: Israel's Most Decorated Soldier	167
Twelve • Barak Attempts Peace	185
Thirteen • Barak on Defense	201

Conclusion	212
Appendix: Military Politicians in the United States and South Africa	221
Chapter Notes	228
Bibliography	243
Index	245

Acknowledgments

There are a number of people I would like to thank for their role in producing this book. First, I'd like to thank George Colbert, the artist from New York who drew the maps of the peace agreements and of the 1982 Israeli invasion of Lebanon (originally used in Howard Sachar's *A History of Israel from the Rise of Zionism to Our Time*) for permission to reprint them here. Thanks also to Jennifer Rowley for putting me in touch with Mr. Colbert. I would also like to thank the Israeli National Photo Collection for providing the photos used in this book. Thanks to Jeff Bezos and Amazon for facilitating my purchase of the books used in my research, which would have been impossible twenty years ago. I would like to thank my parents, James and Rita Mitchell, for providing me the financial assistance to research and write this book, as well as my two previous books. Their frugality and wise investing over the decades made this writing possible.

Preface

In 1968 Israeli maverick journalist and future peace activist Uri Avnery wrote that Moshe Dayan was an "Arab fighter," one type among a class of politicians common among second generation immigrant societies (that is, settler societies) involved in conflicts with the native populations of their lands. As an American interested in history, I was intrigued by this short remark (on which Avnery did not elaborate).

I first started writing on this topic in May 1999, when Ehud Barak was elected prime minister. I then wrote the draft of a book entitled *The Rivals*, organized around the political rivalry for control of the Labor Party between Moshe Dayan and Shimon Peres on the one hand and Yigal Allon and Yitzhak Rabin on the other. I began the book with the Arab Revolt of 1936–1939 and ended it with Peres's failed presidential bid in 2000. I was never quite satisfied with it, and it remained a work in progress. I eventually added Ezer Weizman and Ariel Sharon to the cast of characters. Weizman was in some ways a minor member of the anti–Rabin camp and Sharon was introduced in order to cover the Likud after 1980 when Weizman left. The main theme of the book was that the leading "doves" of Israeli politics were really pragmatic hawks who started out as anti–Arab activists in the security field and eventually became supporters of compromise peace based on the "land for peace" formula of Security Council Resolution 242. (Former military intelligence director General Yehoshafat Harkavi wrote on this topic in a short book published in 1977, *Arab Strategies and Israeli Responses*.)

In 2002 I returned to exploring Arab-fighter politicians by looking at Indian-fighter politicians in the United States in the late eighteenth century and first half of the nineteenth century, and also at African-fighter politicians in South Africa in the second half of the nineteenth century and during the twentieth century. Because the publishing strategy of my publisher, Greenwood Press, changed, the focus of the book was placed on Indian fighters (with an appendix that discussed Arab fighters in Israel). In 2004 I researched and wrote a book looking at the Israeli class of Arab fighters, although I never published it. I had first devoted a paragraph to the topic in my book *Native vs. Settler: Ethnic Conflict in Israel/Palestine, Northern Ireland and South Africa*, and I had read the chapter on Moshe Dayan in Uri Avnery's *Israel Without Zionism* and wanted to explore the topic further. In 2002 I did basic research to see if I could find any other cases of elected military politicians besides those in Israel, South Africa, and the United States. I defined a "case" as at least four figures at the national level who came into politics in at least two separate waves. I looked at all of the British settler colonies and then at the European colonial powers that were democracies, and the search came up negative.

With the announced retirement from politics of Ehud Barak at the start of 2013 and the death of Ariel Sharon a year later, I decided that now would be a good time to pursue a book combining the 1999 and 2004 efforts. The first chapter is devoted to an overview of the phenomenon of military politicians in Israel, while the rest of the book is devoted to a detailed examination of the biographies of four Arab-fighter politicians who were involved in negotiations with the Arabs. Three of these cover all of the Arab negotiations, from the armistice agreements of 1949 through the discussions with King Hussein of Jordan in the late 1960s and 1970s, the Kissinger separation-of-forces agreements and the Sinai II interim agreement in the mid–1970s, the Camp David process from 1977 to 1979 with Egypt, and finally the Oslo process between Israel and the Palestinians from 1993 to 2000. Ariel Sharon was not a participant in any of these negotiations, but he is included because he was in many ways the most successful Arab-fighter politician and had the longest career of violent interaction with the Palestinians of any Israeli Arab fighter. He was also more typical of the Arab fighters on the Israeli Right, and he figures in the careers of the other three figures either as a soldier or as a politician.

The four figures I have chosen are important both because of their successful political careers and because of their importance to Israel's Arab policy. There are two additional politicians whom I could have chosen, but they were left out either because they can be discussed piecemeal or because there is little readily available biographical material for them. Ezer Weizman I will cover in the discussions on Dayan and Rabin. His major importance was as the Likud's first defense minister from 1977 to 1980. Weizman played a secondary role in the negotiations with Egypt by cultivating good relations with the Egyptian leadership, but the actual negotiating was done mainly by Moshe Dayan. The other individual was Yigal Allon of Mapam, Ahdut Ha'Avoda and the Labor Party. He was Israel's first significant Arab-fighter politician along with Moshe Carmel, but he lost out to Dayan in his attempt to make it into the second rank in 1967 and he succeeded only under his former subordinate Rabin in 1974. He played an important role in the negotiations with Egypt in 1975, but a less important role than either Yitzhak Rabin or Shimon Peres. Allon wrote two books, one on defense policy and one on his youth in Mandatory Palestine, and the single biography of him, by Israeli historian Anita Shapira, is devoted mainly to his military career in the Palmach and as Israel's leading field commander in the 1948 War of Independence; Shapira's biography includes only a 23-page epilogue on his subsequent political career. Allon's main importance to Israeli policy was his authorship of the Allon Plan in July 1967 (which I discuss in conjunction with the Dayan Plan). Allon and Carmel are also different from later Arab-fighter politicians in that most of their military careers were spent in the pre-state Hagana militia rather than in the Israel Defense Forces (IDF).

The following four parts of this book are the mini-biographies of the four Arab-fighter politicians I have chosen: Moshe Dayan, Yitzhak Rabin, Ariel Sharon, and Ehud Barak. I put them in roughly chronological order, although I am forced to discuss some events out of order (such as Sharon's final war against the Palestinians before the Camp David summit) to preserve the integrity of the mini-biographies. I have chosen these individuals because they cover all the major negotiations with the Arabs, as well as policy by the two major Israeli parties (Labor and Likud), and because they include the three Arab fighters who reached the top rank of Israeli politics—the premiership—as well as the man who established the precedent for ex-generals dominating the defense ministry starting in June 1967. They also include individuals from the first, second, and fourth waves of Arab-fighter politicians. When discussing them I will make comparisons with American and South African native-fighter politicians when appropriate, as well as with other Israelis.

For each biography, I will have a chapter on the military career of the individual followed by a chapter on the early political career, and then another on the later political career. Usually this will entail a chapter on the political career before becoming prime minister and then as prime minister. But for Rabin it will mean a chapter covering his first ministry and then his career as defense ministry, with his second ministry in another chapter. And for Barak it will mean a chapter on his short ministry in 1999–2000 followed by a chapter covering his return to politics as defense minister.

For each of these politicians (except Barak), there are an abundance of biographies in English. Waiting since 1999 to complete this book has allowed me to acquire many more biographies on Dayan, Rabin, and Sharon. I have also written a book on the Oslo process, *When Peace Fails: Lessons from*

Belfast for the Middle East. The reader can judge whether the wait has been worthwhile.

The purpose of this book is to explore the attitudes of Israel's Arab-fighter politicians toward the Arabs and how they perform in negotiations with them. This entails covering some of the same territory explored by writers on civil-military relations in Israel, such as Amos Perlmutter and Yoram Peri. But the main focus is on former senior soldiers serving in civilian clothes as either defense or foreign ministers and as prime ministers in negotiations. In the two other cases that serve as precedents for Israel (covered briefly in the appendix) we are mostly dealing with individuals who were not professional soldiers but rather professional politicians who served in conscript militias or as volunteers in wartime. In the American case, only Zachary Taylor and Ulysses S. Grant fit the Israeli model of having distinct successive military and political careers—and Taylor's political career only lasted for three years before he died suddenly of natural causes. In the South African case, only the later figures like Magnus Malan and Constand Viljoen (and others) from the Afrikaner Volksfront fit the Israeli pattern, and of these all except Malan had their careers after the end of white minority rule. Only Andrew Jackson, William H. Harrison, Paul Kruger, and Malan negotiated with their respective indigenous populations to conclude treaties (and Harrison usually worked with figures who had no real authority to negotiate). Thus in Israel we are looking at something novel: a group of native-fighter politicians who negotiated with the native population or with the surrounding states made up of native Arab allies of the Palestinians. As a result, it should be possible to draw general conclusions about Israel's Arab fighters as negotiators in a way that would not be appropriate when discussing Indian fighters or Boers/Afrikaners.

This analysis may or may not be of future importance and relevance. Three of these Israeli figures had their main careers in the Labor Party, which does not seem to be capable of returning to power in the near future. The negotiations detailed in this book all took place either at the very end of Labor's three decades of rule in Israel (from 1974 to 1975) or in the brief periods when Labor returned to power in the 1990s. It is not clear today that former generals will play the same central role in the Likud that they played over the decades in Labor. So far four former generals have played major roles in the Likud: Ezer Weizman, Ariel Sharon, Shaul Mofaz, and Moshe Ya'alon. Weizman left the party three years after it came to power over Menahem Begin's policy toward the autonomy negotiations with Egypt. Sharon and Mofaz left the party to form Kadima in late 2005. Sharon is now dead and Mofaz heads a two-man party; unless he can effect a merger with the Likud, his career is over. Only Ya'alon has an ongoing political career.

After May 1967 these former chiefs of staff provided the Israeli public with a sense of security during crises due either to the formation of multistate Arab coalitions against Israel that threatened war or to terrorist attacks. Starting with Dayan, they earned the sobriquet of "Mr. Security" from the Israeli public and political writers as they reassured the public in the face of these threats. They provided the credibility for Israel to make territorial concessions that civilian politicians lacked in Labor. Whether such individuals will be needed to play that same role in the Likud is an open question, for ever since the disengagement from Gaza in August 2005 no Israeli government has given up territory. (Begin's government had four generals in the cabinet when it agreed to give up the Sinai.)

Two of these four, Dayan and Barak, lost their reputations as "Mr. Security." Dayan went on to negotiate with the Arabs without it; he still retained the confidence of the prime ministers under whom he served, Golda Meir and Begin. Barak ultimately managed to regain his reputation as defense minister because he was not negotiating with the Arabs over territory.

Maps

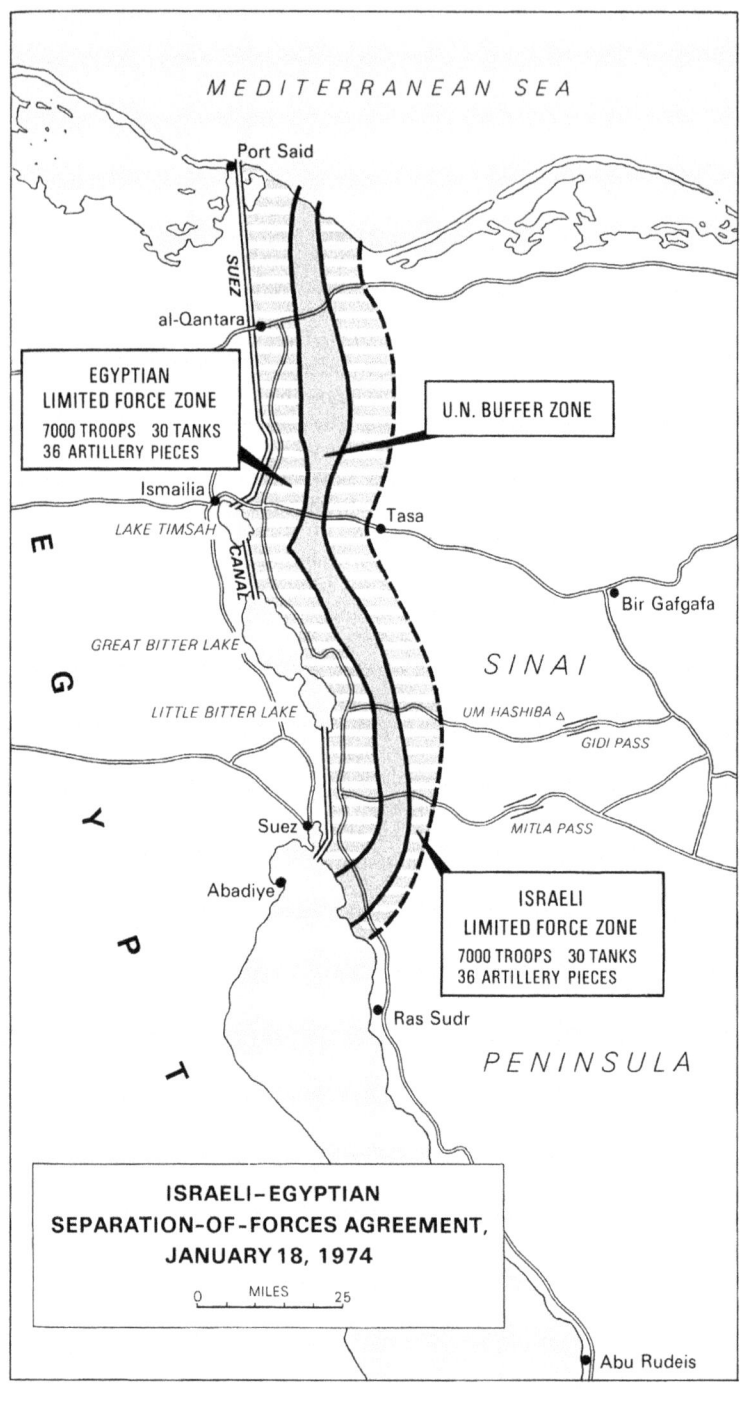

Maps 9

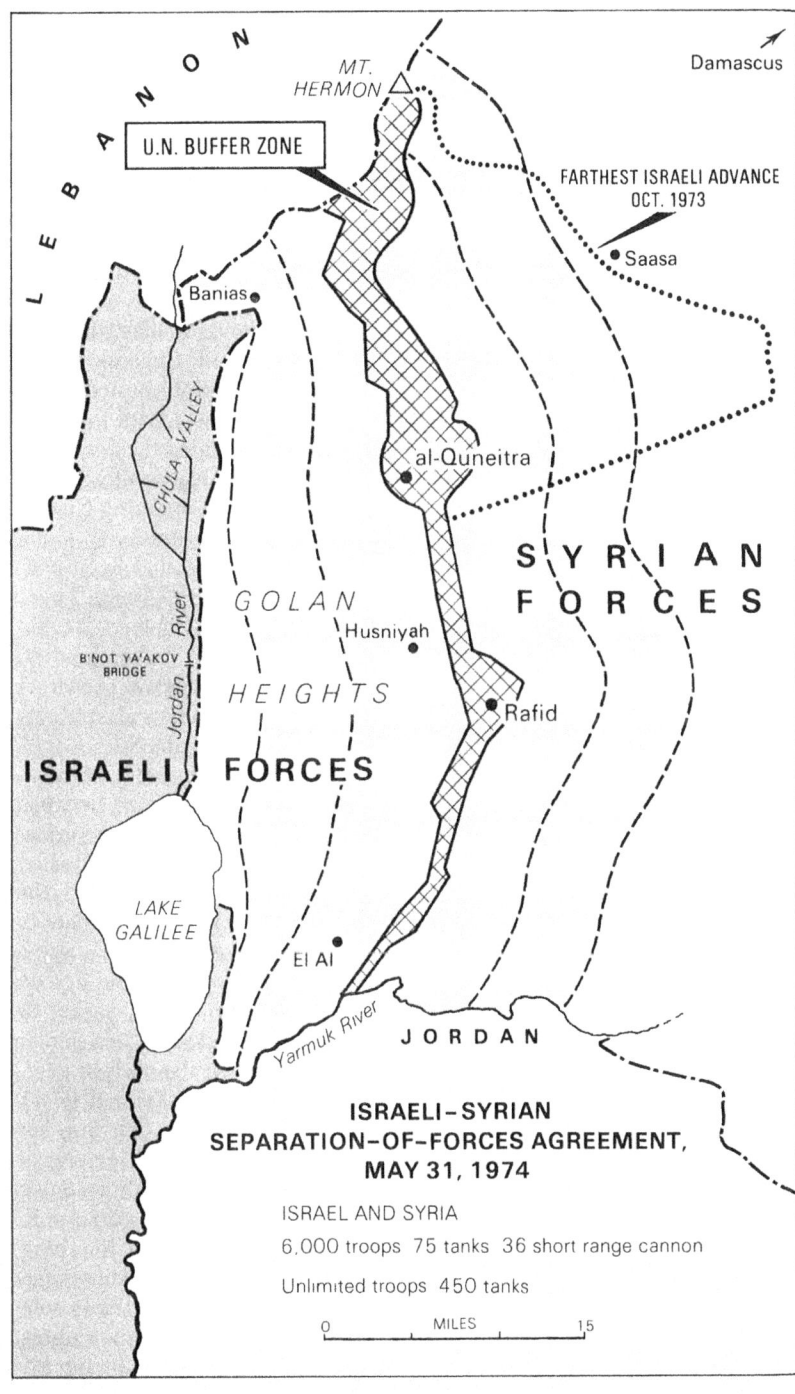

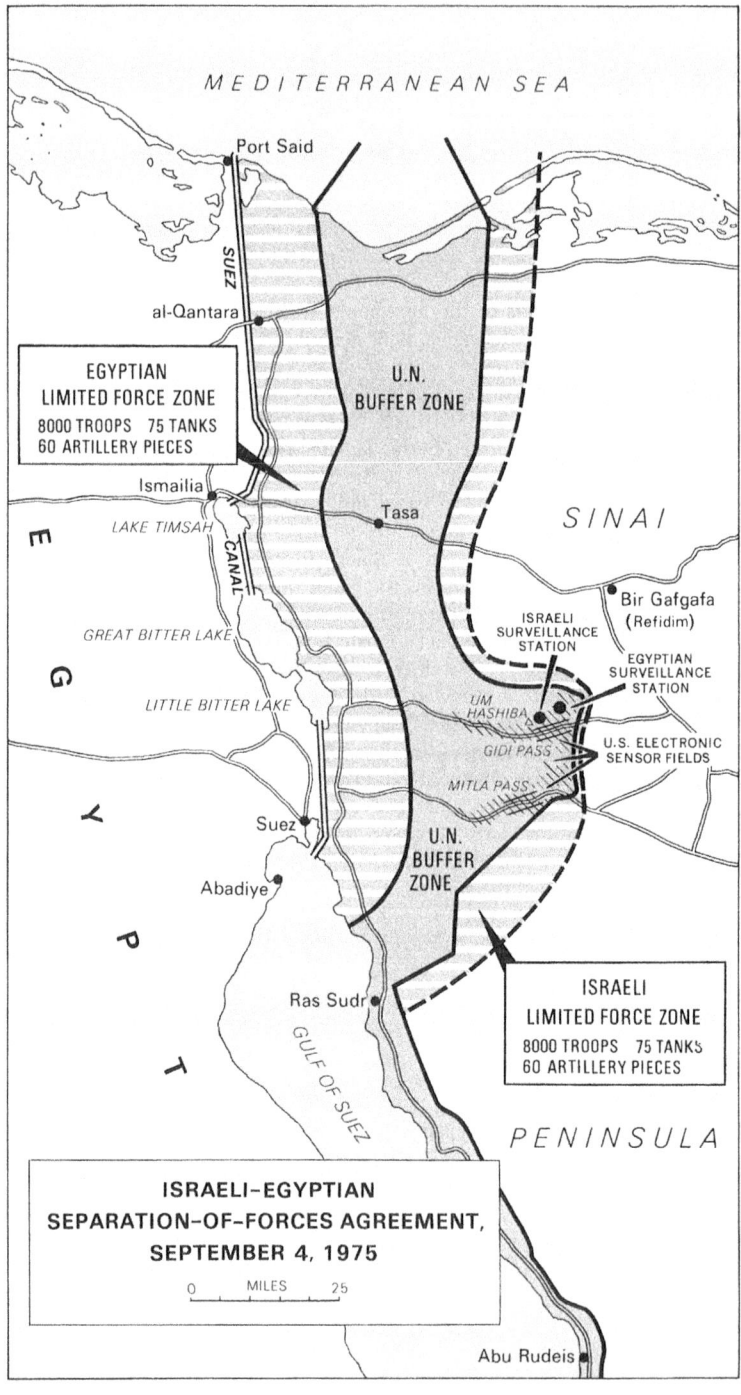

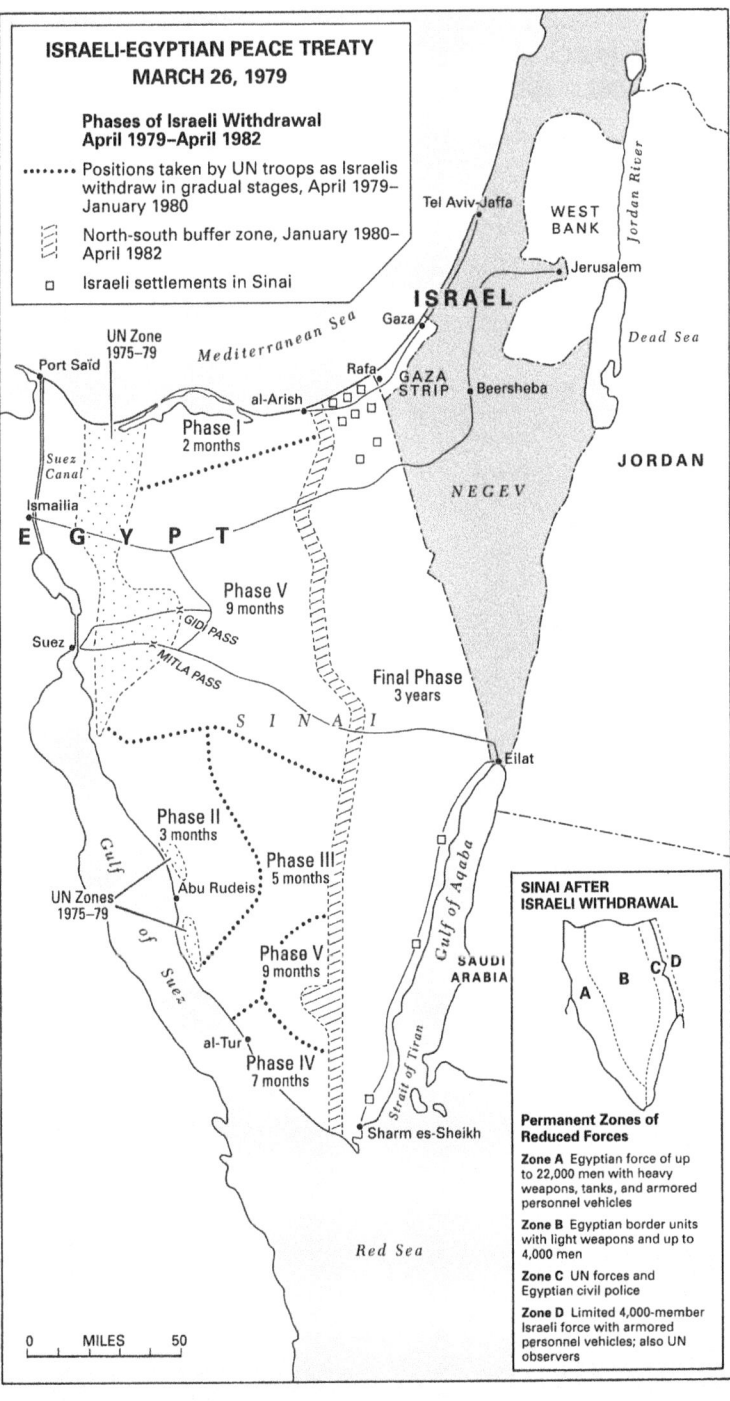

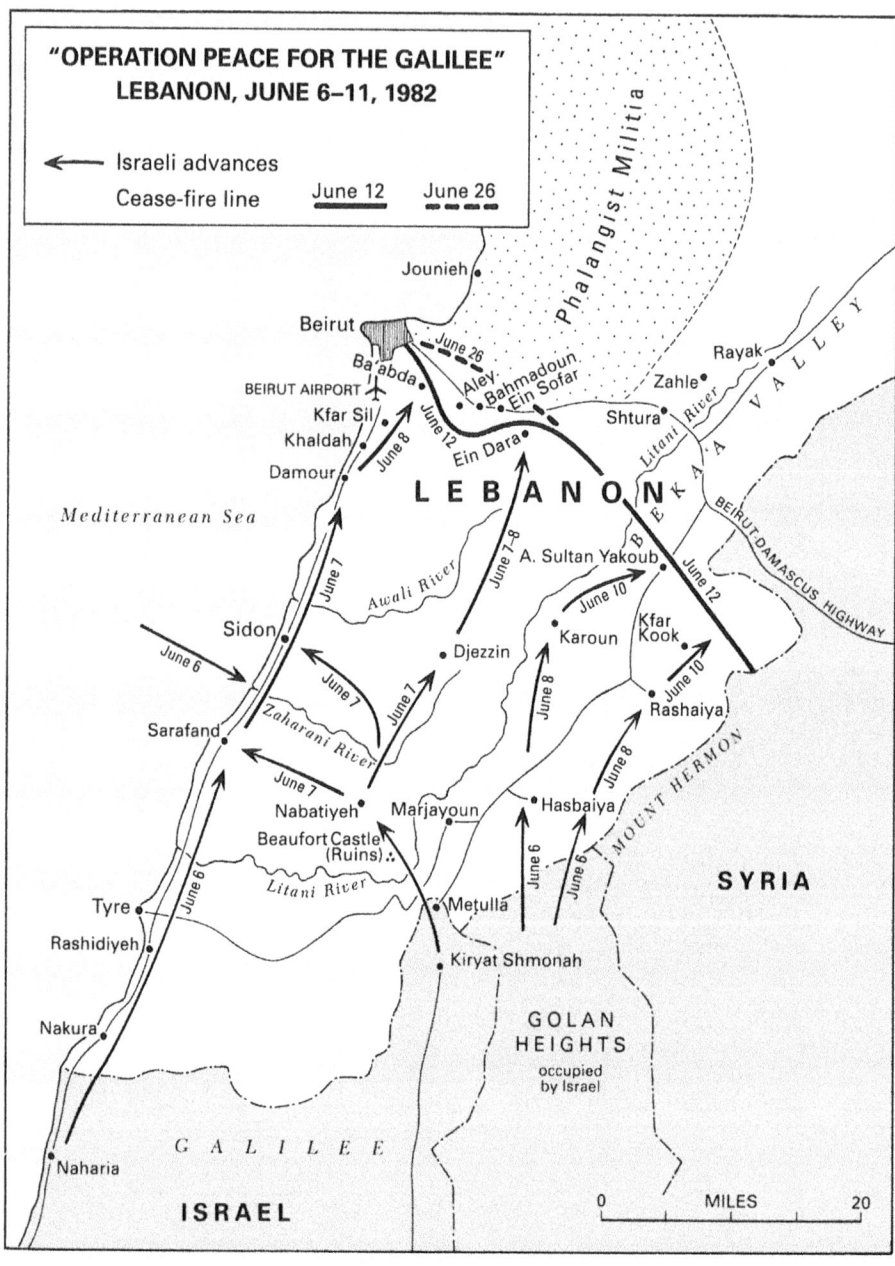

PART I: MOSHE DAYAN, 1915–1981

Chapter One

Israel's Military Politicians

In sixty-five-plus years of independence Israel has had at least five separate generations or waves of military politicians that can be grouped together.[1] The first wave was from 1949 to 1959 and consisted of three main military politicians: Yigal Allon and Moshe Carmel of Ahdut Ha'Avoda (The Unity of Labor)—a party that broke off from Mapam in 1954 and lasted until 1968, when it merged to become part of the Israeli Labor Party—and Moshe Dayan. Allon was the outstanding field general of the War of Independence, in which he commanded offensives during the civil war phase against the Palestinians in the Galilee. He then became the commander of the Central Front during the Ten Days in July 1948 and of the Southern Front for offensives in October and December 1948. (Yitzhak Rabin was Allon's deputy commander.) Carmel was commander of the Northern Front. Along with these two was Hagana commander Israel Galili, who served as deputy defense minister during the War of Independence. Carmel served as minister of transport from 1955 to 1959 and again from 1965 to 1969. Allon served as minister of labor from 1961 to 1967, as minister of immigrant absorption and deputy prime minister from 1967 to 1969, as minister of education and culture and deputy prime minister from 1969 to 1974, and finally as foreign minister from 1974 to 1977. Israel Galili also served as minister of information briefly and then as minister without portfolio in several governments. Ahdut Ha'Avoda was basically a paramilitary party based on the Hagana and Palmakh high command.

The second wave was from 1968 to 1977 and consisted mostly of heroes of the 1956 and 1967 wars. Ezer Weizman, the head of the Israeli Air Force from 1958 to 1964, was the first general on the Israeli Right when he joined Gahal as transport minister in the government of national unity in 1969. He was followed by Ariel Sharon, who entered the Knesset in January 1974 but resigned a year later. Haim Bar Lev and Yitzhak Rabin were the most important politicians for Labor. Yigael Yadin and Meir Amit entered the Knesset in 1977 with the Democratic Movement for Change, which split into two parts in 1979. This was also the period when Moshe Dayan reached the defense ministry. The ministry would be reserved exclusively for former generals and defense technocrats after June 1967, with the exceptions of Menahem Begin in 1980–1981 and Amir Peretz from 2006 to 2007. Each of the two main parties had a single defense technocrat: Shimon Peres for Labor and Moshe Arens for the Likud. Weizman remained in politics until 1993, when he was elected president. Weizman served as minister of transport from 1969 to August 1970, and as defense minister from June 1977 to March 1980. From 1980 to 1984 he went into business and made money. In 1984 he headed his own generals list, Yahad, and the following year he joined the Labor Party.[2]

The third wave was from 1983 to 1988 and consisted of several independent generals. The first of these was Raful Eitan, who retired as chief of staff in 1983 and then joined Tehiya as head of his own faction. In 1984 he entered the Knesset with Tehiya. In 1988 he ran as the head of that faction, Tzomet (Crossroads), in the election and served as minister of agriculture from 1988 to 1992. He won eight seats in 1992 but failed to enter Rabin's government and so was forced to serve in the opposition. In 1996 he entered the Likud and served as minister of internal security in 1998–1999. He failed to win any seats in 1999 and retired from politics.[3]

The other generals list was that of Rehavam "Gandhi" Ze'evi, who formed the Moledet list in 1988. He won only two seats. Moledet ran on the platform of forcibly transferring Arabs out of Israel. He served in Shamir's government briefly in 1990–1991, before resigning. In 1999 his Moledet Party merged with two other parties to form the National Union. In February 2001 he was assassinated in the Old City by Palestinian terrorists from the Popular Front for the Liberation of Palestine hours after he had tendered his resignation from Sharon's government.[4]

The fourth wave was in the 1990s and consisted of Ehud Barak, Amnon Lipkin-Shahak, Yitzhak Mordechai, Amram Mitzna and Avigdor Kahalani. Kahalani, a hero from the First Lebanon War, during which he was an armored battalion commander who fought against the Syrians, retired as a brigadier general from the IDF and ran on the Labor Party list in 1992 and was elected. In March 1996 he formed his own list, the Third Way, which won four seats in the 1996 election. The party was dedicated to keeping the Golan Heights under Israeli control. Kahalani was invited to serve in Benjamin Netanyahu's coalition as internal security minister. In 1999 the party failed to pass the entry barrier and Kahalani's political career was over.

Lipkin-Shahak served as chief of staff after Barak and he ran with

Yitzhak Mordechai and some Likud defectors as the Center Party, which won five seats in 1999. Lipkin-Shahak played a major role in the negotiations in 1999 and 2000 with Syria, at Camp David and finally at Taba. In March 2001, after defecting from the Center Party, he resigned from the Knesset and went into business. He joined the Labor Party in 2003 and was active in the Geneva Initiative. Lipkin-Shahak died of cancer in December 2012 after a long battle with the illness.

Mordechai served as defense minister under Netanyahu from 1996 to 1999. In February 1999 he resigned from the Likud and as minister over a dispute with Netanyahu and joined the new Center Party that Lipkin-Shahak was forming with Ron Milo and Dan Meridor, two former Likud politicians. He served as minister of transport in the Barak government. Mordechai was forced to resign from the party in 2001 after he was indicted for sexual assault against two women during his military service. He was convicted and served time in prison.

Mitzna rose to become commander of Central Command at the start of the Intifada. He then took a year's study leave in the United States, which Rabin thought of almost as desertion in time of war. Mitzna would not be promoted further with Rabin as defense minister. He served as head of the IDF's planning branch in 1990, and ended up retiring from the IDF in 1993; he was elected Labor mayor of Haifa that same year. He was later reelected mayor in 1998. In 2003 he became the Labor candidate for prime minister, and the party was reduced to 19 seats in the Knesset. Peres soon came back to replace him as leader and Mitzna retired to the Negev, where he worked in the development town of Yeruham as appointed mayor.

The fifth wave started in 2000 and consisted of Shaul Mofaz, Moshe "Boogie" Ya'alon, and others. Mofaz was chief of staff after Lipkin-Shahak and became defense minister under Sharon in 2002. He then resigned as defense minister in November 2005 to join Kadima. In Kadima he was the number two person after Tzipi Livni and won control of the party in internal elections in the summer of 2012. He briefly joined the Netanyahu government and then, less than two months later, quit. In January 2013 Kadima was reduced to only two seats. Ya'alon was chief of staff after Mofaz and served under him when Mofaz was defense minister. The two did not get along well. Ya'alon joined the Likud in 2008 and was elected to the Knesset in 2009. He served as strategic affairs minister and deputy prime minister in the second Netanyahu government and as defense minister in the third Netanyahu government starting in February 2013.[5]

Efraim Eitam rose to the rank of brigadier general in the IDF in the last decades of the twentieth century. He contemplated a career in politics within the Likud, but because he was a *ba'al tshuva*, or "born-again Jew," he ended up joining the National Religious Party and being elected to the Knesset in 2003. He pulled the Mafdal out of the Sharon government in 2005 in opposition to the disengagement from Gaza. Before leaving as housing and construction minister, he had introduced a plan to settle the E-1 area of Jerusalem, which would have cut the Palestinian Authority off from East Jerusalem. In January 2006 he was injured while protesting the court-ordered destruction of Jewish housing on Palestinian land.[6]

Unlike the United States and South Africa (see appendix), Israel has only two tiers of government: municipal and national. Israel's military politicians have to either become mayors of major cities or be elected to the Knesset and then appointed a minister to be on the political fast track. Within the government, there are basically three tiers of ministries: the premiership at the top; the defense, foreign, and finance ministries at the next level; and the other ministries at the bottom. Military politicians usually do not serve as finance ministers. Instead, they serve as some sort of infrastructure or transport minister and then hope to get appointed to either the defense ministry or the foreign ministry, and eventually to the premiership. At particular key moments, as in 1974 or 1999, circumstances may develop when a general can go all the way to the top.

There is a noticeable trend. Before 1967 it was unusual for generals, including chiefs of staff, to join any party other than Ahdut Ha'Avoda, which merged with Mapai and Rafi in 1968 to form the Israel Labor Party. Moshe Dayan went into politics because he was a charismatic war hero. After 1967 it became normal for retiring chiefs of staff to join the Labor Party, as they were assured a seat in the Knesset (and often a ministry as well). The Likud was dominated by "the fighting family" of paramilitary veterans from the Etzel and Lehi underground organizations of the 1940s and by their offspring, the princes. Only genuine war heroes like Sharon or Weizman could have a real shot at the top jobs in the Likud.[7] This continued up until 2000, with most former generals joining the Labor Party for professional opportunistic reasons; those who did not joined other parties out of genuine ideological conviction. But after 2000 and the outbreak of the Al-Aksa Intifada, former chiefs of staff began joining the Likud. This was because they were more likely to serve as defense minister or prime minister someday in the Likud than in Labor, which was in decline after 2000.[8]

In politics, name recognition is of particular importance. The political candidate whose name is well known to the public has an immediate advantage over the candidate whose name is unknown. In democracies that are at peace for long periods of time, as in Western Europe after 1945, the names of generals are generally unknown to the general public, except for those of veteran generals from World Wars I and II who continued to serve after the war. In Europe the aristocracy tended to dominate both the military and the church and left politics to the business and professional classes. This was not true in the United States and South Africa, which had no hereditary aristocracy (among whites), and so a tradition of war heroes serving in politics took hold in these two countries. It also took hold in Israel for similar reasons, but because of the greater threat and frequency of wars it became more institutionalized.[9] Those war heroes with particularly stellar military records became known in Israel as "Mr. Security." The four subjects of this book are examples of this phenomenon, (as are presidents Washington, Jackson, Taylor, Grant, and Eisenhower in America and Paul Kruger, Louis Botha, and Jan Smuts in South Africa), and all four individuals dominated the negotiations between Israel and its Arab neighbors from 1974 to 2001.

The equivalent for an American politician becoming governor in the United States is an Israeli Arab-fighter politician becoming the head of his own list for the Knesset. Arab fighters tend to form these lists at three different points in their careers: at the start, in order to leverage their way into a ministry in a Labor or Likud government; in the middle of their careers when switching parties—as Sharon and Weizman did—and at the end of their careers after they have gone as far as they can in either Labor or the Likud. Sharon was forced to form his own list because the Liberals would not take him back after he resigned from the Knesset. Weizman formed his Yahad Party after a change in his ideology meant that he could no longer remain in the Likud and he had to "cleanse" himself before entering Labor. Some spend their entire political careers in their own lists, or at least outside of the two main parties.

Based on historical precedents overseas (see Appendix), it appears very likely that military politicians will continue to play a major role in Israeli politics until a stable peace is established with the Palestinians, and then possibly for a decade or two after that.

Chapter Two

General Dayan

Moshe Dayan, when he was born in May 1915, was the first child on the first kibbutz (or communal village) in the Jewish *yishuv* (colony) in Palestine. He was named after a friend of his father, Moshe Barsky, a fellow kibbutz member who was murdered by Arab thieves while getting medicine for the settlement. Dayan's father Shmuel had immigrated to Palestine in 1908 at age eighteen and joined Degania, the first kibbutz located at the southern tip of Lake Kinneret (or the Sea of Galilee), two years later. His mother, Devorah, came to Palestine in 1913.[1] Dayan set a common pattern among the soldier politicians I will be discussing: from his father he inherited a sense of duty and patriotism, and from his mother a love of the arts (in Dayan's case, this was poetry, which became one of the three great non-professional interests in his life, along with sex and archaeology).[2]

Dayan's childhood was a strange foreshadowing of his later life as an adult, starting with his birth. At age three he contracted trachoma, an eye disease common among the Arab peasants in the region. Because this was during World War I and the Russian Jews were considered enemy aliens by the Ottomans, there were movement restrictions that made it difficult for his mother to take him to Jerusalem to find medical treatment. He temporarily went blind in the eye that he later lost.[3] Dayan would later have problems with his remaining eye in his old age. When he was five, the first widespread ethnic strife between Jews and Arabs broke out and several of the buildings in Degania B, the satellite commune, were burned. A year later Shmuel moved the family to the Jezreel Valley and helped found Nahalal, the first *moshav ovdim*, or worker's cooperative, in Palestine. This would be Moshe Dayan's home as a young adult, until he began his political career, and where he would be buried.[4] Later these two types of settlements, the kibbutz and the moshav, would become the background of the Labor Zionist movement in which Dayan would spend his political career. His father would also become a member of the First Knesset in 1949 and serve for the next two decades.⁵

As a child Dayan was aggressive and violent—a way of acting out his sense of abandonment by his parents. His father Shmuel was often away from home on labor movement business as a means of escaping from his distant wife, while Dayan's mother was a narcisstic woman who initially spoke no Hebrew or Yiddish, as she grew up in a wealthy family in Russia and spoke only Russian. As a result, Moshe took out his rage on his cousin Shulamit. He was unpopular because he put on airs of superiority and tried to beat his rivals into submission. He was not noted in his youth for being particularly intelligent or an original thinker.⁶

In 1934 he was brought home unconscious after being clubbed while sowing seed in one of his father's fields. He had been attacked by a Bedouin friend who was invited to his wedding the following year. The dispute was part of the arguments that were common over grazing rights, with Arabs asserting their traditional right to graze their livestock everywhere and the Jews asserting their rights of ownership to specific fields.⁷

In 1935 he married a pretty young girl named Ruth Schwartz from a prominent Jerusalem family. He would remain married to her for thirty-six years, happily for the first two decades, unhappily for the remainder. She would connect him to his future partner in the Camp David accords, Ezer Weizman, who married Ruth's younger sister Reuma and, like Moshe, became a general, a war hero, and a professional politician. Ruth was on Nahalal to study agriculture. In her memoir she claimed to have earlier been the girlfriend of Zvi Spector, who was higher up in the Hagana than Dayan and who was killed in a famous incident in which his small craft was lost in the Mediterranean off the coast of Lebanon in 1941. Zvi was the father of one of Israel's leading fighter aces, Brigadier General Yiftach Spector.⁸

In 1936 Dayan joined the Jewish Settlement Police, a force created with approval of the British Mandatory authorities to protect the Jewish rural settlements from Arabs. He started out serving as a guide for British officers because he knew the Lower Galilee and Jezreel Valley so well. The Arab Revolt, which would last for three years, had broken out in April 1936 with a general strike of Arab workers enforced by the Mufti Haj Amin al-Husseini's agents. The following year, after attending a sergeant's course, he was promoted to sergeant. During the course he met Yigal Allon, who was two years younger than him, for the first time. Dayan was an introvert by nature and Allon an extrovert, and so the two seemed to take an immediate dislike to one another that would last for over thirty years. "There was an insufferable fellow there who spoiled the whole course for me. His name is Moshe Dayan," wrote Allon in a letter.⁹

In 1938 Captain Orde Wingate, who had served in the Sudan and would die as a major general leading the Chindits in Burma during World War II, formed the Special Night Squads to combat the Arab Revolt by taking the fight to the enemy. Wingate was an Evangelical Protestant who believed in Zionism, spoke Arabic, and loved to quote the Bible, which he always carried with him. Wingate became known as "the friend" to the Jews and Israeli historians because he was the main supporter of the Zionists among the British troops stationed in Palestine in the late 1930s. He taught his squads to fight at night, set up effective ambushes, and infiltrate an area without being seen. Dayan considered Wingate a genius and learned as much as possible from him.[10]

In November 1938 Allon and Dayan were both deputy commanders under Yitzhak Sadeh, the future Palmakh commander and a veteran of the Red Army, in the establishment of Kibbutz Hanita, a settlement established about five miles inland from the Mediterranean coast on the border with Lebanon. Hanita was one of the "tower and stockade" settlements created by the Hagana. Under Ottoman law, which Britain retained during the Mandate, if a building was erected with a roof on within 24 hours, it could not be torn down but must be left. So the Hagana would organize a convoy of trucks, each carrying a section of a prefabricated building or a wall to protect the settlement, and men would be brought in from all over the Yishuv to establish a new settlement. Most of the settlements were set up to control strategic terrain or mark out the future borders of the state. A famous picture was taken with Sadeh in the center with his arms around Allon and Dayan, and the caption on the back in Hebrew referred to them as "the future general staff." Sadeh became the first commander of the Palmakh in 1941 and Allon the second commander in 1945. Allon was the leading field general in the War of Independence, Sadeh was the commander of the Israeli army's only armored brigade and Dayan actually became the chief of the general staff in December 1953. While at Hanita, Allon was noted for his approachability, whereas Dayan was noted for his distance from his subordinates.[11]

In the summer of 1939 Allon and Dayan were both instructors in a Hagana platoon leaders' course in the Lower Galilee. In October 1939, while on training maneuvers for the Hagana, the semi-official armed wing of the Jewish Agency in Palestine that had been created in 1920 as a result of the first Arab–Zionist riots, Dayan was the leader of a group of Jewish soldiers that was intercepted by a British patrol and arrested after a local Arab had reported them. One of the men was armed with a pistol, which was a hanging offence at the time. Official Hagana policy was not to admit to anything under interrogation, but Dayan saw no point in this. He confessed that they were Hagana members and therefore pro–British, with the common enemy of Arab nationalism. The group was quickly sentenced to ten years in prison, to be served in the old stone prison at Acre. Dayan at the time had a very young daughter, Yael, who was brought by her mother to visit him in prison. Dayan had served sixteen months in prison when, on February 17, 1941, the men were all released.[12]

The Allies were planning on invading Vichy-French Lebanon and Syria, and the Hagana would provide the local guides for the British invasion force. This was the time when the British allowed the Jews to form the Palmakh (short for Plugot Makhatz, or strike companies) as a 2,000-man permanent force within the Hagana whose members would live on kibbutzim and work in the fields to finance their training. Allon and Dayan were named as two of the six company commanders in the Palmakh. Dayan helped conduct the interviews of the new recruits to the force. Yitzhak Rabin was one of those whom he decided was combat material.[13]

Dayan was part of a fifteen-man combined Australian and Jewish Palmakh group that was the spearhead of the force. It crossed into Lebanon after dark on the night of June 7, 1941, with the object of capturing a local police station and bridge. Dayan helped seize the police station the next morning and then went up on the flat roof of the one-story building to get a better view of the area. While looking through a pair of binoculars he was severely wounded. Sunlight had glinted off the binoculars and a sniper shot the lens, driving the eyepiece into Dayan's left eye socket. He quietly and stoically bore the pain for several hours until he could be evacuated to Hanita. He had lost the eye immediately and the cheekbones under it were damaged, as well as the fingers of one hand. The Australians accompanying him were very impressed with his bravery.[14]

The wound was painful and kept him out of combat for the next seven years. He went to Paris for an operation, but it was a failure. For the next seven years he worked mainly as a farmer and partly as an intelligence officer in the Hagana. In 1941–1942 he was responsible for setting up a network of informers who would provide information if Palestine were overrun by General Erwin Rommel, which appeared quite possible during both 1941 and 1942, up until the Battle of El Alamein in October 1942. During this time Dayan hitched a ride with a convoy to Baghdad and saw the city, which he found disappointing after all the stories about its glorious past.[15]

After Lehi (the Stern Group) assassinated Lord Moyne, the British official overseeing the British Empire in the Middle East, in Cairo in November 1944, Jewish Agency leader David Ben-Gurion declared a "war" against both the Etzel (Irgun) and Lehi in reaction. Hagana intelligence was responsible for finding the leading figures in the two underground organizations, kidnapping them, interrogating them and then handing them over to the British for detention. Even though it was Lehi that had carried out the assassination, Ben-Gurion had the Hagana concentrate on the Etzel, as it was the greater political threat to the Jewish Agency, having declared its own revolt against the British in February 1944. Dayan was involved in this intelligence operation and regarded it as a rather unpleasant duty. Menahem Begin, the leader of the Etzel and later the prime minister when the Camp David negotiations took place, did not hold it against Dayan, as did some Likudniks decades later.[16]

When the War of Independence moved into its conventional stage on May 15, 1948, after the British evacuation, the Israeli declaration of independence, and the Arab invasion by the armies of five Arab countries, Dayan was working at Hagana headquarters without a command. General Ya'acov Dori, the first Israeli chief of staff, dispatched him to Degania, his birthplace, to help advise the defenders against the Syrian army. Dayan arrived along with one of the Israel Defense Force's (IDF) four antique, French World War I-era 75 mm cannons. The Syrians were not expecting much resistance when suddenly their few tanks were greeted by cannonfire and Molotov cocktails. The Syrians fled, and this gave rise to Dayan's "bird theory" of the Arabs' fighting ability—a little noise and they would fly off.[17]

After this he was put in charge of organizing a new battalion out of Lehi veterans, kibbutz and moshav members, Tel Aviv soldiers, and overseas volunteers (mostly from South Africa). It was designated the 89th Commando Battalion and was equipped with jeeps armed with machine guns and American halftracks. While the new unit was still in training, word arrived that the Etzel arms ship *Altalena* was off the coast of Israel. Dayan was ordered to go to the coast and prevent it from unloading its arms. Dayan did not use his Lehi company on this mission, but rather took some men from his other three companies to Kfar Vitkin. They encountered the ship off the shore with a few men on land unloading crates of weapons. A few shots were exchanged and the men ashore fled back to the ship. Six Etzel men were killed and eighteen wounded on the beach by Dayan's men. The *Altalena* managed to offload about a fifth of its cargo of arms donated by the French government to Israel. From this point it sailed to Tel Aviv and became the responsibility of Allon and Yitzhak Rabin (we will take up the rest of the story of the *Altalena* later).[18]

Dayan spent about a week in continuous combat during the War of Independence in July 1948, when he took part in Yigal Allon's offensive against Ramle and Lydda (Lod) in the central coastal plain, haSharon, known as Operation Dani. Dayan used his battalion as shock troops to force the Arabs to surrender. They managed to recover a Jordanian Arab Legion armored car with a two-pounder (37 mm) cannon from a ditch and used that to lead their attack. Later the attack would be one of those battles from the war that was taught in IDF officer training courses as the type of action officers were expected to emulate. Only one of a dozen battalion commanders who took part in the offensive, Dayan was the one who stood out.[19] During the offensive Ben-Gurion, who had had a close relationship with Dayan since the late 1930s, ordered Dayan to Jerusalem to discuss taking over the military command in Jerusalem. Dayan was annoyed to be called out during the middle of a battle. He went to Jerusalem, spoke with Ben-Gurion, and agreed to take over but not until after the end of Operation Dani. Operation Dani was commanded by Dayan's old rival, Allon, who was the Central Command head, and Yitzhak Rabin was his assistant commander, while Dayan was only a battalion commander. Dayan was probably made front commander because he had no political party backing him, as did those affiliated with the Palmakh.[20]

The 89th's participation in Operation Dani lasted from July 11 to July 15. Then Dayan was ordered by Chief of Operations Yigael Yadin to take his battalion to the south and participate in the offensive in the Negev against the Egyptian army. The unit arrived at its forward operating base on the 15th and participated in an attack on the 16th and 17th; on July 18 Dayan was promoted from major to lieutenant colonel and called away to take over command of the Jerusalem front.[21] In the 1948 war the IDF had set up four regional commands during the first ceasefire in June 1948: Southern Command (the Negev), Jerusalem, Central Command, and Northern Command. Except for Jerusalem, which was eliminated after the War of Independence, these commands remain in place today and generals are rotated around them so that chiefs of staff (CGSs) and their deputies are familiar with the challenges on all fronts.[22]

In Jerusalem, although he organized a couple of attacks against the Jordanians, Dayan's responsibilities were mainly diplomatic rather than military. In September, following the Lehi assassination of UN mediator Count Folke Bernadotte, who had been involved with the rescue of Hungarian Jews from the SS, during World War II Dayan moved against the Etzel and Lehi camps in Jerusalem, where they had retained an independent existence because Jerusalem was not part of the territory granted to Israel under the UN partition plan of November 29, 1947. Dayan forced the men to cease operations and integrate into the IDF.[23]

After the Ten Days offensives of July, there were two more periods of active fighting: in October in the Galilee against Arab irregulars and the Lebanese army and in the Negev against the Egyptians, and again in the last

President Chaim Weizmann with Lt. Col. Moshe Dayan during the president's visit to Jerusalem, December 1, 1948. Israel state photograph archive.

week of December and first week of January 1949 against the Egyptians inside the eastern Sinai region. Dayan concluded a ceasefire agreement with his Jordanian counterpart, Lt. Col. Abdullah el-Tal, on November 30, 1948.[24]

From early January until late March Dayan took part in the negotiations with the Jordanians conducted in Jerusalem, meeting with King Abdullah I a dozen times. Because Dayan had grown up around Arabs, spoke some colloquial Arabic and knew Arab customs, and regarded the Arabs as rivals for control of Eretz Israel/the Land of Israel rather than as Middle Eastern incarnations of European anti-semites (as did many of the Jewish leadership in all parties), he was ideal as a military officer for diplomatic assignments.[25] His first diplomatic assignment had been escorting the body of accidentally slain General David Marcus (a.k.a. Mickey Stone) back to West Point, New York, for burial. After using a surplus dress uniform purchased in a clothing store, he had flown the body back to the United States. At that time, he managed to meet with an American Jewish officer, Abraham Baum, who had taken part in a raid in March 1945 as part of General George S. Patton's army. The officer gave Dayan advice about carrying out commando raids that Dayan put to use during Operation Dani.[26]

A five-course dinner in Amman was followed by an all-night negotiating session between the Israeli armistice delegation and the Jordanian leadership on March 23, 1949, during which maps were initialed. Dayan flew to the island of Rhodes to sign the armistice agreement with Jordan on April 3. In June the Israeli general staff appointed Dayan to head the Israeli delegation to the Mixed Armistice Commissions, which supervised the armistice agreements and marked out the actual ceasefire lines on the ground. In this role he achieved minor territorial gains for Israel and control over its main railroad line. After Israel's last armistice agreement was signed with Syria in July 1949, Dayan was featured on the cover of *Life* magazine, the first time that his famous eye-patch appeared on the cover of an international news magazine.[27]

Somewhere between the sergeant's course in 1938 and his appointment as Jerusalem military commander in late 1948, Dayan developed a sense of charm—the ability to make others feel important—as a defense mechanism. He was able to mingle with others and smile while mentally ignoring all those who were not important to his advancement. This trait remained with him until the end of his political career.[28]

On October 9, 1949, Dayan was appointed head of the Southern Command to succeed Yigal Allon, who was sent abroad to France on study leave. During the War of Independence there was an anomalous situation in which the IDF's primary striking force, the Palmakh, was loyal to a party, Mapam, that was a rival to Ben-Gurion's Mapai Party. Ben-Gurion was determined to bring the IDF under his control by purging those Palmakh commanders whom he considered to be too political and promoting officers loyal to Mapai. In the elections to the first Knesset in February 1949 Mapam had featured a number of IDF figures on its list, such as Allon and Northern Commander Moshe Carmel. Mapai had Dayan and three other IDF officers run on its list in safe places and then resign their seats after being elected. After this election it was made illegal for serving officers to run for the Knesset.[29]

The officer handing over control of Southern Command for Allon was Yitzhak Rabin. Rabin remembers Dayan in his memoirs as being particularly abrupt, but this was probably a combination of Dayan's nature and Rabin's resentment. Rabin had bypassed Dayan in rank and position within the Palmakh/Hagana in the mid-1940s. He had much more combat experience than Dayan, but as Allon's loyal deputy he was considered too close to Ahdut Ha'Avoda. Ben-Gurion used "affirmative action" to jump Dayan over many officers more senior to him. But if one looks at Dayan's standing in the Palmakh before he lost his eye in 1941, one can view this as a restoration of rank after Dayan had proved himself in combat during Operation Dani in July 1948, and then as a front commander in Jerusalem. Allon resigned from the IDF after the end of his study leave once it was made clear to him that he had no future in the IDF.[30] A half-century later Dayan's nephew Uzi, son of Moshe's younger brother Zorik, who was killed in April 1948 in a battle with Druze mercenaries, suffered from political influence in the opposite direction and had his career cut short in the number two position in the IDF as deputy chief of staff.[31]

In early 1952 Dayan attended a senior officer's course in Britain. On June 1, 1952, he was made head of the Northern Command. Six months later he was made deputy chief of staff under Mordechai Makleff, who agreed to stay on for a year to give Dayan enough experience to take his place chief of staff.[32]

In June 1953 Dayan pioneered the policy of reprisal raids as a response to Palestinian terrorist attacks. The policy was to hit Arab military or economic targets in the country (Jordan, Egypt) from which the terrorists were operating. This was intended to force the country to suppress the Palestinians and put an end to the raids. Dayan recognized that there were two possible outcomes to this policy: it would work or it would lead to war. Dayan actually favored war with Egypt because he believed that sooner or later Israel would be forced into a second round of war with its Arab neighbors. He preferred that this arrive at a time of Israel's choosing rather than at its enemies' pleasure, and he really wanted a change to the border with Egypt to give Israel a buffer between Egypt and the Gaza Strip.[33]

Dayan chose Ariel Sharon, who was then a reserve officer studying in Jerusalem and who had served under him as an intelligence officer in Northern Command, to head Unit 101, a commando infantry unit designated to carry out these raids. Dayan would personally brief Sharon before each reprisal raid and would usually wait at IDF headquarters or in the field to debrief Sharon upon his return from each mission. As a result, Sharon built a much closer relationship with both Dayan and Ben-Gurion then his rank warranted.

Dayan made it his personal mission to restore the Palmakh ethos to the IDF. It had been lost after the Palmakh was purged and many veterans quit or were forced out of the IDF. He decided that all senior officers would have

Defense Minister Dayan touring southern front with Ariel Sharon (far left rear) in September 1967. Photograph by Ilan Bruner, Israeli Government Press Office.

to undergo a basic paratrooper jump course and earn their jump wings as a means of inculcating this spirit in the IDF. Dayan underwent his course in the summer of 1954 and sprained his ankle in his final jump, so that he was forced to sport crutches at the Kirya, as the IDF headquarters in Tel Aviv is known.[34]

Dayan spent two hours reviewing intelligence reports every morning when he arrived at work. He then spent most of the rest of his day touring bases, meeting with officers, and reading. Because reading with only a single eye caused eyestrain, he preferred to receive oral reports. Dayan was not a micro-manager but oversaw a few major policy lines that he had decided upon, such as reprisal raids, the training of infantry units in basic skills, preparations for the war with Egypt and, after the war, the integration of armor and jet aircraft into the IDF. He drove home every night when he was not in the field and back to work in the morning, often speeding in the knowledge that no military policeman would give him a ticket.[35]

In December 1953 Ben-Gurion temporarily retired from politics by going to Kibbutz Sde Boker in the Negev, where he herded sheep and read philosophy. (Ironically, as this was a kibbutz founded by former Lehi members, the bodyguard assigned to him was one of the assassins of UN mediator Folke

Bernadotte.) Moshe Sharett (formerly Shertok), who had been the foreign minister, now became the prime minister, and Pinhas Lavon, a Mapai apparatchik, became the new defense minister. Lavon wanted to prove his toughness by approving ever more daring operations, which made Dayan uneasy, as he was used to Ben-Gurion serving as a check on his impulses. Lavon and Dayan thus became rivals.[36]

Lavon approved a scheme to have Egyptian Jews who had been recruited as Israeli agents set off bombs in Western facilities in Egypt in an attempt to cause a rift between Cairo and Washington. While Dayan was touring the United States, studying its combat units, one of these agents was caught when an incendiary bomb accidentally caught fire in his pocket and he was arrested by the police. Under interrogation he confessed and the spy ring was rolled up. This became known as *esek habeesh*, or the affair of the mishap. An investigation was eventually launched into who in Israel gave the order to activate the unit and this became known as the Lavon affair (*parashat Lavon*). The three leading suspects were head of military intelligence Benjamin Gibli, Dayan, and Lavon. Eventually Lavon was forced to resign as defense minister and Ben-Gurion was brought out of retirement to return to one of his two former jobs.[37]

In February 1955 Israel carried out a major reprisal raid against Gaza, causing major casualties to the Egyptians. As a result of this, President Gamal Abdul Nasser decided to actively support the Palestinians in their struggle by training and equipping volunteers to serve as guerrillas to infiltrate Israel. These became known in Arabic as *Fedayeen*, or "self-sacrificers," for their willingness to risk their lives. In August 1955 the first fedayeen raids into southern Israel occurred. Dayan threatened to resign in order to win permission for a reprisal raid that was more extensive than what Sharett wanted the IDF to carry out.[38]

The following month Haim Laskov became deputy chief of staff and, by agreement with Dayan, took up many of the administrative duties, freeing up Dayan to concentrate on preparing for war against Egypt. On September 27, 1955, Nasser publicly announced a major arms deal with Czechoslovakia that involved modern artillery, Soviet tanks, and MiG-15 fighters. This threatened to tip the balance of power in the region in Egypt's favor. Dayan wanted to strike before Egypt had a chance to receive the equipment and absorb it into its military by training its armed forces in how to use the new arms.[39]

In October 1955 Dayan went on a long-delayed vacation to Italy, Switzerland, and France with his wife Ruth. Ben-Gurion sent word that he wanted Dayan to cut short his vacation and return to Israel for discussions. On the flight back Dayan was seated next to an attractive young blonde named Rahel

Rabinovich, who became the great love of the second half of his life. She became his mistress and then in 1972, after he had divorced Ruth, she became his second wife. On November 2, 1955, Ben-Gurion presented his new government to the Knesset with himself as prime minister and Sharett back as foreign minister.[40]

Dayan knew in late 1955 that Ben-Gurion was not yet ready for another war with Egypt, so he tried to escalate the situation against the wishes of both Sharett and Ben-Gurion. On December 11, 1955, Ariel Sharon led an attack on a Syrian military post on the eastern edge of the Kinneret designed to provoke an Egyptian response after Syria had entered into a defense pact with Egypt. Dayan wanted to either provoke Egypt into war with Israel or, failing that, demonstrate that Nasser was a paper tiger who would not honor his agreements. Sharon's men killed 37 soldiers, captured 30 prisoners, and killed 12 civilians.[41]

The raid badly impacted American relations with Israel. Secretary of State John Foster Dulles cancelled a meeting with Sharett to discuss possible American arms sales to Israel, as President Eisenhower probably was not too eager to sell arms to Israel and risk the much larger Arab arms market, much less give Moscow an opportunity to increase its influence in the Middle East. So Shimon Peres, who was then director general of the defense ministry under Ben-Gurion, began to explore the possibility of acquiring modern arms from Britain and France. France was the best prospect, as Nasser was supporting Algerian nationalists who were fighting for independence from France. Thus the two countries had a common enemy and Peres, who was born in Poland and had immigrated to Palestine as a boy, spoke much better French than English at this time.[42]

Dayan began preparing the Israeli army for war against Egypt. In January 1956 he started appearing at Defense Fund drives to collect public donations for purchasing military equipment. On January 15 he briefed all senior officers of the rank of colonel and above regarding his assessment of the situation with Egypt and the military balance. In April 1956 there were momentary border clashes with Egypt along the demilitarized zone, but the crisis passed. On April 30, 1956, Dayan gave an eulogy at the graveside of Roi Rothberg, killed the previous day by fedayeen, in which he stated that it was the mission of his generation to defend the land against the Palestinians from whom they had taken it.[43]

Peres reported to Dayan that, in his opinion, the French were ripe for a military alliance with Israel against Egypt. In a two-day conference in late June in France, Dayan, Peres, and military intelligence head Yehoshafat Harkavi negotiated a working alliance with the French brass. Dayan now began attempting to deescalate the confrontation with Egypt long enough for Israel to absorb French weapons into the IDF and bring Britain into an alliance. In mid–September Sharon carried out a major reprisal raid against a Jordanian police station south of Hebron. This was meant as a feint to shift attention away from Egypt and onto Jordan as a possible target for Israeli military action. In the raid Meir Har-Zion, a commando whom Dayan had come to admire as the best soldier in the Israeli army, was severely wounded in the throat and had to retire from the army.[44]

On October 16–17, in a two-day conference in Sevres outside Paris, Dayan, Peres, and Ben-Gurion worked out with the French leadership and Foreign Minister Selwyn Lloyd of Britain the mechanics of a tripartite war against Egypt. Israel would begin by attacking Egypt and moving toward the Suez Canal. London and Paris would subsequently issue an ultimatum calling on both sides to withdraw from the canal area and then use noncompliance as a pretext to intervene militarily and attempt to overthrow Nasser. Lloyd appeared disgusted by the whole affair, probably due to the prospect of collaborating with Israel. Ben-Gurion was initially noncommittal and allowed himself to be talked into the plan by Dayan and Peres. During the conference Dayan doodled to relieve tension.[45]

The Sinai War (known in Europe as the Suez War) began on October 29 with the drop of part of Sharon's paratrooper brigade at the Parker memorial just outside the eastern end of the Mitla Pass in western Sinai. The rest of the brigade then raced across the Sinai in half-tracks to join up with the paratroopers while armored forces began attacking Egyptian forces along the border. The Egyptians began pulling back into the Sinai, and by November 2 Israeli forces were along the northern half of the Suez Canal and along the southern half the following day. By November 4 Israeli units competing against one another had reached Sharm al-Sheikh, which controlled the Straits of Tiran and the entrance into the Red Sea from the Gulf of Akaba, from both directions. The following day Israeli forces landed on islands in the straits and Anglo-French paratroopers finally arrived. The joint Anglo-French naval task force had been slow in steaming south to Egypt, and there was a major public reaction in both countries in opposition to the intervention. This meant that the European troops were unable to carry out all of their military objectives before a ceasefire was forced on them and Israel by combined superpower pressure.[46]

Dayan failed to court-martial Sharon for disobeying orders or deliberately misinterpreting them and sending a major force into the Mitla Pass. The Egyptians had fired down upon the advancing troops, who lacked air cover and hence were a large part of the Israeli casualties of the campaign. Dayan later wrote as justification for his leniency that "it is better to fight with galloping horses that need to be reined in than to prod and urge oxen that refuse to budge." Sharon remained at the same rank for several years until he was finally promoted to general under Chief of Staff Rabin. Opponents of Sharon's Lebanon war blamed Dayan for not sacking Sharon, as Meir Amit and others urged. But this decision paid dividends for Israel in 1967 and 1973. Dayan was furious with Southern Command leader Assaf Simhoni for attacking with too large a force prematurely and thus taking the risk of betraying Israeli intentions. But Simhoni's light plane crashed in a sandstorm after the war and thus Dayan was spared from having to decide how to deal with him.[47]

Dayan spent most of the war from October 31 onward embedded with Colonel Haim Bar Lev's armored brigade. (Bar Lev eventually became chief of staff after Rabin.) Dayan saw the value of armored forces up close and spent his remaining time as chief of staff after the withdrawal from Sinai transitioning the IDF from an infantry force based on Palmakh ideals to a blitzkrieg force more in line with German Wehrmacht concepts pioneered in 1939–1942. Besides ordering more tanks and jet aircraft, he also started to modernize the World War II surplus navy.[48]

As a battalion commander in the 1948 war and later as chief of staff in the 1956 war, Dayan developed a reputation for personal bravery and fearlessness. Avner Falk interprets this as part of his narcissism—a denial of the possibility of death because of his specialness. It would help to build his personal charisma, which would serve his political career well later in 1967–1973.[49]

Starting in early December American financial pressure on Israel led Ben-Gurion to order Dayan to pull the IDF out of Sinai. The retreat was carried out at the slow pace of 15 miles per week, with mine removal providing the excuse for the pace. Dayan had all units carry out a thorough reconnaissance of the Sinai in case Israel was forced to return in the future. In Gaza Dayan traded basic foodstuffs with the Bedouin for 70 Roman amphorae that were dug up. This was a renewal of Dayan's interest in archaeology that began when he was head of the Southern Command. In the 1960s, when he was defense minister, it would become an obsession and almost cost him his life.[50]

The Sinai War made Dayan an international celebrity, and he became more popular in Israel than Ben-Gurion. This caused problems for Dayan. One day an Italian journalist asked Ruth Dayan how she felt about her husband's affair with Rahel Rabinovich, assuming that she knew about it. She was deeply embarrassed and the marriage collapsed. Dayan basically wanted his wife's permission to carry on the affair with Rahel. He told her that she could have a divorce if she wanted but that he could not change; however, she enjoyed being married to a celebrity and did not ask him for a divorce until 1971.⁵¹

In December 1957 Dayan went on study leave from the IDF for a year and became a student at Hebrew University, studying Middle East politics and international relations. But he rarely attended classes, preferring to conduct gabfests in the student cafeteria and to conduct affairs with students. By mid-1958 Dayan was gravitating toward the Young Guard faction within Mapai. The Old Guard, led by Levi Eshkol and Golda Meir, banned him from making public appearances until his formal release from the IDF on November 1, 1958. They resented Ben-Gurion's attempt to introduce new blood into the party on his side at their expense.⁵²

In 1959 Dayan went on a speaking tour of Mapai branches around the country for the 1959 Knesset campaign. For the election Dayan was in thirteenth place on the Mapai list, just behind Abba Eban, who had recently retired from the Israeli foreign service after serving as ambassador to the United Nations and to Washington. In the election Mapai won 47 seats, up seven from 1955, and had over three times as many votes as the next party, Herut.⁵³

Ben-Gurion appointed Eshkol as his finance minister and Meir as his foreign minister. The following year the Lavon affair reopened, and Lavon became Ben-Gurion's chief rival in the party. Dayan served as agriculture minister from December 1959 to November 1964. In late 1961 Mapai began drawing closer to Ahdut Ha'Avoda, and there was pressure for Dayan to give up his ministry so that it could be offered to his rival, Allon. But Dayan resisted the pressure. He did not attend party steering committee meetings and spent his free time digging up archaeological sites. In 1962–1963 his political relationship with Ben-Gurion began to cool because Dayan disagreed with Ben-Gurion's handling of the Lavon affair and his demands for an independent judicial investigation rather than a party investigation. This eventually forced Ben-Gurion to resign in June 1963, with Eshkol taking his place as prime minister.⁵⁴

Dayan's main innovation as agriculture minister was a program to get Israeli farmers to grow a variety of tomato that Dayan dubbed the "moneymaker," as it was popular in Europe. Dayan figured this would help Israeli farmers and earn foreign currency for the state. But the variety was not popular with Israeli housewifes, who refused to buy it. Farmers did not want to grow one variety of tomato for domestic sales and another for export and so refused to cultivate it; thus, the moneymaker became a money loser.⁵⁵

Eshkol's elevation curtailed Dayan's influence within the cabinet. But Dayan still preferred to remain active in the government's inner circle. When

Ben-Gurion quit Mapai in 1965 to form his own independent party, Rafi, Dayan did not want to follow him but felt compelled to do so out of a sense of personal loyalty. There was a division of labor within the party: Ben-Gurion determined policy, Peres ran the party administration and managed the election campaign, and Dayan provided the charisma.[56]

Rafi was excluded from Eshkol's coalition government because of the acrimony between Ben-Gurion and Eshkol. With only ten seats, Rafi was too small to force its way into the coalition. So Dayan began a two-year period of opposition. He used this "break" from politics to publish a memoir of the Sinai War, *Sinai Diary*, based upon his office diary. The book was a best-seller in Israel in 1965 and was translated into several foreign languages. It was the first of three memoirs that he would publish.[57]

The following year Dayan went to Vietnam for two months in April and wrote a series of articles about the American war effort. He prepared for this task by meeting with a number of American Vietnam experts; then he met in the field with numerous American army and Marine officers and was embedded with the Marines. While in Saigon he ran into Ruth one evening by chance—she was in Southeast Asia consulting—and they had a romantic evening that was one of the last pleasant times in their marriage, but he was not really happy that she had shown up. The articles, however, revived his reputation within Israel and added to his international reputation.[58]

Chapter Three

Defense Minister Dayan

Most histories begin the crisis that led up to the Six-Day War of June 1967 on April 7, when Syrian shelling of three Israeli kibbutzim on the border of the two countries led Israel to respond with airstrikes to silence the Syrian artillery. The Syrians scrambled their aircraft, and in the ensuing dogfight six Syrian fighters were shot down. This created a crisis on the border, with Moscow telling Damascus that the Israeli army was massed along the border and planning to invade. Jerusalem invited the Soviet ambassador to Israel to tour the border and see for himself, but he refused. Dayan had been very critical of the confrontation in the Knesset Foreign Affairs and Defense Committee, where he argued that this would force Nasser to take more provocative steps. such as closing the Straits of Tiran or attempting to bomb the Israeli nuclear reactor at Dimona.[1]

In November 1966 Egypt and Syria had concluded a mutual defense treaty and Israel had invaded the village of Samua south of Hebron in a massive reprisal raid with tanks and mechanized infantry. Israel officially admitted to destroying 41 houses in the village, but Jordan publicly claimed that 100 houses had been destroyed—although an internal Jordanian document said only sixty. The American military attaché in Amman who visited the village afterward supported the Jordanian figure. This led to increased tension in the region.[2]

Dayan became aware of the threat of war when during the military parade in Jerusalem to celebrate Israel's nineteenth anniversary, Rabin received word that the Egyptian army had moved units into the eastern Sinai. The next day Rabin hosted all the former chiefs of staff for a function at defense headquarters in Tel Aviv. He asked them to predict what Nasser would do next. Dayan told him that Nasser would demand the removal of the UN peacekeeping force that had been put in place following the end of the Sinai War. He then predicted that Nasser would go further and close the Straits of

Tiran, as he had in 1955, providing Israel with a *casus belli* (legal case) for war. Dayan's predictions came true the next day. Dayan probably had insight into Nasser's thinking from his attempts in 1955–1956 to provoke Nasser into war.[3]

On May 20 Dayan asked Prime Minister Eshkol for permission to tour the units on the Southern Front. Eshkol gave it to him and Rabin ordered his officers to show everything to Dayan. Before heading south to make the inspection, Dayan telegraphed his daughter Yael, who was overseas, to return home at once. On her father's advice, she attached herself to Ariel Sharon's armored division as a journalist to cover the war. Dayan met with Rabin on May 22 to discuss the situation and what Israel should do. Rabin said Israel could destroy the Egyptian air force with a preemptive attack, but Dayan argued that the present government would never allow this. Dayan's main impression was of how depressed Rabin appeared to be.[4]

On May 23 Dayan toured the Southern Front and spoke with Southern Commander Yehoshua Gavish. He told Gavish that Israel would win the war but suffer massive casualties—20,000 to 30,000 killed. General Avraham Yoffe, one of the three division commanders in the south, told him the next morning that Rabin was sick with nicotine poisoning and had asked Weizman to take over command.[5]

On the next day, May 24, Dayan was mobbed by civilians in Beersheba where he was walking. They wanted him to be defense minister. The following day he asked his brother-in-law, Chief of Operations Ezer Weizman, to allow him to return to active duty. He was then 52—still young enough to serve as a reservist. Dayan wanted to replace Gavish as Southern Commander. He knew the southern geography by heart from his previous periods as front commander and chief of staff, but Rabin did not want a subordinate he could not control. Dayan informed Eshkol that same day that he had requested to be reinstated.[6]

During the final two weeks before the war there was increasing pressure on Eshkol to form a wider war cabinet—a government of national unity, similar to what Britain had during World War II—to deal with the threat. Education Minister Yigal Allon had been in Moscow trying to defuse the situation, but he was back in Israel on May 25. By this time there was already popular pressure on Eshkol to appoint Dayan as defense minister. It took some time for Eshkol to adjust to the idea of appointing someone else to act in this position. He, like Ben-Gurion during Israel's first two wars, was both prime minister and defense minister. Beyond that, his natural inclination was to name Yigal Allon, the hero of the 1948 war, as his defense minister. In addition to having much more combat experience than Dayan, Allon had studied defense theory in both Paris and London with people like writer Liddel Hart. But because Allon was in the Soviet Union, he was not initially available, and then Eshkol resisted until it was too late.[7]

Women in Mapai demonstrated to have Eshkol appoint Dayan as defense minister. Dayan became the candidate for defense minister of both the National Religious Party and Herut in addition to his own Rafi Party; this easily outweighed the support for Allon from Ahdut Ha'Avoda and parts of Mapai. The decisive figure in the NRP was Rabbi Moshe Haim Shapira, who preferred Dayan to Allon because he thought that the former would *prevent* war. Herut leader Menahem Begin had first urged Eshkol to step aside in favor of former Prime Minister Ben-Gurion, but everyone else thought that Ben-Gurion was past his prime and too old. So Begin settled for Ben-Gurion's junior partner in the Sinai War as defense minister. On June 1, 1967, Eshkol agreed to form a national unity government—the first of many in Israel's history—with Rafi and Herut entering the government and Dayan as defense minister.[8]

On his first full two days as defense minister, Dayan reviewed the general staff plans for the war. He came to three main decisions. First, Israel would bypass the Gaza Strip so as not to lose momentum by dealing with refugees. Second, Israel would stop short of the Suez Canal so as not to force the closure of the canal. Third, opening the Straits of Tiran would be a major objective of the war. Israel would concentrate offensively against Egypt while remaining on the defensive opposite Jordan and Syria. These plans would not all work out in practice.[9]

During the war Dayan commuted back and forth between the cabinet in Jerusalem and defense headquarters in the Kirya in Tel Aviv. He competed for influence with Allon and Rabin, who both had access to Eshkol. Rabin countermanded Dayan's instructions regarding Gaza, possibly because of pressure from Allon or simply due to his own memories of not having conquered the Strip in 1948–1949. And IDF forces did advance to the banks of the Suez Canal. Dayan's main influence on the conduct of the war was on the Golan, where, at six in the morning on June 9, he unilaterally gave Northern Commander David Elazar the order to capture the Golan after having argued in the cabinet a few hours earlier against taking the plateau. He bypassed both Eshkol and Rabin, presumably in the knowledge that Rabin had previously argued in favor of taking the Golan. Aside from all this, Dayan's real contribution to the war effort was to raise both civilian and military morale on the eve of the war. "Dayan provided a powerful drive for the readiness to fight," wrote his brother-in-law Ezer Weizman in his memoir.[10]

Dayan was a volatile personality with a tendency to change his mind

Three. Defense Minister Dayan

frequently and to act before he had thoroughly thought something through. On the positive side, he was willing to correct his mistakes. On the negative side, he was often unwilling to admit that he had made any mistakes and pretended that whatever he did was the best decision at the time. Shortly after the Six-Day War Dayan had the three existing bridges over the Jordan River dynamited in order to demarcate Israel's eastern border. Then, shortly afterwards, he had two temporary ad hoc bridges constructed to allow trade between the West Bank and Jordan.[11]

Dayan himself entered the Old City of Jerusalem with Rabin and Central Commander Uzi Narkiss. He later issued a statement saying that Israel had returned to its birthplace, never to leave again. This was in line with the melancholy song "Jerusalem of Gold" by poet Naomi Shemer, which had appeared a few weeks before the war and then became identified with the conflict, with a new verse being added to indicate how everything had changed. Because of the fear that had gripped the Israeli public during the *hamtana*, or "waiting," before the war, many Israelis gave a divine or messianic interpretation to events. Dayan was not really responsible for that, but he did not do much to resist this interpretation. Orthodox Judaism had since biblical times seen irreligious figures as instruments of God's will, and Dayan, with his womanizing, fit that tradition well.[12]

The Israeli government spoke of returning both the Sinai and the Golan in exchange for peace, but never said the same about the West Bank. For the next twenty years, the preferred negotiating partner for Labor Zionism regarding the Palestinian question was Jordan. There were two versions of the Jordanian option, both equally unacceptable to King Hussein, who was either unwilling or unable to make any territorial concession to Israel: territorial compromise (the Allon Plan) and functional compromise (the Dayan Plan). A little over a month after the war, Allon publicly announced his plan. It called for Israel to split the West Bank with an Arab partner (initially conservative local leaders from the West Bank and then, after he did not get any results, with Jordan), so that Israel would retain between 30 and 40 percent of the West Bank in the Jordan Valley and Dead Sea areas, while the populated areas in the interior would be returned to Jordan through a linkage at Jericho. Dayan called simply for the territory to stay intact, with Jordan handling political representation and administrative functions while Israel handled security. The Allon Plan became the unofficial plan of the Labor Party, with Israel's settlement activities being guided by this proposal.[13] Dayan's plan was the more realistic option in that it would allow Jordan to continue to support the Palestinian residents of the West Bank while simply not resisting Israel's military rule over the territory. Jordan did continue to pay the salaries of

West Bank teachers and other officials until July 1988; because Israel was legally obligated to also finance the occupation, these officials drew double salaries.

Dayan favored an invisible occupation in which Israeli bases would be located in rural areas, out of sight and out of mind of the population, and the population would continue to receive services through local officials, who would provide them with Israeli funding and supervision. But successive Israeli governments saw the West Bank as an Israeli colony. Initially it would be a market for Israeli agricultural and industrial products, and cheap Israeli products and jobs in Israel for Palestinian workers served to raise the living standards of the Palestinian population in the first decade of the occupation. Then it became an Israeli settler colony.

Under Labor, settlement took place in the mainly empty Jordan Valley, where settlements were set up in order to help prevent infiltration of guerrillas and guard the approaches against Arab armies. There were also some minor returns of Jews to places from which they had been expelled in 1948: the Etzion Bloc near Bethlehem and the Jewish Quarter of the Old City and Hebron (from which Jews were expelled in 1929). This was a sort of Jewish right of return, while the Jews adamantly denied any Arab right of return to Israel. But starting in 1974–1975, after Dayan was out of office, Gush Emunim (the bloc of the faithful) began erecting settlements in the heart of the West Bank. These were only a handful until the Likud came to power in 1977, and then the trickle became a flood.[14]

Dayan appointed Shlomo Gazit, a former head of military intelligence, as coordinator of activities in the West Bank. Gazit claimed that Dayan's occupation policy rested on three pillars: an invisible occupation, normalization, and a wise penal policy (this meant releasing prisoners periodically after they had spent a few years behind bars for security offenses so that they did not become martyrs).[15]

Repeatedly between 1968 and 1977 King Hussein met with a variety of Israeli government leaders and ministers in "secret" meetings to which he usually piloted himself by helicopter. Hussein always came to these meetings accompanied by Riad al-Masri, who was at various times foreign minister and prime minister, and other times simply an influential and trusted advisor; the Israeli leaders who met Hussein included Dayan, Allon, Eshkol, Golda Meir, Rabin, and Peres. Most territorial offers made by Israel were in line with the Allon Plan, but some were more generous than others. Hussein rejected them all because he did not feel that he could safely accept anything less than a 100 percent return of the territories lost in 1967. But the meetings were not a complete waste of time. In them the two sides would discuss security matters, including fedayeen operations and Jordanian efforts to stop them, Israeli policies toward the Palestinian population and other matters (such as regional political developments). Besides providing for security cooperation, the meetings served to educate the two leaderships about the red lines and thinking of the other side. Whereas many Americans, British, and Israelis admired King Hussein and referred to him as the "plucky little king" (or PLK, for short), Dayan thought that Hussein was a spoiled playboy who had lost half his kingdom by entering into a war that he should not have, and then refusing to accept realistic offers from Israel.[16]

In 1968 the three separate labor parties (Ahdut Ha'Avoda, Mapai, Rafi) joined together to form the Israeli Labor Party. Levi Eshkol was a sick man in 1968, burdened with a weak heart, and the succession battle was lining up. The three separate parties soon dissolved into distinct camps around the succession: the Dayan camp consisted of Rafi and Mapai supporters who had remained loyal to the party in 1965, and the Allon camp of Ahdut Ha'Avoda and the Mapai Old Guard. When Levi Eshkol died suddenly of a heart attack in February 1969, Golda Meir was brought out of retirement to serve as a compromise candidate for prime minister that both camps could accept. Dayan sent a message to General Yosef Geva, director general of Allon's office of immigrant absorption, stating that he was not a candidate for the top job because he was happy as defense minister. But Allon did not trust Dayan. "Do not believe that sly fox," Allon told Geva.[17]

In Dayan's first few years as defense minister, his first task was fighting the War of Attrition. This is not usually numbered among Israel's major wars, partly because there is no widespread agreement about its starting point or who was included on the Arab side. The broadest dating of the war extends from June 1967 to August 1970, and includes the fighting in the Suez Canal area and Israeli air strikes into Egypt, the anti-fedayeen campaign along the Jordan River, and occasional actions on the Golan. A more restricted date range has the war starting in October 1968—when Egyptian artillery hit Israeli positions with a major barrage and Israel retaliated against Egyptian oil refineries—and continuing until August 1970, with the conflict limited to the Egyptian front. Another, shorter version has the war from March 1969, when President Nasser officially declared a war of attrition, until August 1970. All agree upon the August 1970 end date because that is when a ceasefire between Egypt and Israel, mediated by Secretary of State William Rogers, went into effect. The widest definition is mainly used as a means of recognizing military service; most analysts use one of the latter two definitions.

Dayan behaved as defense minister much as he had as chief of staff: concentrating on a few areas of policy that interested him while leaving most administrative tasks to his subordinates. He toured units along the Suez Canal, oversaw the construction of the fortifications of the Bar Lev line in 1968–1969, went along with units on patrol against fedayeen infiltration in the Jordan Valley and toured the Golan Heights. The idea was to get a first-hand understanding of the security challenges that the troops in the field were facing, along with how well the commanders in the field were coping with them. He was nearly killed when he was caught in an Egyptian military barrage in October 1968.[18]

One of the biggest changes that occurred during Dayan's tenure as defense minister was the conversion of the IDF from European, mainly French, arms to American weapons. Before the Six-Day War, President Johnson had agreed to sell Israel A-4 Skyhawk attack jets. These began to arrive in Israel in 1968. They were followed by F-4 Phantom fighter-bombers a year later. The Israeli army also began converting over from British Centurion tanks to American M-60 Patton tanks and M-60A1 tanks, which were both a step up from the M-48 Patton tanks that Israel had bought from Germany (with American approval) a few years earlier. In small arms, the IDF began to convert from the Belgian 7.62 mm FN automatic rifle to the American M-16 automatic rifle. Eventually Israeli infantry soldiers would end up with a combination of Israeli-designed Galil assault rifles, M-16s and captured Kalashnikov AK-47 assault rifles.[19] Much of this involved the integration of weapons that Rabin had chosen for the IDF when he was chief of staff. But the process of conversion sped up after France imposed an arms embargo on Israel at the start of the Six-Day War and then, after lifting it, reimposed it in December 1968 after Israel blew up numerous Arab passenger jets at Beirut International Airport as a reprisal for Arab government support for Palestinian terrorism.[20]

Security policy was decided by Meir's "kitchen cabinet," consisting of herself, Dayan, Allon, Finance Minister Pinhas Sapir, Foreign Minister Abba Eban, and Minister of Information Israeli Galili. Because Golda Meir was herself a hawk and territorial maximalist, as were Ahdut Ha'Avoda members Allon and Galili, and Eban and Sapir were doves, Dayan was the centrist voice on security policy. But all agreed that Israel would not give up any territory without a formal peace agreement with any of its Arab neighbors. But because Dayan was unwilling to push for his views, he would usually simply offer his view or advice to Meir and then defer to her. It was a pattern that started when he was chief of staff and then agriculture minister under Ben-Gurion, and it would continue while he was foreign minister under Begin. Possibly because he changed his mind so often, Dayan may have subconsciously not trusted his own judgment and so preferred to have someone over him making the final decision.[21]

Dayan believed in using overwhelming force in reprisals in order to gain the upper hand. He supported the escalation of the use of air power against Egypt during 1970 after Ambassador Rabin indicated that this would not be a problem as far as Washington was concerned. On the Israeli side the War of Attrition was mostly fought by the Israeli Air Force (IAF) and by commando units—Israel's version of the U.S. Navy Seals—and Sayeret Matkal (headquarters reconnaissance) and other special forces units. Ehud Barak and the Netanyahu brothers got plenty of action during the War of Attrition. The Egyptians fought it mainly with artillery and air defense units, most of them manned or supervised by Soviet advisors. The Soviet Union escalated its involvement in the region with its input of pilots, air defense units and other personnel starting in January 1970.[22]

During his time as defense minister Dayan engaged in his two main leisure activities: having romantic intrigue and exploring archaeology. It was due to an archaeological mishap that Dayan found himself in the hospital as Israel was engaging in its largest military action since the 1967 war. In March 1968, the IDF invaded Jordan in a major reprisal known as the Battle of Karameh. The Jordanian army decided to fight alongside Fatah, and it was the Jordanians who caused most of the Israeli casualties. While all this was taking place, Dayan was lying in a hospital fighting for his life after a dig site caved in on him. A companion managed to pull him out, but not before he sustained several cracked ribs and a damaged larynx that prevented him from speaking for several months. In the hospital he was visited not only by Jewish well wishers but also by Arabs, something that, after the Intifada, would be inconceivable for any Israeli leader.[23]

In his six years as defense minister Dayan was involved in a number of international negotiations. The first were the negotiations among Egypt, Jordan and Israel mediated by UN mediator Gunnar Jarring. These never really got off the ground and went nowhere. Next were the negotiations among the same three countries mediated by American Secretary of State William Rogers in an attempt to reach a comprehensive solution to the conflict. These took place in 1969 and, once again, did not really go anywhere. Finally, in 1970, Rogers decided to focus on ending the War of Attrition between Egypt and Israel by concentrating on that single front. After a dogfight between Soviet MiG pilots and Israeli F-4 Phantoms over Egypt that resulted in six Soviet aircraft being downed on July 30, Cairo decided that it would agree to Israeli terms and call a ceasefire. Egypt, however, cheated on the ceasefire by moving up its surface-to-air missiles after the ceasefire went into effect. Herut withdrew from the government of national unity in response to Meir's acceptance of the ceasefire because she did so under UN Security Council Resolution

242, which called for Israel to give up conquered territory in exchange for peace.[24]

The following month was the infamous Black September in Jordan, when Palestinian terrorists hijacked three civilian airliners to an abandoned airfield in Jordan and blew up the aircraft after removing the passengers. At this point the Jordanian army intervened and a civil war broke out between the army and the Palestinian fedayeen. Syrian tanks intervened and invaded northern Jordan, but the Syrian air force under Hafiz al-Assad refused to intervene after the Jordanian air force attacked the tanks. Assad wanted the intervention to fail so that the government would appear weak and he could seize power, which he did two months later. A former Iraqi general who was part of the Jordanian military likewise pulled off an intelligence deception to keep the Iraqi army units stationed in Jordan from intervening. The net result was that the Palestinians were thoroughly defeated, and the fedayeen organizations like Fatah, the Popular Front for the Liberation of Palestine (PFLP) and the Democratic Front for the Liberation of Palestine (DFLP) were forced to relocate to southern Lebanon, which then became Fatahland.[25]

During the crisis President Nasser of Egypt suffered a fatal heart attack. His successor was Muhammad Anwar al-Sadat. Sadat, who was one of the original Free Officers who carried out the 1952 coup that overthrew the monarchy, was regarded as a weak and comic figure. No one in Israel initially took him seriously. He announced that 1971 would be the Year of Decision in the confrontation with Israel. Then, in July 1972, he expelled from Egypt most of the Soviet advisors who had entered three years before. Israel interpreted this as making him less able to go to war, but the opposite was true.[26]

Israeli military intelligence, Aman, and the Mossad had a doctrinal belief that Egypt could not win a war against Israel because of Israel's air superiority. So as long as Egypt was unable to neutralize the Israeli air force, Egypt would not go to war. It never occurred to anyone, including Middle East analysts from the Central Intelligence Agency in Washington, that Egypt might go to war with no intention of winning militarily just to shake up the political situation. Dayan, however, was worried about intelligence reports of Egyptian movements, and so he called for a partial mobilization in May 1973. Nothing happened and the IDF demobilized.[27]

The Mossad had a secret agent in Cairo, who just happened to be Nasser's son-in-law. In reality, this source was probably either a double agent working with or known to Egyptian intelligence, and used to mislead Israel.

Sadat had recruited Assad for a united attack on Israel on October 6, 1973, which fell during both the Muslim holy month of Ramadan and the Jewish holy day of Yom Kippur—the Day of Atonement—when most Jews were in synagogue and many soldiers were on leave from the Egyptian and Syrian fronts. The two Arab militaries had to compromise on the time of attack so that neither had an optimum time. The war began at 1:55 p.m. (after the Israeli agent told his handler the day before that the war would begin at 6 p.m.).

Dayan was alerted to the report by Chief of Staff David "Dado" Elazar, who proposed a mobilization on both fronts for a preemptive strike. Dayan did not want a preemptive attack or a general mobilization, as he wanted it to be clear that the Arabs were the aggressors so that Israel would have support in Washington and guaranteed resupply of arms. Dayan, as he did whenever he had a major disagreement with Elazar, took the issue to Meir. Meir refused permission for a preemptive strike but allowed the mobilization to go ahead.[28]

Sooner than Israel expected, hordes of Egyptian infantry crossed the Suez Canal in rafts, using water cannons to erode the Israeli physical barriers along the east bank of the canal. The small "forts" of the Bar Lev line were soon surrounded and most of the infantry inside were either killed or forced to surrender. Only a few of the forts remained intact after three days. The Egyptians had practiced the crossing for months and carried it out almost flawlessly.

On the Golan the Israeli tank crews were forced to retreat. Dayan, at the Kirya headquarters, quickly decided two things. First, his "bird theory" of Arab fighting capabilities, developed 25 years earlier in the May 1948 Degania defense and during Operation Dani, no longer applied; the Arabs were both confident and competent. Second, he decided on October 9 (by which point the IAF had already lost 10 percent of its combat aircraft) that because of the much shorter distances in the Northern Command, a Syrian breakthrough out of the Golan had to be prevented at all costs. If the Syrians broke into Israel proper, they could possibly cut the country in two and threaten Haifa, Israel's third largest city. If the Egyptians broke out into the Sinai, they could be destroyed in the desert by the IAF or by Israeli armor. As a result, most reserves were rushed initially to the Golan to stabilize that front, while the IDF organized a secondary defense line in the northern Sinai from which to organize a counterattack against the Egyptians.

Traditional American and Israeli accounts of the war published in the 1970s have Dayan panicking and falling apart. He is said to have told Meir in a call from the front, "The Third Temple [code for the state of Israel] is in danger." Avner Cohen, Israel's leading nuclear historian, and others have claimed that Israeli nuclear weapons were on stand-by to be delivered by aircraft on the Golan. Dayan's defenders claim, however, that he was simply much quicker than others to realize the seriousness of the situation, and that much of the failure of the first few days was caused by other generals operating under old assumptions that were now passé.[29]

Dayan visited the front to see how things were developing, briefed editors of the major dailies on the course of the war, and took part in the discussion of senior officers on where to end the advance into Egypt. When touring the front he refused to give actual orders, which he allowed to flow down the chain of command, but instead gave "ministerial advice." (Such advice, however, could be overlooked until actual orders came through.) He left it up to Elazar to manage the war and discipline officers when necessary.[30]

The IDF was forced to develop new tactics to deal with Soviet anti-tank missiles, which were deployed in large numbers with forward infantry units along the Suez Canal, and with Soviet surface-to-air missiles (SAMs), which were integrated in a layered defense to provide overlapping protection against Israeli aircraft for several miles on both sides of the canal. Eventually the IDF abandoned its purely armored formations and went back to using combined arms attacks, in which mechanized infantry in armored personnel carriers or halftracks would accompany the tanks and use machine-gun fire and mortars to suppress Egyptian infantry. The Soviet Sagger anti-tank missiles were wire guided and had to be directed by the firer; thus, if the crew could be killed or forced to take cover out of sight of the target, the missile would crash harmlessly into the ground or veer wildly away.

After a week the IDF had not only stabilized the Syrian front but also driven deep into Syrian territory so that Damascus was within range of Israeli 175 mm guns. On the Egyptian front, things didn't go so well. A major Israeli counterattack on the third day of the war failed, resulting in major losses. Israeli Southern Commander Shmuel Gonen had taken over command from Sharon in July 1973, and so was new to his position. After the failed attack Dayan suggested to Elazar that Sharon and Gonen switch places so that Sharon would resume his old command and Gonen would resume a command level that he had already mastered. Elazar rejected that suggestion, along with one to simply relieve Gonen of command and instead placed former chief of staff Haim Bar Lev as an additional layer between Gonen and Elazar so that Bar Lev would have to approve all of Gonen's major decisions.[31]

But on October 14, under pressure from Assad to relieve Israeli pressure on the Syrians, the Egyptian army launched a major attack from its bridgeheads on the eastern side of the Seuz Canal. They ended up losing about 250 tanks. The following night, in the early hours of the morning, General Sharon led a very quiet crossing of the canal at a point between two Egyptian armies—in combat the dividing line between two units is often a vulnerable area, as there is a tendency by each unit to assume the other has responsibility for security. Once the bridgehead had been established and secured, large numbers of Israeli tanks and infantry were ferried across the canal. The Israeli tanks were then free to go on the hunt and destroy Egyptian SAM units, which in turn opened up holes in the Egyptian air defenses that could then be exploited by the IAF.[32]

By this time, October 14, American resupply (in the form of C-5 Galaxy aircraft stuffed full of tanks and munitions) was arriving in an air bridge from the United States. And replacement A-4s and F-4s were being flown across the Atlantic to the Azores and then on to Israel. With the knowledge that losses of tanks and planes would be made good, commanders were free to risk them in attacks.

Israel had actually asked for a ceasefire on the Egyptian front on October 12—against the advice of Secretary of State Henry Kissinger. But Sadat turned the request down.[33] Sadat remained ignorant of the serious nature of the Israeli crossing of the canal for several days. This allowed the IDF to conquer much of the area of the Egyptian Second Army along the west bank and to surround the Egyptian Third Army along the east bank. The IDF had been attacked by numbers of tanks, artillery tubes and aircraft similar to those the Axis Powers employed in Operation Barbarossa against the Soviet Army in World War II. But instead of taking two years to turn the situation around, the IDF had done so in only two weeks.

Kissinger resisted Soviet pressure for a ceasefire for several days until October 22, when one was finally negotiated in Moscow. The following day, Israel used the Egyptians' attack on Israeli vehicles—sent forward to provoke just such a reaction—as an excuse to launch a major assault on the Egyptian city of Suez. Finally, on October 24, eighteen days after the start of the war, a ceasefire went into effect.[34] It was Israel's longest non-static war since 1948—in fact, the longest period of sustained maneuver combat since May–June 1948.

Egypt and Israel set up negotiations after the war at Kilometer 101 in order to work out arrangements for resupplying Egyptian units surrounded by the IDF. Nixon had ordered Meir to allow a resupply on October 25 after Dayan initially refused. The negotiations made quick progress and Kissinger decided to shut them down so that they would not preclude his own mediation, which he felt was necessary in order to both end the Arab oil embargo against the West and help effect a change of alliances within Egypt from the Soviet camp to the American camp.

Kissinger spent the first two months after the war arranging a ceremonial

Geneva Conference on the Middle East hosted by the two superpowers, which he would then use as cover for his own shuttle diplomacy in the region. Israel favored such a conference because it met a basic Israeli demand of meeting the Arabs face to face and forcing them to deal with Israel as a reality. This would be useful for Labor's election campaign. The conference met just before Christmas for two days and never reconvened.[35]

Elections had originally been scheduled for October 1973, but because of the war they were rescheduled for December 31, 1973. Ariel Sharon had formed the Likud from four smaller parties of the right the month before the war. Labor lost five seats in the election, and so, with just under 40 percent of the vote, the Labor Alignment ended up with 51 seats to 39 for the Likud on its first time out—up from 29 for Gahal in 1969. Meir formed a new government with Dayan still as defense minister and Abba Eban as foreign minister.[36]

In October, Kissinger returned from Moscow with a ceasefire and met with Dayan. Dayan respected Kissinger but feared his power, and was afraid that the Arab oil embargo would come before the need for an interim agreement in Kissinger's calculations. In 1971 he had proposed to Meir that Israel pull back to the passes in the Sinai in exchange for a non-belligerency agreement with Egypt. Alon and Galili had wanted a much shorter pullback that was unrealistic and Meir had then been opposed to the idea. Now, two years and a war later, Meir gave Dayan permission to propose a separation-of-forces agreement that would allow Egypt to keep limited forces on the east bank of the Suez Canal. On December 1, 1973, Dayan presented the idea in Washington to Kissinger as an Israeli suggestion.

On January 4, 1974—only four days after Israel's election—Dayan again presented the separation-of-forces agreement to Kissinger, this time as a formal Israeli proposal. Kissinger listened very carefully and decided that the situation was ripe for a round of blitz "shuttle diplomacy" between Jerusalem and Egypt in order to conclude an agreement. The negotiations, which will be covered in greater detail in the next chapter, made quick progress and an agreement was signed on January 18, 1974.[37]

On February 3, 1974, Lieutenant Motti Ashkenazi, who had been in command of one of the Bar Lev forts that did not surrender to the Egyptians, began a protest vigil outside government offices (*kiryat hamemshala*) in Jerusalem. Six weeks later there was a mass protest rally of 25,000, comprising mainly young reservists and the parents of those killed and wounded in the war. "One could not remain indifferent," wrote Dayan. "In any case, I was certainly affected."[38]

On November 21 as a result of public pressure, Meir appointed an inde-

Three. Defense Minister Dayan

Meir government members vote for new Rabin government, June 3, 1974. From left to right: Defense Minister Dayan, unknown, Prime Minister Golda Meir, Labor Minister Yigal Allon. Photograph by Moshe Milner, Israeli Government Press Office.

pendent commission headed by the president of the Supreme Court, Shimon Agranat (the body was later named the Agranat Commission), to hold hearings on the responsibility for the conduct of the war. It was to deal with the intelligence failure that led to Israel's surprise and the preparation of the IDF for war. Under the rules negotiated for the commission, a minister would not be found culpable if he was following the professional advice of an IDF senior officer charged with responsibility for a particular activity. (The commission's report did not tackle the issue of ministerial responsibility, under which a government is deemed responsible for actions taking place under its authority.) The Agranat Commission issued its preliminary report on April 1, 1974. It placed most of the blame for Israel ill-preparedness, and for the heavy initial losses, on Chief of Staff Elazar and Aman head Major General Eliyahu Zeira. Four intelligence officers were either sacked or forbidden to work in the intelligence field. Southern Commander Gonen was relieved of command pending the final report.[39]

Dayan told Meir several times he was willing to step aside as defense minister and serve as a sacrificial lamb in order to allow her and the party to continue to function. But she had confidence in him and rejected his offer when she formed a new government in January 1974, and again after he tendered his resignation following the preliminary report of the Agranat Commission and the adverse public reaction to the failure to censure Dayan.

Dayan initially wanted his Rafi faction to stay out of the government in March, but after seeing an intelligence report on a possible Syrian attack he decided to rejoin the government. The attack never materialized and Dayan was accused of inventing it. On April 11, Meir resigned, and it was decided to hold an election for the new leader of the Labor Party. Rabin narrowly beat Peres.[40]

The government of Meir and Dayan stayed on as a caretaker government while the leadership election was held and a new government was formed. They agreed to give up power as soon as the Israeli-Syrian separation-of-forces agreement was negotiated and finalized. The agreement was signed in Geneva on June 3, and the next day Dayan left the ministry after just over seven years as defense minister. This has so far remained a record in the post–1967 period.[41]

Chapter Four

Dayan as Negotiator

For the last six years of his public career (not counting his run for the Knesset at the head of his own party in the last months of his life) Dayan was involved in negotiations with Arabs, as he had been early in his military career, a period that overlapped by about six months his time as defense minister. Dayan was involved in two sets of negotiations with Egypt—one that lasted for ten days, and a second that lasted for about eighteen months from start to finish—and one with Syria that lasted for about five weeks.

Henry Kissinger was involved in negotiations between Israel and its Arab neighbors from November 1973 to August 1975. Early on he developed and perfected what came to be known as "shuttle diplomacy," or "step-by-step diplomacy." Every month Kissinger would make a trip to the region and speak to the governments of the parties that he was interested in bringing to an agreement. He would also meet with King Hussein of Jordan, America's closest Arab ally in the region, and with the Saudi royal leadership, as well as either the Algerian leadership or the Moroccan monarch. The idea was to build support for his diplomacy among the leaders with whom he was negotiating, and to get a feel for regional thinking regarded the conflict. Later he would apply this same technique in his unsuccessful African shuttle diplomacy aimed at ending the conflicts in Rhodesia and Namibia in 1976.[1]

When Kissinger decided that the two sides were close enough together to reach an agreement, he would clear his calendar for ten days or two weeks and head out to the region in his Boeing 707. Just aft of the cockpit Kissinger had a seating area where he could meet with his top advisors; there was also a copier and teletype communications equipment aboard the plane, as well as a sleeping compartment for the secretary. The back half of the plane was reserved for the reporters who accompanied him on his shuttles. There were no freelancers on board—all the journalists came from the leading television networks and the major American newspapers and wire services.

Typically, Kissinger would arrive in Israel in the late afternoon at Ben Gurion International Airport, about halfway between Jerusalem and Tel Aviv. He would be picked up at the airport by the Israeli foreign minister and chat with him on the way to Jerusalem. When they arrived, they would head straight to the government meeting room. There would be fruit and other snacks around the table, and Kissinger would begin by describing what had happened since they last met. The ministers would then discuss what the government's new position should be, with each minister having his say (Meir was the only female minister). Although the most relevant ministers were the prime minister, the defense minister and the foreign minister, because of Israel's system of multiparty coalition government, many other ministers were important in order to win wide support for any agreement in the Knesset.

There might be a break for a catered dinner around eight or nine. Then negotiations would continue until sometime after midnight. Kissinger would go to his suite at the King David and catch a few hours of sleep before rising for a late breakfast over telex reports. After this, he was off to the airport with the foreign minister to catch a flight around 10 a.m. to Cairo, Suez, Ismailiya or wherever Sadat would be hosting him the next day (or Damascus during the Syrian shuttle).

The journalists would spend their time shopping and filing stories over the wire service while Kissinger was busy meeting with the government. They had a set time to be at the airport, and Kissinger's plane would wait for no one. Kissinger would wander to the rear of the plane and brief the press as a whole under the very thin disguise of "a senior American official" or else invite a particular reporter up to the front of the plane for an interview. Because Kissinger wanted only favorable media coverage and seats on the plane were at a premium, he played by "Vegas rules": what was seen and heard on the plane stayed on the plane, except for authorized leaks and briefings. So details like Kissinger's nervous habit of stuffing himself with food when things were not going well had to wait to be revealed when reporters wrote their books after he was no longer in office.[2]

Kissinger supplied relatively few of the ideas that went into the final agreements reached between Israel and its Arab neighbors. Instead, he relied on the Israeli government—mostly with Dayan supplying the ideas in the first two sets of agreements—on Sadat, and on his own staff, which included Assistant Secretary of State for Near East Affairs Joe Sisco. Kissinger mainly contributed the atmospherics and controlled the pace of the bargaining. If he thought that Israel was conceding too quickly, he would advise the government and pocket part of the concession for later use so that a situation did not arise in which the Arabs suddenly upped their demands beyond the ability of Israel to deliver. When he thought that Israel was not conceding enough or was moving at too slow a pace, he would give the Israelis a lecture about how they would suddenly find themselves isolated; there would be dire consequences, he told them, and he would be helpless to do anything to save them from their own shortsightedness.[3] Another of his important functions was to educate both parties about the constraints and limitations on the other side so that neither side would expect too much from the other. And he would entertain both sides with amusing stories about their opposite numbers and, if need be, about his own government and his experiences with the Chinese, the Russians, the Vietnamese, and so forth.[4]

Kissinger had several things going for him as a mediator. As a diplomatic historian and someone who had been involved in numerous negotiations as national security advisor during Nixon's first term, he had lots of negotiating experience to fall back on. He also had a theoretical understanding of the dynamics of negotiations. While the theory of international mediation was pretty underdeveloped when Kissinger first embarked on his shuttle diplomacy, he seemed to have a natural grasp of the process and produced much material for subsequent studies.[5] He had tremendous stamina, which came in handy during the marathon negotiating involved in the Israeli-Syrian separation-of-forces agreement. As Rabin later remarked, Kissinger could show up at any hour and look like he had just had ten hours of sleep. Kissinger also had the backing of the two presidents he worked for, and autonomous decision-making power. Nixon was struggling with the Watergate affair when Kissinger was involved in his first two negotiations in the Middle East and was desperate for any achievement that might stave off impeachment. Gerald Ford, when he came into office in August 1974, was relatively inexperienced in foreign policy, but he knew Kissinger personally and knew better than to try to restrain the secretary. Kissinger had an over-sized ego that did not allow him to believe that anything was beyond his powers once he had decided that it was humanly possible. This combination of knowledge and experience, drive, self-confidence and presidential support made him a formidable negotiator. He also had the resources of a superpower in its prime at his disposal to influence or coerce the negotiating parties.[6]

From the Yom Kippur ceasefire until Christmas 1973, Kissinger was mainly focused on arranging the Geneva Middle East Conference, which was attended by the two superpowers, Israel, Egypt, and Jordan (but not by Syria— President Hafiz al-Assad refused to accept UN Security Council Resolution 242, upon which the conference and subsequent diplomacy was based). The conference arrangements mostly involved Israeli Foreign Minister Abba Eban and not Dayan. Dayan's diplomatic work really began in January 1974.[7]

Kissinger had two main goals for his shuttle diplomacy: first, to get the Organization of Petroleum Exporting Countries (OPEC) to lift its boycott of sales to Western countries without appearing to give in to Arab blackmail; second, to get Egypt to join the Western camp by cutting its ties with Moscow after Sadat realized that he could more easily recover the Sinai through American diplomacy than through Soviet arms. The subsequent agreement with Syria was mainly intended to provide diplomatic cover in the Arab world for Egypt's agreement and for future agreements. If Kissinger could also lure Assad into cutting or lessening his ties with Moscow, that would be a bonus.[8]

Israel had three main aims in negotiating with its Arab neighbors. First, it wished to recover its prisoners of war. The exchange was made conditional on the diplomacy (and it was Meir's main reason for going along with the process). Second, Israel needed to please Washington and keep American arms and aid coming. Third, it was important to separate Egypt from the other confrontation states and take it out of the military balance between Israel and the Arabs. This was an aim pursued mainly by Rabin, but it might have been a major consideration for Dayan as well.[9]

Because of the previous talks at Kilometer 101, the negotiations with Egypt went quite smoothly. Dayan was quite engaged in this shuttle exercise. The negotiation concerned the Suez Canal area and Dayan wanted an agreement so that the Egyptians could reopen the canal and thereby have an incentive not to go back to war with Israel. The Egyptian-Israeli separation-of-forces deal was the model for subsequent agreements, with its architecture of a buffer zone in the middle surrounded by symmetrical limited-forces zones in which there were strict limits on the number of tanks and on the number and size of artillery tubes—a five-zone model. Dayan played a very useful role in the negotiations on January 15 in adjusting the lines and the force limitations to take Egyptian objections into account. After the Egyptian-Israeli agreement was signed in Geneva in January, Kissinger turned his attention to the Syrian front.[10]

In February Kissinger worked out with Assad the mechanics of an exchange of information on Israeli prisoners held by Syria, which would be released once an agreement was signed, along with the timing of Israel's transmission of a proposal to withdraw its forces. Jerusalem, however, was not really eager for an agreement with Damascus. Over the decades the Syrians had cultivated the image in the Arab world of being the most ideologically radical of Israel's neighbors, while at the same time the least competent militarily. And the Syrian Ba'ath (Renaissance) Party was the most radical of the various ideological trends in Syria. So while the Israeli government was ready and willing to believe that Sadat now wanted peace, it did not believe that the same was true of Assad. And while negotiations were under way, Israel engaged in artillery duels with the Syrians inside Syria and Syrian commandos attacked IDF positions. Because of the narrower territory of the Golan compared to the Sinai, Israel had much less room to maneuver. Jerusalem was quite willing to withdraw from all the territory captured during the Yom Kippur War, but Damascus also wanted to recover some of the territory lost in 1967.[11]

After his February trip to the region, Kissinger returned to Washington with little agreed on except for the mechanics of the prisoner information exchange. In mid–March the Arab oil producers in OPEC announced that the oil embargo against the United States was being provisionally lifted. On March 29 Dayan brought to Washington a plan for an Israeli withdrawal to a line east of Kuneitra, along with a request for a thousand tanks and 4,000 armored personnel carriers. Kissinger informed Dayan that Assad would not accept this line but told him not to give up any settlements in the Golan in the meantime. By the end of April Kissinger felt that he had achieved enough to justify a return to the region in order to wrap up an agreement. He flew to the Middle East on April 28.[12]

Damascus was demanding all of Kuneitra, plus three hills that overlooked the city, which was the capital of the Golan. Soon the negotiations became centered on the hills and the city. On May 15 Kissinger began introducing his own proposals into the talks in an attempt to break the stalemate between Jerusalem and Damascus. On May 19 Assad said he would allow Israel to keep the three hills if Israel would promise not to station any artillery that could reach Kuneitra on the hills. On May 23 Assad agreed to a larger UN peacekeeping force in the buffer zone, as Israel wanted, along with a ten-kilometer-wide buffer zone and fifteen-kilometer-wide limited-forces zones. On May 26 Kissinger began to have his staff draft the final agreement and Assad attempted to reopen some issues that Kissinger thought were already settled (this was really a probe to see how resolute Jerusalem was, and he backed down the following day). On May 28 Assad gave his private assurance to Kissinger that he would not allow terrorist attacks on Israel from his lines. The following day Kissinger announced that an agreement had been reached.

Two days later Israeli and Syrian military representatives signed the agreement in Geneva. The agreement consisted of a short public agreement, a map, and letters between the U.S. government and the leaders of the two sides specifying the private assurances that had been made by the other side. In the Israeli-Syrian agreement there was an extra layer of two limited-range artillery zones adjacent to the limited-forces zones for a total of five areas altogether.[13]

During the midst of these negotiations, Dayan had to deal with two separate terrorist attacks in northern Israel. The first was on the northernmost town in Israel, Kiryat Shmona, on April 11, before the negotiations had begun in earnest. A three-man terrorist squad from George Habash's Popular Front for the Liberation of Palestine (PFLP) infiltrated the town and attacked a school, which turned out to be empty. So they left and entered an apartment building, going from apartment to apartment and murdering the residents. Before the three were killed in a barricaded room on the top floor, they had killed 16 civilians, half of them children.

On May 15, 1974, three terrorists belonging to the Democratic Front for the Liberation of Palestine (DFLP), a splinter organization from the PFLP, infiltrated the town of Ma'alot in the western Galilee, about 20 kilometers east of Nahariya. The three attacked a bus of women from a factory, killing several, and then went door to door and started killing anyone who answered. They subsequently took over a school building holding 100 students and four teachers. The terrorists demanded the release of their comrades held in Israeli prisons. The government agreed to release the prisoners, but it wanted the release to be simultaneous—it did not trust that the terrorists would release the children once their comrades reached Damascus. So Israeli paratroopers and Sayeret Matkal commandos stormed the building and killed the terrorists. But because they made a mistake about which floor they should enter on, when they threw a phosphorus grenade they gave the terrorists time to kill several of the hostages while they waited for the room to clear of smoke. The terrorists killed more than 20 of the hostages and wounded 68, including a girl who had signaled to Dayan to get back as one of the terrorists took aim at him while Dayan was observing. Dayan's nephew Uzi, a reservist major, took part in the rescue attempt.[14]

So between dealing with these terrorist attacks (and the public criticism of the deaths associated with them), with the attacks on his presence in the government, and with his normal duties, Dayan was rather distracted during the negotiations with Syria. He was not nearly as useful as he had been earlier, and as he would be in the negotiations with Egypt to come as foreign minister.

As soon as Dayan was released from the defense ministry, he felt it was time to set about writing his memoirs. It was unlikely that he would ever be prime minister or even return to a major cabinet job within the Labor Party, and he had his performance in three wars as defense minister, one as chief of staff and one as a battalion commander and then front commander to write about.

Dayan wanted his daughter Yael, a professional novelist and writer, to ghostwrite his memoir. She was working on a novel of her own and thought that, based on his first memoir, *Sinai Diary,* he was a good writer and did not need assistance. But he blackmailed her into helping him by threatening not to write the book at all. In the end she wrote mostly about his childhood, presumably based upon what she knew from being told as a child and from his first wife's memoir. After a few weeks of correcting her first drafts and having her expand on certain points, Dayan took over and wrote the bulk of the book. Although the memoir has the usual faults of the genre—such as one-sided recollections of controversial events—it did not have the defensive tone and the bitterness and rancor of Rabin's memoir, which appeared only three years later. It is considered one of the more interesting memoirs by Israeli statesmen, largely because Dayan was directly involved in so many important events in Israel's history from before independence until the aftermath of the Yom Kippur War. It took him about eighteen months to write the book.[15]

Dayan also wrote *Living with the Bible,* a book based on his personal memories, his antiquities and the Bible, relating biblical heroes like Joshua with modern-day Israeli figures. This was a bridge between his memoirs and his antiquities, which he now displayed in a large garden.[16] Dayan had married Rahel Rabinovich in the summer of 1973 and seemed satisfied after two decades of living a wild life of celebrity, power, and sex. Through Rahel he was able to enjoy some of the finer things in life, such as expensive wines, nice furniture and hanging out with the nonpolitical elite.[17]

Occasionally Defense Minister Shimon Peres would call him and ask for advice on some matter. The most important of these instances was when Peres tracked Dayan down at an expensive restaurant in Tel Aviv during the Entebee hostage crisis and dragged him away from his bowl of soup and guests. At a side table Peres related the rescue plan to Dayan, who pronounced it a great plan. Dayan had earlier offered to go to Uganda and meet with President Idi Amin, but Rabin had vetoed the idea out of fear that Dayan would be taken hostage. Between 1974 and 1977 Peres kept Dayan up to date on political developments, and in 1977 he kept Dayan in a realistic spot on the Labor Knesset list.[18]

Dayan attended Knesset sessions occasionally (the author observed him at one in 1976), but he was generally bored by politics. In September 1975 he voted against the Sinai II agreement that Rabin, Allon, and Peres had negotiated. Dayan claimed that Israel had given up too much for what it had gotten back, but many observers wrote off his opposition as ego. There was a similar case with American arms control negotiator Paul Nitze a few years later. In the Nixon administration Nitze had helped to negotiate the SALT I arms control agreement. As a Republican, he was absent from the Carter administration, which negotiated the SALT II agreement with the Soviet Union. Like Dayan returning to power to negotiate the Egyptian-Israeli peace treaty, Nitze returned during the Reagan administration to negotiate the Intermediate Nuclear Forces (INF) agreement in 1987. In both cases, it was Dayan's ego thinking that if he was not personally involved, the best possible deal could not have been obtained.[19]

Rabin was forced to call early elections for May 1977 after he decided to punish the National Religious Party (NRP) for voting against the government in a non-confidence vote. Ironically, just as Shimon Peres had assumed power as acting prime minister after Rabin resigned over his wife's illegal bank account, time finally ran out for the Labor Party, and after 29 years of Labor Zionism being in power in Israel—and another 15 before that in the Yishuv—arrogance and corruption caught up with it. But Prime Minister Menahem Begin needed an interlocutor to deal with the outside world. As someone branded a terrorist by both the British and Ben-Gurion, Begin needed someone to give his government credibility. On May 7, 1977, Begin phoned Dayan at Zahala and offered him the post of foreign minister in his government. Ezer Weizman had earlier tried to recruit Dayan for the Likud, and Begin and Dayan entered into secret negotiations about a change in party, but they could not reach an agreement before the deadline to register came. Dayan registered as a Labor candidate only minutes before the deadline.[20]

Dayan was convinced that Egypt was ripe for peace with Israel and that Begin needed someone with his experience and expertise to negotiate the treaty. It was this, rather than simply a desire to return to power and attend diplomatic functions—which actually bored Dayan—that motivated his acceptance of Begin's offer. Dayan became an independent in Begin's coalition government after it was formed by the Likud, the NRP and Agudat Israel. Begin had a narrow majority without Dayan, and once the Democratic Movement for Change joined a few months later it was a wide margin. Many Labor voters and members felt betrayed by Dayan because he did not return his seat. But Dayan would justify this "betrayal" with the results that he obtained for Israel in his two and a half years in power. Dayan made his acceptance conditional on Begin agreeing not to annex the West Bank, as called for in the Likud platform, while negotiations for a peace agreement continued.[21]

Dayan functioned as foreign minister in the same way that he had previously functioned as defense minister and chief of staff: he concentrated on implementing or monitoring a few key policies that were of great interest to him and left the administration of the ministry to others. This is not surprising; after developing a leadership style that worked for him, there was little

Outgoing foreign minister Allon (left) and incoming foreign minister Dayan at Israeli Foreign Ministry in Jerusalem, June 21, 1977. Photograph by Yaacov Saar, Israeli Government Press Office.

incentive to change, particularly at age 62—early retirement age in the United States. Dayan concentrated above all on the peace process with Egypt. In the first instance, this meant getting the word out to Egypt that Israel was interested in a full peace treaty. No longer would Israel passively wait by the phone for a call that might never come, as it had done (or claimed to have done) after the June 1967 war. This time Dayan and Begin would actively seek out peace with Egypt.[22]

The first step was finding countries that had ties with both Egypt and Israel and had leaders who might pass on a personal message to Sadat about Israel wanting peace. Dayan met with several foreign leaders in the summer and fall of 1977, but the only real mission that produced results was a secret meeting with Hassan al-Tuheimi, an eccentric political advisor to Sadat, in Rabat, Morocco, on September 4. Morocco had had fairly close covert ties with Israel since the early 1960s, when the Mossad began training Moroccan intelligence agents. In 1976 Rabat had offered to serve as a mediator between Israel, on the one hand, and Egypt and Syria, on the other. The al-Tuheimi meeting came about as part of this.[23]

Dayan traveled to Morocco via Europe wearing a disguise, as had Rabin

Official dinner at the Knesset, August 9, 1977. From left: Foreign Minister Dayan, Mrs. Vance, Prime Minister Menahem Begin, Secretary of State Cyrus Vance. Photograph by Moshe Milner, Israeli Government Press Office.

before him. Despite later media reports after Camp David, Dayan made no promises about returning of all of the Sinai to Egypt at the meeting. He merely stated that Israel's openness to withdrawal would depend upon what Egypt was offering in exchange. Al-Tuheimi returned to Egypt and reported to Sadat. A month earlier Begin had traveled to Bucharest, Romania, to meet with Romanian dictator Nicolae Ceausescu, who had friendly relations with Israel. Begin asked him to pass a message on to Sadat, which Ceausescu did, along with the observation that Begin seemed to be a strong leader.

President Jimmy Carter wanted to make his mark on the Middle East by achieving peace between Israel and the Arabs. But, influenced by the Brookings Institution special report on Middle East peace from 1976, and by National Security Advisor Zbigniew Brzezinski who had helped to draft the report, he saw peace in terms of a comprehensive agreement arrived at in an international conference, in which Israel would give up all the territories captured in 1967 in exchange for peace. Begin met with Carter in July and presented an Israeli peace plan. Dayan then met with Secretary of State Cyrus Vance, Brzezinski and Vice President Walter Mondale in Washington in September. Mondale played the bad cop in the meeting, grilling Dayan about

Israeli settlements in the Palestinian territories. Carter then said he wanted to reconvene the Geneva Conference, which had last met in December 1973. The following month Dayan worked out with Vance the language for the reconvening of the conference.[24]

When Sadat got word that Carter was planning on reconvening the Geneva Conference, he became worried. This would reintroduce the Soviet Union into the diplomacy of the region, where it could use its radical allies (like Syria) to prevent any progress. There had been a Cold War between Cairo and Damascus since September 1975, when the Sinai II agreement was signed. Sadat decided to preempt Washington and Moscow by getting himself invited to Jerusalem for bilateral negotiations. In a speech to the Egyptian National Assembly on November 9, 1977, Sadat declared that he was ready to travel to the ends of the earth to prevent a single Egyptian soldier from dying in combat—even to the Knesset in Jerusalem. Begin was made aware of the speech by a reporter who happened to catch it on the radio. Four days later Begin told a French delegation in Tel Aviv that he was officially inviting Sadat to Jerusalem. He then issued a formal invitation through the American embassy in Tel Aviv, which transmitted it to the American embassy in Cairo and from there to Sadat.[25]

Sadat was received at Ben Gurion Airport on the evening of November 19, 1977, and traveled by limousine in a special convoy to the Knesset in Jerusalem. At the airport he was greeted by members of the cabinet and former Prime Minister Golda Meir. He traded banter with Meir and Agriculture Minister Ariel Sharon. He was also greeted by Defense Minister Ezer Weizman, who was on crutches after a serious traffic accident. Weizman used his crutch like a rifle to give Sadat a military salute. It was the beginning of a special political friendship between the two that would last for the remaining four years of Sadat's life. The streets were lined with Egyptian flags, which had been hurriedly produced, and all of Israel's major newspapers issued special editions with a headline in Arabic welcoming Sadat. At the Knesset, Begin and Sadat both spoke in English in their respective speeches, setting down their terms for peace. During his speech, Sadat declared that he wanted a return of all the Arab land captured in 1967.[26]

Begin and Sadat agreed to set up two committees, one military and one political, made up of both Israelis and Egyptians, to work on the various issues related to peace. But beyond this, nothing much of a practical nature was accomplished because of the ceremonial aspects of the visit. Two weeks later Dayan again met with al-Tuheimi at the royal palace in Marrakesh, Morocco.[27]

On Christmas Day 1977, Begin, Weizman and Dayan flew to Ismailia,

Defense Minister Ezer Weizman and Foreign Minister Moshe Dayan at the presidential residence in 1977. Photograph by Yaacov Saar, Israeli Government Press Office.

Egypt, for preliminary talks with Sadat. Dayan was worried about the total lack of ceremony on the Egyptian side, in contrast with the Israeli reception a month earlier: no anthem, no Israeli flags, no official ceremony. The Israelis also noticed the ubiquitous huge portraits of Sadat, evidence of the cult of personality that existed in all Arab military regimes, and reminiscent of the personality cults of the totalitarian leaders of the 1930s, which held such bitter memories for the Jews. Little was accomplished at the meeting.[28]

When the two committees started work the following month, Begin managed to inadvertently offend Egyptian Foreign Minister Ibrahim Kamel by addressing him as "young man," which is insulting in Arabic. The delegation was promptly recalled to Cairo.[29] A political rift between Jerusalem and Cairo lasted for half a year, with no negotiations and no progress. Weizman managed to keep the peace process from collapsing completely by developing a personal relationship with Defense Minister al-Gamassy and with Sadat himself.

The first ray of sunshine in the cloudy atmosphere was a meeting that Dayan held with Foreign Minister Kamel and U.S. Secretary of State Vance at Leeds Castle, England, on July 17–18. Dayan was charmed by the medieval atmosphere of the castle, and he came away from the meeting convinced that the Egyptians were serious about wanting peace even though little real progress was made. Dayan threatened to end the peace process unless the Egyptians backed down from their demands and they did. This convinced Dayan that it was worth carrying on.[30]

In early August 1978 Carter invited both Begin and Sadat to meet with him at the presidential retreat at Camp David, Maryland, for a summit negotiation the following month. The basic problem was that, under Begin and the Likud, Israel was prepared only to offer autonomy to the Palestinians in the territories and not to withdraw. However, Israel was prepared to withdraw from the Sinai. Egypt wanted to recover the Sinai from Israel but did not want to be seen as making a separate peace with Israel for fear of being accused of selling out the Palestinians. So a means had to be found to disguise the fact that this was a separate peace, and Israel would have to be convinced enough of the genuineness of the peace agreement to withdraw from its settlements adjacent to Gaza in northern Sinai and from Sharm al-Sheikh. The success of the summit would depend on whether Sadat was prepared to exchange the West Bank for the Sinai and a few Israeli promises, and whether Carter was willing to give up his dream of a comprehensive peace.[31]

Foreign Minister Dayan with President Anwar Sadat of Egypt in the latter's cabin at Camp David, September 1, 1978. Photograph by Moshe Milner, Israeli Government Press Office.

The summit opened on Tuesday, September 5, and lasted for thirteen days. This was longer than Carter and the American team had anticipated. There was a basic asymmetry between the Egyptian and Israeli teams: Sadat was moderate while all his advisors were uncompromising, whereas on the Israeli side Begin was the rigid one and his advisors were flexible. This meant that the American team had to work through Sadat on one hand, and through Dayan, Weizman and Justice Minister Aharon Barak on the other. Sadat and Begin had absolutely no personal chemistry and were kept apart after an initial meeting out of fear that they would cause the summit to collapse. At the summit the Israeli moderates had different roles: Weizman kept the personal chemistry going and smoothed over any ruffled feathers with Sadat; Dayan came up with compromise proposals to find ways out of dead ends; and Barak translated Dayan's ideas into legal treaty language while drafting along with Vance. Even though both Brzezinski and Begin spoke Polish (the former's father was a Polish diplomat in the interwar period), they used only English at the summit. Brzezinski was probably the most rigid personality on the American side, with his dislike of Begin and his support for a comprehensive peace. The individuals who probably worked the hardest at the summit were Carter, Barak, Dayan, Weizman, Vance and Osama al-Baz, a political advisor in the foreign ministry.

Carter came up with the idea of keeping a common draft that would be updated with input from the other two teams when the ideas had been accepted by the opposite side. This meant that everyone was working off of a common document. Carter, Vance and Weizman had to keep Sadat from being talked out of compromises by his advisors, who had their own careers invested in the inter-Arab state system and did not want to see Egypt become isolated within the Arab world. Two separate documents were drafted at the summit—a draft Egyptian-Israeli peace treaty and the guidelines for autonomy—and these collectively became known as the Camp David accords.

A major sacrifice on Begin's part was his agreement to allow a free vote of conscience on the proposal to remove Israeli settlements in the Sinai when the Knesset voted on it. Weizman got Sharon to phone Begin from Israel and tell him that the Sinai settlements were expendable. With the United States agreeing to pay the costs of Israel building new air bases in the Negev Desert to replace those lost in the Sinai, the issue of Israel's withdrawal from the Sinai was taken care of. The day before the agreement was reached, Sadat threatened to leave, and when the Israeli team said it would leave as well he allowed himself to be convinced by Carter to stay on.[32]

Shortly after the agreements were announced at the end of the summit, Foreign Minister Kamel resigned citing opposition to the agreements. He was eventually replaced by Boutros Boutros-Ghali, a Christian Copt whose grandfather had once been a prime minister under the British. Because he was a Copt, Boutros-Ghali had to settle for the title of acting foreign minister rather than foreign minister. He was a professional diplomat who specialized in African affairs, and hence might have been more flexible than those senior diplomats who had spent their careers in the Arab world. In Israel, the Camp David accords were put before the Knesset for a vote, and it was 84 in favor and 19 against, with 17 abstentions. Most of the negative votes and abstentions came from within the ranks of the parties of the coalition government. Moshe Arens, a future Likud foreign and defense minister, voted against the accords, and Yitzhak Shamir, the Knesset speaker and future foreign minister and prime minister, abstained.[33]

During the next six months Dayan attempted to nail down the remaining areas of disagreement and keep from moving backward in the face of a consensus within the coalition that Israel had already made enough concessions and should make no more. The major remaining issues were, first, the guarantee of a supply of oil to Israel once it gave up the Sinai oil fields and, second, the primacy of the peace treaty ahead of competing Egyptian agreements

From left: Foreign Minister Dayan, his wife Rahel, and Henry Kissinger at Golda Meir's funeral, December 12, 1978. Photograph by Nati Harnik, Israeli Government Press Office.

with other Arab governments and with the Arab League. On the oil issue, there was a complication because the Iranian revolution in January 1979 meant that Israel could no longer buy oil from Iran. So Egypt agreed to sell Israel oil from the Sinai at market rates for a ten-year period indirectly by first selling it to the United States (this was later changed to fifteen years). In March 1979 Carter flew to the Middle East and engaged in shuttle diplomacy between Cairo and Jerusalem. Begin played hardball during these final negotiations and the Egyptians backed down from their demands, and a compromise was found on Article 6 that gave precedence to the peace treaty while allowing the Egyptians to claim that it did not. Dayan played a key role in finding a solution to the Article 6 problem by discovering a compromise and lining up a majority in the government for his position. "I resolved the crisis," he told his wife.[34]

After the peace treaty was signed in Washington on March 26, 1979, Dayan undertook a tour of the Far East. Upon his return he had a major physical examination in mid–May to deal with some health problems he had been experiencing. He was diagnosed with a weak heart, anemia and a growth in his colon. This growth turned out to be cancerous and Dayan had it surgically removed in late June 1979. Dayan was also slowly going blind and had nearly walked into a tree at Camp David during the summit in September 1978.[35]

Begin named Yosef Burg, the leader of the National Religious Party, as head of the Israeli team attending the autonomy negotiations with Egypt. Burg was a Central European who had little knowledge of Arab culture. But as head of one of the parties most opposed to giving up the West Bank and in favor of its settlement by religious settlers, he was a more suitable political choice to lead the delegation for what Begin had in mind. Over the summer Begin had gradually become estranged from Dayan, as the latter had served his purpose—ensuring good relations with Washington and negotiating a peace treaty with Egypt. Dayan had accomplished his major goal as foreign minister and now was feeling exhausted from his illness. So on October 2, 1979, he submitted a letter of resignation to Begin. On October 23 he became a one-man faction in the Knesset.[36]

Dayan spent the final two years of his life doing two main things. For the first time since the mid–1950s, Dayan became a family man, playing with Rahel's grandchildren. He also worked feverishly to write and finish his peace process memoirs both before he died and before he went blind. He also formed a think tank dedicated to pushing for the negotiation and implementation of autonomy. In December 1980 he proposed in the Knesset that Israel negotiate autonomy with Jordan and then force it on the Palestinians. In the spring of 1981 he converted his think tank into a political party, Telem, mainly at the urging of his colleagues, and campaigned across the country in May and June 1981. As time went on, fewer and fewer people showed up to see him. Telem ended up with only two seats—one for him and one for Yigal Horowitz, who had been a member of Rafi and then of Ben-Gurion's State List in 1969, and subsequently La'am in the Likud. Dayan's health deteriorated rapidly after the election, and he died of a heart attack on October 15, 1981.[37]

Most of his personal fortune he willed to Rahel, leaving very little for his children (and this only at the urging of Rahel). He thought that they were young enough to still retire comfortably, but that he owed it to his wife to ensure her comfort after the 26 years she had spent with him. This made his children bitter, but his personal relations with them had long before broken down.[38]

Dayan's legacy is rather difficult to determine because he was continuously changing his opinion on things, as he did in June 1967 over whether to conquer the Golan. One biographer, American journalist Robert Slater, wrote a decade after Dayan's death that he was mainly remembered for his flexibility during his negotiations with Arabs.[39] But this was mainly with Egypt and not with the Palestinians or with Jordan or Syria. It was too early for the Palestinians to be ready for peace, and too late for Dayan to adapt and change. Had he lived for another decade, he might have adapted and changed as Rabin did. He died at a time when only the fringe Shelli Party and some in Mapam were really advocating negotiations with the PLO. His military legacy, which he shares with Zvi Zur and Rabin, is the creation of the IDF that fought the Six-Day War, the War of Attrition, the Yom Kippur War and the First Lebanon War. Dayan also started the conversion of the IDF from an infantry-heavy force to a blitzkrieg force organized around armor, mechanized infantry, and a tactical air force.

Part II: Yitzhak Rabin, 1922–1995

Chapter Five

General Rabin

Yitzhak Rabin was born in Jerusalem on March 1, 1922, to parents who had recently immigrated to Palestine from Russia. His father, Nehemiah, had first gone to the United States and lived in the Midwest before relocating to Palestine in 1917. His mother, Rosa, born in a wealthy merchant family in a small Russian town, immigrated to Palestine in 1919 after encountering anti-semitism among the revolutionaries she was treating as a nurse during the Russian Revolution. The two met during the defense of Jewish Jerusalem during the Arab riots in 1920 and married the following year.

Rosa became an active Labor Zionist and befriended several important figures, including Golda Myerson, who as Golda Meir would work with Rabin. However, Rosa contracted cancer and died at age 47 in 1937, while Rabin was a student at Kadoorie Agricultural School. He remembered her fondly all of his life. As a result of her death, he grew closer to his father.[1]

Originally Rabin wanted to study hydrology—water engineering for agriculture—and planned to attend the University of California. But in the autumn of 1938 he joined the Hagana, recruited by Yigal Allon, who was then a sergeant in charge of military training at Kadoorie. After the British closed the school due to the Arab Revolt, Rabin followed Allon to Kibbutz Ginnosar in the Lower Galilee and spent six months there undergoing further training. He then spent another six months at Ramat David in the Upper Galilee before returning to Kadoorie in the fall of 1939. He graduated from the school in August 1940.

In the spring of 1941 he was recruited into the Palmakh after being questioned by Moshe Dayan and recommended by Allon. In June 1941 Rabin participated in the invasion of Syria as part of the company led by Dayan, although he was not with Dayan when the latter lost his eye. That autumn Rabin commanded the first course for Palmakh section commanders at Kibbutz Alonim. In 1942 he underwent a course on sabotage and scouting. The following year he became a platoon commander at Kfar Giladi near the Lebanese border.²

In 1944 Rabin met his future wife, Leah Schlossberg, on Allenby Street in Tel Aviv. She was then a fifteen-year-old high school student. Rabin recruited her into the Palmakh when she graduated from high school in 1945, the same year the organization was made illegal by the British. The two were then stationed together at Kibbutz Ein Harod, where she underwent training.³

In 1945 Allon took over command of the Palmakh from Yitzhak Sadeh, a veteran of the Russian Revolution. Most of the commanders were influenced mainly by their immediate superiors, who had trained them using what they knew of precedents from resistance movements in Europe, particularly the Yugoslav Partisans and the French Resistance (Maquis).

In the 1940s in Palestine there were three separate underground organizations within the Jewish Yishuv (Colony, or community). These were the Hagana, founded in 1920 during the Arab riots (but really active only in 1929 during the Arab pogrom), which functioned as the military arm of the Jewish Agency of David Ben-Gurion; the Irgun Zvai Leumi (National Military Organization), or Etzel, founded in 1937 by a breakaway faction of the Hagana and affiliated with the Revisionist Party and especially its youth movement, Betar; and the Lohemei Herut Israel (Fighters for the Freedom of Israel), or Lehi, founded in 1940 by Avraham Stern as a splinter organization by radicals within the Etzel. The Lehi had carried out a short armed struggle in Tel Aviv in the winter of 1942 before being suppressed by the British. In February 1944 Menahem Begin, newly arrived from a prison in Siberia in 1942, declared a revolt against the British Mandate. While the Etzel and Lehi waged an all-out struggle against the British for three years, from late 1944 to late 1947, the Hagana and Palmakh—the standing army of the Hagana militia—equivocated. The Hagana was allied to the British during World War II, but then entered into an alliance with the other two undergrounds, which was known as the Hebrew Resistance Movement (Tnuat haMered haIvri, or Tami, in Hebrew), in the summer of 1945. The alliance lasted for only a year, until the bombing of the King David Hotel by the Etzel in July 1946 led Ben-Gurion to cancel it.⁴

During the period of the revolt the Palmakh was active in two areas: illegal immigration and sabotage of communications. On October 10, 1945, Rabin participated in a Palmakh rescue of illegal refugees kept in a British camp. After breaking into the camp the Palmakh volunteers led the refugees to two kibbutzim, where they mingled with the established members. Rabin carried a small child on his shoulders who urinated on him out of fear. This scene was re-created in Leon Uris's novel *Exodus*, with Arie Ben-Canaan, the novel's hero, being a mixture of Dayan and Rabin. In the 1960 movie version Ben-Canaan was played by Hollywood star Paul Newman.[5]

Rabin was given the assignment of storming a British police station in Jenin in June 1946. After personally conducting the reconnaissance for the operation, Rabin was on his way to Haifa by motorcycle to report back to Allon when he crashed into a truck. After waking up in a hospital, he was sent home to Tel Aviv to his father's apartment to convalesce. Through his eagerness and carelessness he missed the Palmakh's one major operation before the War of Independence: the June 18, 1946, simultaneous attack on the eleven bridges connected Palestine to the surrounding countries. Ten of the bridges were destroyed or badly damaged.

As a result of this attack, the British made mass arrests ten days later on June 29, known as Black Saturday. Rabin, his father and a friend were arrested by the British. He was imprisoned for five months. After his release in November 1946, he went to see Allon and Israel Galili, then the Hagana commander, about applying to study hydrology at the University of California. "You are free to do what you want," replied Galili. "The world war is over but *our war* has just begun." Rabin took the hint and cancelled his plans to study abroad. This probably marked the point when he became a professional soldier.[6]

In the spring of 1947 Rabin was made a battalion commander in the Palmakh, over a year before Dayan got that assignment, and at age 25 compared to Dayan's 33.[7] He was in charge of guarding the water pipeline that ran to eleven new settlements in the Negev Desert. On November 29, 1947, the UN Special Committee on Palestine's partition plan was voted on and adopted by the United Nations. This immediately set off a war that lasted for over a year—off and on—with several ceasefires in the second half. The first half, from December 1947 to May 1948, consisted initially of terrorism, and then a civil war fought between the three Zionist paramilitary organizations listed earlier and two irregular Arab guerrilla armies. This phase ended on May 15, 1948, with the invasion of the newly declared state of Israel by conventional armies from Egypt, Iraq, Jordan, Lebanon, and Syria, as well as contingents from Saudi Arabia and Yemen.

In the War of Independence, Rabin started out in the spring of 1948 in charge of one of the three new Palmakh brigades, the Harel Brigade, in Jerusalem. Harel was in charge of protecting the convoy route from Tel Aviv to Jerusalem. During the first phase of the war the Palestinian strategy was to cut off the isolated Jewish settlements and urban centers with Arab contingents stationed in the surrounding Arab villages. Initially the Zionists had to worry about British troops (who had been their allies during the Arab

Revolt of 1936–1939) intervening to disarm Jewish soldiers both because British foreign policy interests in the Arab world demanded a pro–Arab tilt and because Jewish terrorism by the Etzel and Lehi had alienated the British army. The Hagana created homemade armored cars by welding sheets of armor plating onto the sides of trucks in order to protect them from sniper fire from Arab villages.

On April 3, Uzi Narkiss led a company of Rabin's men to retake the strategic village of Kastel, after it had previously been lost to the Arabs for lack of men and then abandoned by them to loot. Abd al-Khader al-Husseini, a member of the clan that the Mufti of Jerusalem came from and the leader of the Palestinian irregular forces, wandered back on to the battlefield, not realizing that the Jews had retaken the village. He was spotted by a machine gunner and shot dead. This had a critical effect on Palestinian resistance in the final six weeks of the Mandate.[8]

Between April 15 and April 20, 1948, the Harel Brigade was in charge of guarding the Jerusalem corridor. The brigade managed to get three convoys through to Jerusalem during these five days, and they captured three Arab villages. The convoys contained between 250 and 300 vehicles each and snaked for ten miles. Rabin had a talent for painting his unit's situation in the bleakest terms in order to get equipment and reinforcements from headquarters. Only two days before Rabin's unit took over, a convoy had been ambushed in Sheikh Jarrah in East Jerusalem and doctors and nurses from Haddasah Hospital murdered in revenge for the massacre by a combined Etzel-Lehi force at the village of Deir Yassin days before that.[9]

In the final convoy, Yigal Allon and David Ben-Gurion arrived to brief Rabin on a new operation that he was to carry out—Operation Jebussi. His men were to capture the village of Nebi Samuel near Jerusalem and the Sheikh Jarrah neighborhood in East Jerusalem. The attack on Nebi Samuel on April 26 failed completely, with heavy casualties (including the company commander). Rabin's men did capture Sheikh Jarrah, but then were ordered out of it by the British, as it was to be part of their evacuation route at the end of the Mandate three weeks later. At first Rabin refused to evacuate despite British promises not to turn the neighborhood over to the Arabs, but after the British opened fire on him he relented.[10]

Immediately before the declaration of independence and the Arab invasion, the Harel Brigade was ordered to capture the Arab village of Bet Mahzir, which served as a base for Arab attacks on the convoys. The units assigned took three days to capture the village, which Rabin blamed on battalion commander Yosef Tabenkin. But according to Uzi Narkiss, who was in charge of the attack and would be Central Command head in June 1967, the attack was

Palmakh leaders gather, May 1, 1948. Yitzhak Rabin is second from left, and Yigal Allon is center left. Israel state photograph archive.

delayed first because of fog, then because the men refused to fight in daylight, which deprived them of their natural advantage over the Arabs. When the declaration of independence was read officially over the radio, Rabin was listening until an exhausted soldier who was trying to sleep yelled at him, "To hell with it—turn the radio off!"[11]

The first target of the British-officered and -equipped Arab Legion of Jordan during the Arab invasion on May 15 was the Old City of Jerusalem. It was quickly captured. Four days later, on the night of May 19, Rabin's brigade broke into the Jewish Quarter of the Old City through the Zion Gate and delivered supplies and ammunition to the beleaguered defenders. The previous night they had captured Mount Zion outside the gate, with a failed attack by the Etzioni Brigade on the Jaffa Gate having provided the cover. The breakthrough force was too small to hold out and retreated after having delivered the supplies. A new attack on two separate gates was planned for ten days later. But just as it was about to begin, the representatives of the Jewish community in the Old City surrendered to the Arab Legion. All males between 14 and 70 were taken prisoner and led away to captivity, and the women and young children were allowed to pass through the lines to western Jerusalem.[12]

Rabin's last big battle before the first ceasefire was the second Battle of

Latrun on June 10. After the failure to capture the police fortress on top of the hill at Latrun in late May and again on June 8–9, Ben-Gurion was becoming obsessed with the mission of taking the fort. David Marcus (a.k.a. Stone), whose body Dayan would later escort back to West Point, ordered Allon to make a third attempt on the night before the ceasefire was scheduled to go into effect. Allon protested because the IDF was in the process of scouting the "Burma Road," an alternate supply route to Jerusalem that did not depend on capturing Latrun. After declaring angrily that "Allon should be shot!" Ben-Gurion ordered the attack. Rabin's Harel Brigade attacked the wrong hill in the dark and half the fighters were lost. When Ben-Gurion wrote up his version of the exchange with Rabin for the official record, he left out the part about shooting Allon.[13]

Between mid-April 1948 and the June ceasefire, the Harel Brigade saw some of the toughest fighting anywhere. Harel's two battalions lost 220 men, with another 617 wounded and 220 suffering from severe fatigue. Rabin's aloof manner—he, like Dayan, was an introvert—did not make him a natural choice for leading troops that were under such demands. Many came to resent him. In particular, Rabin had poor relations with one of his battalion commanders, Yosef Tabenkin, whose ambitious extroverted nature clashed with Rabin's. By the time of the first ceasefire, 1,100 of the Palmakh's fighters from the start of the war were already dead. Fortunately for Rabin, he was unaware of this.[14]

During the first ceasefire, from June 11 to July 10, the Harel Brigade was refitted as much as possible. Allon decided that he wanted Rabin as his deputy commander for Operation Dani, and Joseph Tabenkin was appointed the new commander of the Harel Brigade. Rabin would spend the rest of the war serving under Allon on the Central and Southern Fronts.[15] His first big challenge came even before the ceasefire was over.

The *Altalena*, the Etzel arms ship that Dayan had forced to go to sea at Kfar Vitkin, sailed south toward Tel Aviv. On June 22 the ship anchored opposite the Ritz Hotel, which was serving as Palmakh headquarters in Tel Aviv. Allon was summoned by Hagana leaders to deal with the open violation of the ceasefire. Allon arrived on the scene, put Rabin in charge without fully briefing him about the background of the controversy, and then left after only a few minutes.

The ship had set sail from France after Begin tried to stop it from sailing due to the UN truce, which prohibited the import of arms and soldiers. Sailing had been delayed because Algerian dock workers refused to load the arms for Israel and Begin had attempted to get Israel to pay for the weapons before the French government decided to simply donate them. Once it had sailed,

Begin negotiated with the Israeli provisional government. He demanded that 20 percent of the arms go to his men in Jerusalem, and the other 80 percent to Etzel volunteers within the IDF, claiming discrimination against his men in the distribution of weapons. Prime Minister Ben-Gurion agreed to the 20 percent demand, but said that the remainder would have to go to the IDF to be distributed based on need. No agreement was reached.[16]

Rabin had only forty men under him, most convalescing after having been wounded in the war. After the Etzel commander, Begin, refused to surrender the ship and its arms, Rabin's men and the Etzel members traded fire with machine guns, rifles and grenades. Finally, after ten hours of battle, the ship was sunk by one of the four "Napoleonchik" 75 mm cannon the IDF had in its ordnance. Initially the cannon fired three warning shots after Etzel volunteers set up a machine gun on the deck of the ship. When the gun was not promptly removed, a fourth shot was fired into the hold of the ship, setting it afire. Begin was forced to swim to shore, where he wisely went into temporary hiding and refused to declare a civil war despite the urging of Israel Eldad, ideological guide of Lehi. Ben-Gurion later declared, "Blessed be the gun that set that ship on fire, it will have its place in Israel's war museum."[17]

Rabin took part in the planning for Operation Dani, the operation in which Dayan gained his reputation as a field commander. After Dayan's battalion had passed through Lydda (Lod), the Arabs, who had promised they would not resist if they were allowed to remain in peace, attacked. After a few members of the Arab Legion arrived on the outskirts of the town in a jeep, the town's population mistook this for a counterattack by the Arab Legion. A boy ran out of the mosque where much of the town's population had taken refuge and threw a grenade at the Israeli guards. At this Arabs emerged from the mosque and the houses and began shooting at the surviving Israelis. Moshe Kelman, commander of the Third Battalion, ordered his men to retake the city. The insurgency was put down in a very bloody fashion, including using a British PIAT anti-tank weapon against the town's main mosque.

Before Operation Dani began, Ben-Gurion had met with Allon and Rabin. When they inquired as to what they should do with the populations of the two main Arab towns after they were captured, Ben-Gurion made a waving gesture with his hand that both men took to mean that the Arabs were to be expelled. When Rabin published his memoir in 1979, the two paragraphs describing this incident were removed by the Israeli censor after Yigal Allon personally appealed to him (Allon claimed that it would damage the reputations of the IDF and the state). However, the translator of the book leaked the text of the censored paragraphs to the *New York Times* and it appeared on October 23, 1979, in the paper; journalist David K. Shipler also published the paragraphs in his book, *Arab and Jew*.[18]

On August 23, Rabin married Leah in a ceremony in Tel Aviv and then rushed off to meet Allon at the nearby Worker's Restaurant. Allon, who during the second ceasefire switched from the Central Command to the Southern Command, asked Rabin to be his deputy commander for the Southern Front. Allon was already planning an operation against the Egyptians and needed Rabin's assistance.[19] By this stage the Syrians, the Iraqis and the Lebanese had largely been knocked out of the war, along with one of the Palestinian guerrilla armies. Remaining were the other irregular army, Fawzi al-Kawukji's Arab Liberation Army, the Arab Legion, and the Egyptian army. These forces were all limited to their present size and suffered from desertion. The Israeli army, the IDF, created after statehood by forcibly merging the Etzel and Lehi paramilitary groups with the Hagana/Palmakh, continued to grow as immigrants and volunteers, both Jewish and Gentile, arrived from abroad.[20]

When the second ceasefire ended in mid–October, Israel opened with simultaneous offensives in the north against the Arab Liberation Army and in the south against the Egyptian army. Ben-Gurion had pushed to have the IDF conquer the West Bank, but the IDF high command (including acting chief of staff Yigael Yadin, Allon, and Rabin) all favored an offensive against the Egyptians in the Negev to clear them out of that region. The operation was decided upon on October 6 and launched nine days later. After a week Operation Ten Plagues was over, with Israel having captured Beersheba and the strip between Yad Mordechai and Ashdod on the Mediterranean coast. By the end of the operation the Egyptian army was boxed up in the Faluja Pocket. On November 11 Rabin had a chance to talk with a young Egyptian liaison officer, Major Gamal Abdul Nasser, who would later play a major role in his future. Nasser told him, "You know, we are fighting the wrong enemy, at the wrong place, at the wrong time. Our main enemy is the British and our main problem is how to gain real independence."[21]

Israel decided to launch one final offensive against the Egyptians in mid–December 1948 in an attempt to drive them completely out of Palestine. On December 1, King Abdullah I had proclaimed the Hashemite Kingdom of Jordan by annexing the West Bank to Transjordan (after Dayan had concluded a ceasefire with the Arab Legion). This freed up the IDF to concentrate on the Egyptian army in the Negev. The goal was the town of El Auja, which was a problem because the Egyptians controlled the main north-south route. But Yadin knew of an old Roman road that led to El Auja. Rabin was sent to survey the route and see if it would take armor. He said that it would and was praised for his accurate assessment. The offense began on December 22,

From left: Deputy Chief of Staff Yigael Yadin, Southern Commander Yigal Allon, and Col. Yitzhak Rabin, November 28, 1948. Photograph by Hans Pinn, Israeli Government Press Office.

and after a week the IDF had—without orders from Ben-Gurion—plunged across the border into the Sinai. The Israelis were now on Egyptian soil.

On January 9, 1949, Ben-Gurion ordered the IDF out of Sinai immediately after five British Spitfires that had been conducting reconnaissance were shot down by Israeli pilots (one of whom was future IAF commander Ezer Weizman). Allon went to IDF headquarters in Tel Aviv to protest personally to Ben-Gurion. Two days before, however, Egypt had agreed to attend armistice negotiations with Israel on the island of Rhodes. Ben-Gurion counted this de facto recognition of Israel by an Arab government as more important than any territory that would be conquered in the Sinai.[22]

Because Allon wanted to be ready to resume the offensive against Egypt if necessary, and because he was opposed to concessions, he sent Rabin in his place to Rhodes. Rabin was forced to wear a necktie for the first time in his life and had no idea how to tie one. He had it tied for him by someone in his unit, who fixed it so that he could slip it over his head at will. But after Rabin arrived at his hotel, he discovered, to his horror, that one of the hotel's staff had untied the tie in order to iron it. Rabin missed the first session of the negotiations because he was afraid to show up without a tie. After Yadin inquired about the reason for his absence, Rabin confessed his ignorance and Yadin personally retied the tie. While getting a haircut at the hotel barber shop, Rabin had to pull the tie off over his head in the presence of one of the Egyptian delegates, causing Rabin much embarrassment.

Israel was forced to give up the gains it had made in Sinai and around Gaza. Rabin was upset, and when he asked, he was told that his signature did not have to appear on the armistice document—so he refused to sign. The armistice was signed without him on February 24.[23]

Upon returning to the Negev, Rabin plotted a route for two Israeli brigades, the Negev and the Golani, to race south across the Negev to the Gulf of Akaba. This was the last operation of the War of Independence.[24] Rabin had been actively involved in combat operations for eleven months— from mid-April 1948 to mid-March 1949. He then had a decision to make: After eight years, would he remain in uniform or seek admittance to the University of California to study hydrology?

On September 14, 1948, Ben-Gurion had summoned the leading officers in the Palmakh to IDF headquarters and announced that he was abolishing the Palmakh command, which since the formation of the IDF in May 1948 had been responsible only for administrative functions and not operational decisions. The Palmakh headquarters was abolished by November 1948, and the three Palmakh brigades were eliminated as Palmakh units in the spring of 1949. Ben-Gurion purged the ranks of senior Palmakh officers because he feared a loyalty to a competing power center. In October 1949 Dayan took over the Southern Command from Rabin, Allon being absent on study leave in France. Allon, Moshe Carmel (the Northern Command head during the 1948 war), and Israel Galili all quit and went into politics. Initially they were part of Mapam with HaShomer HaTzair, but in 1954 they split to form Ahdut Ha'Avoda as a separate political party.[25]

On October 14, 1949, the Palmakh veterans held a dinner in Tel Aviv. Ben-Gurion had issued an order banning officers on active duty from attending. Rabin, as the senior Palmakh officer in the IDF, was the person with the biggest dilemma: Should he dishonor his former comrades by not attending, or attend and thereby risk his future military career? Ben-Gurion decided to help him out by inviting him to dinner at his home. Rabin went to Ben-Gurion's house, but excused himself and left in enough time to attend the Palmakh dinner. After this, Ben-Gurion blackballed Rabin and slowed his promotion within the IDF. But eventually he forgot about the incident—or deliberately misremembered it, as he often did—as Rabin proved that he was not a political general.[26]

Five. General Rabin

About this same time the Negev Brigade was deactivated, leaving Rabin without a command. So he volunteered to be an instructor at the battalion officer's course organized by Haim Laskov, a Hagana veteran. The course was used to create a new military doctrine for the IDF out of the combined experiences of the Hagana, the Palmakh and those officers who had served in the British army during World War II. When Laskov left the course a year later, Rabin, who had been promoted to colonel, took over as head instructor. In early 1951 he was appointed director of military operations for the IDF by Chief of Staff Yigael Yadin. During these early years Rabin was working 18 to 20 hours a day.[27]

In 1950 Rabin's first child, a daughter named Dahlia, was born. Two years later Rabin moved his growing family out of his in-laws' apartment, where they had been living since he and Leah married in 1948. They moved into a home in Zahala, a suburb of Tel Aviv popular with young army officers—hence the name: "Zahal" is Hebrew for IDF.

In November 1952 Dayan sent Rabin to a staff-officer's course in Britain. In the IDF's early days, most of its senior officers attended professional military courses in Britain or France (for those who spoke French), and only gradually did the IDF switch over to sending its officers to the United States to complete their professional training in the 1960s. In Britain, Rabin made the acquaintance of a Jordanian officer whom he later met again after peace was concluded between the two countries in 1994. By chance, the course commander was the officer who had arrested Rabin in 1946. He invited Rabin for coffee one day and, after a chat, made a condescending comment about the wild character of the Israelis. Rabin suffered from his poor command of English (Dayan had experienced the same thing when he visited England on his honeymoon in 1935).

Dayan, who had taken over from Makleff as chief of staff, denied Rabin permission to stay on in England for another year after his study year ended. But he did allow Rabin to accompany him when he went on a tour of U.S. Army installations in 1954. By then Rabin was chief of operations for the IDF. Dayan also promoted him from colonel to major general, but the promotion did not take effect for a year.[28]

Rabin was probably upset when Dayan became chief of staff in December 1953, as he felt that he deserved the position more than Dayan. Dayan made sure to appoint Rabin as Northern Command head in April 1956 so that he would not take part in any war with Egypt. In 1957, Rabin again attended an officer's course abroad—this time an orientation course on new weapons and military doctrine for foreign officers at Ft. Bliss, Texas. Rabin, as Northern Commander, had a policy of having a senior staff officer present at every operation near the Syrian border in case there was an incident and someone had to make quick decisions.[29]

After Zvi Tzur was named to follow Dayan as chief of staff, Rabin went to see Ben-Gurion and managed to extract a promise from him that he would be next in line to be chief of staff when Tzur's term expired. Dayan had called Rabin, Tzur, and Meir Amit into his office in late 1957 and told them that he was going on study leave and was recommending that Tzur be his successor. He suggested to Rabin that he take study leave—a hint that Rabin's usefulness to the IDF was at an end. Rabin decided to take his chances on being appointed next time. After Ben-Gurion retired as prime minister for the final time in June 1963, Rabin went to see Prime Minister Levy Eshkol, who promised to honor Ben-Gurion's promise to him. Rabin claims in his memoir that Peres blanched after Rabin told him that he was guaranteed the chief of staff position by Ben-Gurion.[30]

In May 1959 Rabin became head of operations, then the second highest position in the IDF, the post higher up from the one he held in 1951. A month before, a botched mobilization exercise had led to the forced resignation of two senior officers after it was not made clear to the public and other countries that the mobilization was only an exercise. Rabin was one of the prime beneficiaries of this mini-purge. Rabin traveled extensively for the IDF to Europe and the United States in order to examine new weapons that the IDF might be interested in purchasing in the future. He also wrote doctrinal articles that became required reading for junior officers. In January 1961 he was appointed deputy chief of staff while remaining head of operations. This was almost a guarantee that he would be appointed chief of staff if he did not screw up. He was widely considered the most capable staff officer in the IDF at this time—an Israeli Eisenhower.[31]

• • •

It is easy to assume that the feud between Rabin and Peres that lasted for twenty-some years (from 1974 to 1993) was simply an inheritance of the Dayan-Allon feud that had begun in 1938. But Rabin had his own, personal reasons to dislike both Dayan and Peres. Rabin had much more command and staff experience than Dayan when the latter was named Jerusalem Front commander in July 1948. Later Dayan prevented him from participating in the Sinai War by exiling him to the north. And the personal relations between these two shy introverts were not good. On Dayan's part, he probably disliked Rabin because of both Rabin's association with Allon and his own association with Ben-Gurion. And since Rabin favored an American orientation in arms purchases and Peres favored a French orientation, Peres, who was director of the defense ministry in the 1950s and had Ben-Gurion's ear, would naturally have preferred someone who was affiliated with Mapai and favored the French side as chief of staff.[32]

The way things worked out with Rabin as chief of staff during the Six-Day War, one might expect that Rabin would be grateful for the delay in his promotions and at least forgive those whom he held responsible for it. But Rabin seems to have been a personality who bore grudges, and his friendship with Allon, who had nursed a grudge against Dayan from the start, would only have encouraged him to continue in his resentment. Interestingly, the grudge appears to have been much stronger on the part of Allon and Rabin than on the part of Dayan and Peres. Dayan was generally indifferent to most people outside of his small circle of friends. He probably did not regard Rabin as any less entitled to be chief of staff, and later prime minister, than anyone else. Peres appears to have been the same. He had a burning ambition to be prime minister that was never properly fulfilled, but he probably did not hate Rabin.

The third major rivalry that Rabin had was with Ezer Weizman, and this did not come about until Rabin was chief of staff and Weizman was his deputy. Weizman became convinced that he was denied the top job in the IDF for political reasons, just as Rabin was convinced that he should have been chief of staff earlier. As a result, Weizman allied himself with Dayan and Peres in their internal struggles with Rabin in the Labor Party, even though he himself was a member of the right for the first half of his political career.

• • •

When Rabin became chief of staff in December 1963, there were two main challenges awaiting him. First, he had to deal with Syria's threat to Israel's national water carrier through diversion of the head waters of the Jordan River in the eastern Galilee. Second, it was necessary to update the IDF'S inventory with more modern tanks and aircraft. Rabin had gained a reputation in the IDF for his analytical skills—in this he was much like Dayan, although less intuitive. In acquiring new weapons, he would first analyze what were the needs of the IDF for the present and near future in terms of likely missions. Then he would look at different weapons systems, such as the French AMX-13 tank versus the British Centurion and the American M-48 and M-60 Patton tanks. After considering the options thoroughly, he would make a decision. By the time Rabin was chief of staff, the Israeli air force's main equipment need was a new attack plane. He compared the existing Super-Mystere, the American McDonnel Douglas A-4 Skyhawk, the North American F-105 Thunderchief, and so on,[33] looking in terms of initial cost, cost and ease of maintenance, bomb load, range, and multiple role possibilities, among other things. He also consulted with the generals under him who had the most expertise in the field, such as the head of the IAF and the head of armored command.[34]

General Israel Tal, the head of armored command, developed the long-range gunnery skills of IDF tank gunners. In the fall of 1964, when Syrian bulldozers began diverting the head waters of the Jordan River, Israeli tanks were lined up at the border and the best gunners in the Israeli armored corps opened fire on the bulldozers. This caused tensions and clashes with Syria, but it ended the Syrian attempt to divert the waters and drain Lake Kinneret. This allowed Rabin to thwart the Syrians without seizing territory, as Dayan had advised him.[35]

Rabin, unlike Dayan, had to deal with only a single prime minister and defense minister as chief of staff—Levy Eshkol. This meant that he only had to keep one man informed of unfolding events. For the sly Dayan, it was probably more useful to have several different personalities—Ben-Gurion, Sharett and Lavon—that he could play against one another.

Rabin's big test came in May 1967, when Moscow attempted to gain political leverage in the region by claiming that the IDF was massing on the Syrian border for an invasion. Nasser decided to exploit the crisis by kicking the UNEF peacekeeping force out of the Sinai and closing the Straits of Tiran to Israeli ships. As the crisis accelerated, everyone, including Prime Minister Eshkol, began deferring to Rabin's authority, and he became in effect the final decision maker. On Sunday, May 21, he met with Ben-Gurion at the latter's home in Tel Aviv. Rabin expected encouragement; instead, he was reproached by Ben-Gurion for being too aggressive and thereby putting Israel in danger. He later met with Dayan, and Dayan also reproached him but praised the readiness of the IDF. Two days later he met with Foreign Minister Abba Eban at Eban's home in Tel Aviv. Rabin explained that Israel needed more time and that Eban had to find a way to buy him that time. Eban felt anything but reassured. The next day Nasser announced the closure of the Straits of Tiran to Israeli traffic.[36]

Rabin was suffering from a lack of sleep, severe tension, and guilt after the rebukes that he had received from Dayan, Ben-Gurion, and Interior Minister Moshe Haim Shapira, head of the National Religious Party. Because of the stress, he was smoking inordinately. On the evening of May 23 Deputy Chief of Staff Ezer Weizman visited Rabin's home. Weizman later claimed twice in public that Rabin suffered a nervous breakdown, and he claimed in his memoir that Rabin had offered him control of the IDF. Rabin denied this in his own memoir—declaring that it was not in his power to make such an appointment. In any case, Weizman talked him out of any thought of resignation and encouraged him to get some rest.

Leah Rabin called a doctor, who gave Rabin a sedative that caused him to sleep until noon the next day. Rabin then returned to work, claiming later that he suffered from nicotine poisoning.[37] He had to put up with the tension for another week, and then Dayan took over as defense minister and Rabin was able to function better, only having to do one job instead of two.

On Sunday, May 28, the cabinet took a vote on whether to go to war, and it split evenly down the middle, nine votes apiece. Two days later Egypt signed a mutual defense treaty with Jordan similar to the one that it already had with Syria. Israel was now facing a united Arab command. Rabin met with Eshkol and told him that he was opposed to making Dayan commander of Southern Command, as he had faith in the ability of the existing commander, Yishayahu Gavish. Rabin suspected that Eshkol wanted Dayan to take the appointment to prevent him from taking over as defense minister. Rabin also did not trust Dayan to obey him strictly, even though Dayan had promised that he would.

On June 1, Eshkol finally decided to form a government of national unity by bringing Rafi and Herut into the government. Dayan was made defense minister and began preparing for the war by studying the existing plans. The next day the government made a secret decision not to go to war before Monday, June 5.[38] Prior to the war most of the senior officers in the IDF were hesitant about going to war out of fear of heavy casualties. The four exceptions were Deputy Chief of Staff Weizman, Quartermaster General Mattiyahu Peled (both of whom were then hawks but became doves during the 1970s and 1980s), and division commanders Avraham Yoffe, who was Rabin's brother-in-law, and Ariel Sharon.[39]

On June 4 the Israeli cabinet voted for a preemptive strike against Egypt and its Arab partners, to begin the next day. At 7:45 a.m. the IAF took off from airfields around the country and flew over the Mediterranean Sea to strike Egyptian airfields while their pilots were at breakfast after their morning patrol. The pride of the Egyptian air force was destroyed, along the airstrips where the planes were lined up, and in the air as the pilots scrambled to intercept the Israelis. By 11:00 the Egyptian air force was finished and the IAF could turn its attention to the Jordanian, Syrian and Iraqi air forces. The major decisions during the war were political: whether to go to war against Jordan and Syria with ground forces. Amman made the choice for Israel by shelling West Jerusalem and moving against the UN observers' headquarters in the biblical field of blood. As related earlier, Dayan decided to wage an attack on the Golan after struggling with himself over the issue. Most troops were involved in only two or three days of fighting, as Israel conquered the Sinai in three days, the West Bank in three days, and the Golan in less than two days.[40]

When Dayan entered the Old City in June 1967, he initially wanted to enter alone, but then thought better of it and had Rabin and Narkiss join him. The entry was symbolic not only because of the present positions of the three men but also because of the roles that they had played in 1948: Rabin was the Harel Brigade commander who did most of the fighting in the city in April and May; Narkiss was the commander of the force that broke into the Jewish Quarter ten days before its surrender in May; and Dayan was the commander of the Jerusalem Command in the second half of the war.

Most of the war Rabin spent traveling between IDF headquarters in Tel Aviv and the cabinet in Jerusalem, but he did tour the Golan before David Elazar made his attack. He cautioned Elazar not to rush things as Dayan had advised, but rather to take his time and do it properly so that no one was unnecessarily killed.[41] Rabin had devoted his military career to seeing that the mistakes that killed so many soldiers in 1948 were not repeated. These mistakes involved a lack of proper equipment and ammunition and the insistence that certain battles be carried out (Latrun) despite being unnecessary.[42]

After the war Rabin accepted an honorary doctorate from the Hebrew University on the IDF's behalf. In his speech Rabin spoke about the unique nature of the IDF. He was approached about accepting the degree by his former boss, Yigael Yadin, who was a professor of archaeology at the university. The degree was granted partly out of gratitude for the IDF's liberation of the Mount Scopus campus, which had been behind Jordanian lines since 1948.[43]

Rabin's term as chief of staff ended in December 1967. Rabin then decided to enter politics like his mentor, Allon, and his rival, Dayan. But first he wanted one more position to prepare himself for a career in elected politics—ambassador to Washington. Rabin had grown up on his father's stories about life in the United States, and had visited the country several times on IDF business. Now he wanted to live in the U.S. and see how policy toward Israel was made, and influence it in a positive direction. He appealed to former foreign minister Golda Meir, who was a family friend, and to Prime Minister Levy Eshkol, making a good case that he was well qualified for the job: What better person to put the case to the American administration for arms sales to Israel and in favor of secure boundaries? And as far as his English was concerned, he was married to a former English teacher who could help him learn the language. Foreign Minister Abba Eban was originally hesitant—he probably wanted to keep the ambassadorship in the hands of a professional diplomat—but he came around.[44]

Rabin arrived in Washington in February 1968, a low point in American history, when the country was torn apart by race riots and protests against the war in Vietnam. Two months after Rabin arrived, Martin Luther King,

Jr., was assassinated in Memphis. Two months after that Robert Kennedy was assassinated in Los Angeles.

Most of 1968 was a period for Rabin to get acquainted with Washington and its various power centers: governmental, media and social. As chief of staff, he had made the acquaintance of Henry Kissinger, then a Harvard professor of government, who was a friend of Yigal Allon, who had taken a course from him in a special summer program run for foreign politicians. Rabin had invited Kissinger to give a talk to senior officers when he was visiting Israel in 1966, and then Rabin met him again before going to Washington. Kissinger would be Rabin's key contact inside the Nixon administration, along with Assistant Secretary of State for Near East Affairs Joseph Sisco.[45]

Rabin spent 1969 and 1970 giving advice to Jerusalem on how to fight the War of Attrition based on his feeling for what the American government would tolerate. He also coordinated with Jerusalem regarding Secretary of State William Rogers's initiative for a comprehensive settlement in the Middle East. Kissinger ended up opposing the Rogers Plan and secretly advised Rabin that it was safe for Israel to ignore it, as President Nixon really did not care about the plan and it was basically the only area of foreign policy that Rogers was allowed to work on. Based on his conversations with Kissinger, Rabin advised Jerusalem that deep penetration air raids by the IAF into Egypt would be tolerated, and he urged Jerusalem to carry them out as a means of retaining escalation supremacy in the war. Rabin also developed his own contacts within the Pentagon, where he was a prized speaker because American generals were eager to apply Israeli expertise to the war in Vietnam.[46]

Rabin began writing his own "pink sheets" of weekly analysis on events in the Middle East that he would then give to the media. This caused friction with Foreign Minister Abba Eban, who believed that all information efforts should be concentrated in Jerusalem. Basically, this was a turf battle, which Rabin ended up winning. Eban lacked allies within the cabinet while Rabin had celebrity appeal in both Washington and Jerusalem. The pink sheets were effective in getting out Israel's message to the media in the capital of Israel's most powerful ally and Meir was not about to end them simply because they annoyed Eban—she might even have considered this a bonus. But as a result Rabin made an enemy of Eban, who then became an ally of Dayan and Peres, whereas he had previously been a supporter of Allon.[47]

A key point of Rabin's time in Washington was the Black September crisis in 1970, when civil war erupted in Jordan. Syrian tanks crossed the border and intervened on the side of the Palestinian fedayeen organizations that posed a threat to the Hashemite regime. National Security Advisor Henry Kissinger coordinated the American response, which consisted of requesting a fly-over of the battlefield by IAF F-4 Phantom fighter-bombers. Because the Syrian air force, led by General Hafiz al-Assad, declined to participate in the battle out of a desire to embarrass the Syrian government, the overflights encouraged the Jordanian army to take on the Syrian tanks and drive them back into Syria. This episode made King Hussein more sympathetic to Israel and demonstrated Israel's value as a strategic asset and American ally. The September crisis also helped to cement personal relations between Rabin and Kissinger, which was important during the latter's shuttle diplomacy in the Middle East in 1975.[48]

In 1971 Rabin was busy fending off demands from Ambassador Gunnar Jarring, the UN special negotiator, for Israel to make territorial concessions without the Arabs promising anything in return beforehand. The following year he interfered in the American presidential election by speaking out for Nixon as good for Israel. This annoyed many American Jews, about 65 to 70 percent of whom traditionally vote Democratic in presidential elections. It also enraged the liberal media and the government in Jerusalem. But Rabin's statement, although impolitic, had little effect on the votes of most American

Prime Minister Golda Meir (center left) and National Security Advisor Kissinger (center right) flanked by Israeli Ambassador Rabin and Leah Rabin in the United States, February 27, 1973. Photograph by Moshe Milner, Israeli Government Press Office.

Jewish voters, and Nixon won the election in a landslide.[49] When Israel needed the administration's assistance the following year to hurriedly replace American military equipment destroyed during the Yom Kippur War, Nixon was happy to comply. He probably would have complied even without Rabin's support because he deemed it in America's best interests to do so, but this way he bore no grudge against Israel when it was time to make his decision. Rabin ended his term in Washington and returned to Jerusalem in March 1973. Three months earlier *Newsweek* had named him one of the two most effective ambassadors in Washington (the other was Soviet ambassador Anatoly Dobrynin). One journalist wrote, "It is fair to say that no other diplomat in recent years here has been attacked so often for displaying such a noticeable lack of diplomacy."[50] This was a testament to the special Israeli-American relationship.

In January 1973 Rabin had announced at a formal dinner in New York that he would be a candidate for the Knesset in October. In 1971 Golda Meir had asked Rabin three times to come home and join the government, but she never had a post for him. She announced that he would be returning by about the end of 1972. When he did return, he began giving speeches to promote his role in the party. He criticized both Meir and Dayan for saying the Palestinians had no right to control their own destiny. The right to national self-determination "cannot be granted or taken away by outsiders," he told an audience. But the controversy over this statement failed to dim his popularity.[51]

During the Yom Kippur War he reported to headquarters in his capacity as a reserve general. He visited critical places on both fronts in the early days with Chief of Staff David Elazar and would report back to headquarters on what he found. He then attached himself to his brother-in-law Avraham Yoffe, a division commander in the 1967 war, to tour the two fronts in a jeep. While visiting units at the front, they took down personal messages and reported back to the soldiers' families that their sons, husbands, and brothers were safe. The war was an especially trying time for Rabin, as it was the first time since 1948 that the country was at war and he had no command responsibility. (This may help to explain his appearance nine years later by Sharon's side during the siege of Beirut.) The Yom Kippur War was also the last time Rabin was in uniform during wartime. Afterward he was a politician. He also headed up an emergency loan effort to get citizens to voluntarily donate part of their income to pay for the war effort.[52]

Chapter Six

Rabin: Prime Minister to Defense Minister

On December 31, 1973, Rabin was elected to the Knesset along with Ariel Sharon and Haim Bar-Lev, the chief of staff who had followed Rabin. The post of labor minister in the new government led by Golda Meir was subsequently assigned to Rabin. When Dayan was planning on not joining the government, he expected that Rabin would be appointed defense minister in his place. In April, when Meir resigned as prime minister, the office was Finance Minister Pinhas Sapir's for the asking. As a senior Mapai member, he was an ideal compromise between the rival Ahdut Ha'Avoda faction, led by Yigal Allon, and Rafi, led by Dayan and Shimon Peres. But Sapir did not want the job, and told Rabin to his complete surprise, that he was Sapir's candidate for the premiership.

When the party leadership contest was held on April 22 the two candidates were Rabin and Peres. Dayan had gotten his brother-in-law Ezer Weizman to leak an account of Rabin's "breakdown" on May 23, 1967, to *Ha'Aretz*. However, Rabin lined up three generals (Aharon Yariv, Ariel Sharon and Israel Tal) to refute the charge and talk about how important his contribution had been to the victory in 1967. Rabin was told by an aide that Weizman's charges had only changed the votes of about 25 to 30 members of the Central Committee of the Labor Party, far fewer than necessary to ensure a Peres victory.

Before the vote the two candidates had met in a restaurant and Peres vowed to support Rabin should he win if Rabin would do the same. Rabin agreed. The final vote was 298 for Rabin and 254 for Peres—Peres lost by only 44 votes, a total that would stick in his craw for three years. But because of the close margin, Rabin was forced to make Peres his defense minister, even though he thought that Peres was totally unqualified because he had never served in uniform (despite having served as head of the manpower branch of the IDF, and later as head of the fledgling navy in 1948). Rabin appointed his old commander Yigal Allon as his foreign minister, forming a troika (or triumvirate) that would rule Israel for the next three years.[1]

Two weeks after Rabin and his government were sworn in, President Richard M. Nixon took a triumphant tour of the Near East encompassing Egypt, Israel, Jordan and Syria in a vain attempt to demonstrate his importance to Congress before it voted on impeachment charges. Nixon told President Assad of Syria that it was American policy that Israel should return to the 1967 border in exchange for peace. He told Rabin that it was better to deal with Hussein now rather than with Yasir Arafat and the PLO later.[2]

Rabin knew that once Vice President Gerald Ford replaced Nixon, Kissinger would be back in the region pressing for another peace agreement. Nixon resigned in early August. Rabin then had the choice of making a peace agreement with either Egypt or Jordan. Jordan was pushing for an Israeli retreat all along the Jordan River. Allon favored an agreement with Jordan, as did Kissinger, before Yasir Arafat and the Palestinian Liberation Organization replaced Jordan as the authorized representative of the Palestinians. But both Rabin and Peres favored an agreement with Egypt. Before forming his government, Rabin had made a promise to the National Religious Party

Prime Minister Rabin with Foreign Minister Yigal Allon (left) and Defense Minister Shimon Peres (right) during Knesset debate in 1974. Photograph by Yaacov Saar, Israeli Government Press Office.

(NRP), the representative of the religious Zionists, that he would hold a referendum before he gave up any part of the West Bank in negotiations. Rabin did not want his government to collapse and Peres, then still a hawk, favored breaking Egypt away from the other Arab countries.[3]

When Gerald Ford took over as president in August 1974, his top priority was moving the country beyond Watergate. This he did by giving Richard Nixon a full pardon a month later, thereby using up much of his political capital. Nixon had already advised Ford before he left that "Henry is a genius, but you don't have to accept everything he recommends. He can be invaluable, and he'll be very loyal, but you can't let him have a totally free hand." Ford took Nixon's advice and kept Kissinger on as his secretary of state because Nixon wanted him to, because Kissinger was popular (which did not bother Ford, who had a healthy ego), and because Ford personally liked Kissinger and respected his diplomatic accomplishments under Nixon. Kissinger had once invited Ford to speak to one of his political science classes at Harvard, and at that time Kissinger impressed Ford with how smart he was. Although Kissinger assured Ford that it was his job to get along with the president rather than the reverse, Ford did tend to give Kissinger a free hand in diplomacy as long as he remained well briefed. On Ford's first day in office Kissinger gave him a global review of policy and then had him meet all of the leading foreign ambassadors to Washington. So the pattern was similar to that which prevailed during the final months of the Nixon administration, when Kissinger negotiated the two separation-of-forces agreements between Israel and its neighbors.[4]

Kissinger promised King Hussein that Sadat would work to defeat any resolution favoring the PLO taking over responsibility from Jordan at the Rabat Arab League summit in October 1974. But Sadat did not like Hussein and wanted an agreement for himself, so he made no effort to prevent the PLO from getting its way at Rabat. Kissinger probably did not push too hard with Sadat, knowing that it was a lost cause. Kissinger was also focused on making sure that Egypt ended up in the Western camp, where Hussein already firmly was. So he naturally preferred an agreement with Egypt over one with Jordan and realized that the former would be much easier to negotiate than the latter (with its potential for causing the collapse of the Israeli government and its replacement by a hardline Likud coalition, as in fact occurred in 1977).[5]

Among academic critics of Kissinger's Middle East diplomacy, there are two main groups. First there are those who challenge the whole premise of shuttle diplomacy and step-by-step negotiations. They argue that Kissinger should have brokered a comprehensive peace agreement, with Israel retreating on all fronts simultaneously, at an international peace conference in the spirit of Versailles, or maybe a Middle Eastern version of the Geneva Conference on East Asia of 1954 that ended the French Indochina War, But at these conferences it was the defeated power that was doing the retreating, not the victorious power. Israel did not trust the Arabs and so had to go slowly to test them, and it could only retreat on one front at a time; for major withdrawals, there would be a space of several years between peace agreements. Israel and its supporters in Washington would not stand aside and let a peace settlement be imposed on Israel by foreigners, which would probably also cause the Arabs to come up with ever-increasing demands. Kissinger understood all this and wrote that, while Washington could win support from the Arab states by helping Israel to return territory to them through peace agreements, it could never afford to make the process look too easy. Kissinger had observed his predecessor's failure at negotiating a comprehensive agreement in 1969, just five years before—and he did not forget the lessons learned.[6]

The second group of critics argue that Kissinger's diplomacy was aimed at peripheral issues, such as the separation-of-forces agreements, rather than at the core issue of the Arab-Israeli conflict—the Israeli-Palestinian dispute. Attributes to this is his unwillingness to negotiate with radical non-state actors like the PLO. But that was the whole reason Kissinger urged Israel to negotiate with Hussein before it was too late. This is reflected in his decision to prioritize the agreement with Egypt over one with Jordan in 1974–1975. Kissinger would argue that he could only go as far as Israel was willing to go, and that the situation was not ripe for an agreement on the Central Front in 1974. But it was ripe on the Southern Front in 1975. Kissinger correctly perceived that the gaps between the Israeli and Egyptian positions in 1974–1975 were bridgeable, whereas they probably were not on the Jordanian front. Jordan wanted an Israeli retreat all along the Jordan River, whereas Yigal Allon, the one senior minister supporting an agreement with Jordan, wanted an agreement centering on a return of Jericho and the interior Arab towns on the West Bank in accordance with the Allon Plan (which King Hussein rejected). Kissinger correctly knew the limits of his own skill.[7]

Israel in the fall of 1974 was looking for a non-belligerency agreement with Egypt in which the latter would end the state of war with Israel in exchange for Israel giving up part of the strategic passes in the Sinai and the oil fields. Anwar Sadat did not feel secure enough to sign a non-belligerency agreement with Israel at that time, but he was willing to concede some of the practical substance of non-belligerency in exchange for a complete Israeli withdrawal from the passes and the oil fields. On December 9, Allon met with Kissinger in Washington and passed on the Israeli proposal for a deal.

Kissinger transmitted this to Cairo, where it was duly rejected. Five weeks later Allon returned to Washington for talks over two days, but he lacked a new proposal. He merely invited Kissinger back to the region.[8]

Kissinger toured the Middle East in early February 1975 on a ten-day trip to assess the prospects for another shuttle. Before he left, Sadat publicly blessed his efforts, although Amman, Damascus, and the Palestinians, as well as Moscow, all remained opposed. Nevertheless, Kissinger felt that the two sides were close enough for serious bargaining with the help of his mediation in a new round of shuttle diplomacy. Kissinger arrived in Cairo on the evening of March 8.[9]

The next day Rabin handed Kissinger a seven-point proposal that failed to include an Israeli line of withdrawal. Rabin was waiting for the Egyptian response to the other six points. Kissinger received from Cairo a topographical analysis of the defense needs of both sides written by Egyptian defense minister Abd al-Gamassy, which had Israel withdrawing to a line within the eastern half of the Sinai. But Jerusalem still insisted on a non-belligerency agreement. Rabin did not really trust Sadat because the Egyptian ruler had, according to him, already betrayed President Nasser by changing Egypt's foreign policy orientation, as well as the Soviets and President Assad by working

Prime Minister Rabin and Henry Kissinger at Blair House, September 11, 1974. Photograph by Moshe Milner, Israeli Government Press Office.

toward another agreement with Israel. Rabin thought that he might be willing to betray Israel just as easily.[10]

The next day Sadat rejected a non-belligerency agreement but agreed to include a declaration on the non-use of force. Sadat also rejected Israeli possession of an electronic monitoring station in the western end of the Giddi Pass, Um Khisheiba. After ten days of shuttling back and forth between the two capitals, with side trips to Damascus, Riyadh and Amman, Kissinger was stalemated. On March 21 Sadat's final word was given to Jerusalem: Israel could not keep Um Khisheiba and the UN mandate would only be renewed for another year. The Israeli government rejected all of Egypt's demands. Kissinger announced the next day that he was suspending his shuttle diplomacy.[11]

When Kissinger returned to Washington on March 24, he publicly announced that there would be a reassessment of the American-Israeli relationship. This was both a method of putting pressure on Israel and a way for Kissinger to vent his frustration at failing to reach an agreement. As part of his reassessment exercise, Kissinger met with a group of Washington "wise men"—veterans of previous administrations—to seek advice (or at least appear to be seeking advice). Among these, George Ball, a former undersecretary of state in the Johnson administration, publicly advocated an imposed comprehensive solution. Over the next several weeks Kissinger met with academic specialists on the Middle East, American ambassadors in the region, and his own policy aides in an attempt to solicit new suggestions.

By the third week in April he had the choices boiled down to three options: first, a return to Geneva and an attempt at a comprehensive settlement; second, a virtually complete settlement but without full withdrawal and final peace; third, a resumption of shuttle diplomacy. Kissinger was basically opposed to using Geneva other than as a showpiece for signing agreements arrived at elsewhere. The second option looked no more realistic than the first, especially in light of Israeli counter-pressure. Jerusalem had worked with the American Israel Public Affairs Committee to mobilize support in Congress for Israel's position. A letter opposing reassessment signed by 76 senators—three-fourths of the Senate—was delivered to Ford on May 21. Reassessment as a means of pressuring Israel was dead. Kissinger now had to find a way to bridge the gaps between the positions of both sides.[12]

In Egypt Sadat could make decisions on his own after hearing advice from his ministers. In Jerusalem, however, the three top ministers in the troika had to agree on a policy. This was much more difficult. President Ford and Kissinger decided to move the two sides closer by meeting with them separately. On June 1–2, 1975, Ford met with Sadat for the first time in

Salzburg, Austria. The two seemed to get along well. Ford sounded out Sadat about another attempt at an interim agreement and Sadat was willing, but his terms were the same as at winter's end. Sadat did suggest that he might be willing to have an American presence at Um Khisheiba to monitor the agreement. Ford returned from Salzburg determined to push the peace process forward to success. Rabin was scheduled to come to Washington June 11–12, 1975.[13]

When Rabin went to Washington in June, he was threatened by Kissinger with a return to Geneva if the diplomatic effort to reach an interim agreement failed. Rabin told him that he was not scared of Geneva. Rabin agreed that Israel would retreat to the eastern end of the pass if the Egyptians met their demands for the substantive equivalent of non-belligerency. On June 27 Ford sent a letter to Rabin, probably drafted by Kissinger, that summed up the state of the negotiations and suggested that Israel reconsider its position before July 11, when Kissinger was scheduled to meet with Gromyko. It was another threat to return to Geneva.[14]

Peres had proposed to Rabin that Israel agree to the stationing of a joint Soviet-American monitoring mission in the pass. Rabin objected to intro-

Rabin and Kissinger on the balcony of the State Department, June 10, 1975. Photograph by Yaacov Saar, Israeli Government Press Office.

From left: Rabin, President Gerald Ford and Secretary of State Kissinger at the White House, June 11, 1975. Photograph by Yaacov Saar, Israeli Government Press Office.

ducing the Soviets into the area, but agreed to Israel discreetly proposing an American monitoring force to Kissinger while he was on vacation in the Virgin Islands. Peres offered to go but Rabin objected, so the Israeli ambassador to Washington, Simha Dinitz, was sent instead. Dinitz flew to the Virgin Islands carrying a large topographical map with the Israeli definition of the eastern end of the pass, which was barely lower than the summit. The sensor proposal was for four American warning stations supervised by three American-manned outposts placed on the roads leading to the pass. Kissinger agreed to the suggestion regarding the sensor stations, but told Dinitz that Israel needed to come up with a definition of the eastern end of the pass that was much lower in elevation.[15]

Ford was reluctant to introduce Americans into an area where they might be vulnerable to attack, but he acquiesced to Kissinger's urging. When told that the force was Peres's idea, Kissinger was relieved because in 1975 Peres was the hawk in the government. By going along with this, he believed that he could sell an agreement to Jerusalem. On July 18 Dinitz presented Kissinger with another Israeli map of the withdrawal line that was much more to Kissinger's liking. Rabin was also looking for an assurance of $2 billion in

Prime Minister Rabin, Leah Rabin and Foreign Minister Allon at Lod Airport before flying to Germany, July 8, 1975. Photograph by Yaacov Saar, Israeli Government Press Office.

American aid to Israel each year, and also for an assurance that the idea of an interim agreement with Jordan had been dropped and that there would be only cosmetic changes on the Golan. Kissinger finally felt that the situation was ripe for another attempt at shuttle diplomacy.[16]

On August 20 Kissinger left for Israel with only three items left to be negotiated. The first was the exact position of the Israeli line of withdrawal. The second was the level of American aid to Israel, and the third was the details of the American monitoring mission in the pass area. Rabin had decided that Israel would sign an agreement in exchange for high levels of American aid. An agreement would keep Egypt out of the Arab coalition against Israel in the event of a future war, ensure that Israel would be strong enough to win in any war, and be so expensive that Kissinger would not attempt to repeat it on the Golan with Syria.[17]

Neither of the two Middle Eastern parties was very enthusiastic about the agreement—in this it resembled more the Israeli-Syrian separation-of-forces agreement of June 1974 than the Egyptian-Israeli agreement of January 1974. Egypt was gaining the status of America's main Arab ally in the region.

Israel had earlier agreed to give Egypt unimpeded access to the Sinai oil fields. But when the maps were examined it was discovered that there was only a single road to the oil fields, and Israel also needed this road as a link with Sharm al-Sheikh. So the two sides agreed to use the road on alternate days, with one day a week set aside for use by the UN peacekeeping force. This occurred without incident for four years, until Israel gave up the whole area to Egypt as part of the Egyptian-Israeli peace treaty in 1979.[18]

The agreement required ten days of shuttling back and forth by Kissinger before it was reached on August 31 and signed in Geneva on September 1. During the shuttle process there were massive right-wing demonstrations in Israel. Several of the protestors used anti-semitic language, referring to Kissinger as "Jew-boy" and "the husband of the shiksa" (a derogatory term for a Gentile woman in Yiddish). The Likud was opposed to Israel giving up any territory except in exchange for a peace treaty. And the right-wing protestors had to stay in practice in case they ever had a peace agreement regarding the territory that they cared about—the West Bank—to protest. King Hussein greeted Kissinger at the Amman airport in a correct but cold fashion, with his band playing only the American national anthem and not the Jordanian anthem. Hussein also received Kissinger at a conference table in his office rather than in some informal manner. Elsewhere, President Assad branded Sadat a traitor to the Arab cause. His treatment of Sadat by itself all but ensured that there would be no follow-up agreement with Israel on the Golan.[19]

In April 1975 the Lebanese Civil War began when a Palestinian bus wandered into the Christian area of East Beirut and was fired upon by one of the Christian militias. The fighting gained strength throughout the year and into 1976—it would finally end in 1990 with a Syrian takeover of most of Lebanon. Initially, Israel and Syria found themselves on the same side: both backed the Maronite Christians against the Palestinians. With both Israel and Syria focused on Lebanon and Jerusalem not offering any territorial proposals that King Hussein was willing to accept, which amounted to anything less than a return of 100 percent of the territory, there was no other Arab partner for Israel that Kissinger could negotiate an agreement with.

In 1976, as the Lebanese Civil War escalated, so did the Angolan Civil War and the African nationalist insurgency in Rhodesia against white minority rule. Kissinger aligned Washington in a coalition with two of the three African nationalist movements in Angola against the third, which was supported by Cuba, the Soviet Union and Yugoslavia. The American coalition included Pretoria, Lusaka, Dar es Salaam and Paris. But a massive Cuban intervention beat a smaller South African intervention, and Kissinger decided to use diplomacy to recover American prestige. He spent April through September 1976 in a failed attempt to mediate a peace agreement in Rhodesia and Namibia, but he did make important progress toward a settlement in both territories.

During this time Rabin agreed to work toward major withdrawals on all fronts in exchange for non¬-belligerency agreements with all of the confrontation states. But the process never got off the ground because the Lebanese Civil War did not deescalate until the American presidential campaign was well under way in 1976, which meant that Ford was focused on reelection and unwilling to take risks.[20]

In late June 1976 Wadia Haddad's Popular Front for the Liberation of Palestine (PFLP) in conjunction with Ilich Ramirez Sanchez (a.k.a. "Carlos the Jackal")organized a hijacking of a French Air France passenger jet to Uganda. The flight had many Israeli and Jewish passengers who were held hostage, to be exchanged for Palestinian prisoners in Israeli prisons. On the night of July 3–4 Israeli paratroopers and Sayeret Matkal forces organized a rescue of the hostages from the Entebbe airport. The rescue force arrived in a C-130 Hercules transport plane that contained a Mercedes-Benz automobile carrying commandos disguised to look like Ugandan dictator Idi Amin Dada and his aides. Surprising the hijackers, the commandos managed to kill them all. The only casualties were the rescue's ground commander, Lieutenant Colonel Yonatan Netanyahu (the older brother of the future prime minister), a passenger who was killed in crossfire and one murdered by Amin's thugs in the hospital where she was located during the rescue.[21]

Rabin spent 1976 quarreling with Peres in an unseemly display of mutual enmity. Whatever position Peres adopted, Rabin regarded it with suspicion and fear that Peres would replace him as leader of the Labor Party. When Rabin wrote his memoirs, he took credit for the Entebbe rescue mission, Operation Yonaton. Most observers, however, credit Peres as defense minister for organizing the rescue and bringing it before the cabinet for approval. This was in sharp contrast with their conduct from 1993 to 1995, when they managed to cooperate on behalf of the Oslo peace process.[22]

Peres had a demonstrated record throughout his political career of being willing to go behind his superiors' backs in pursuit of whatever agenda he was pursuing at the time—both because he believed in the agenda and because he believed in his own advancement.[23] Rabin had a prickly personality and was very insecure during his first term as prime minister because of his lack of political experience in government. His former commander, Allon, had much more experience than he did and was unwilling to take orders from his former subordinate. In addition, Peres was the protégé of Ben-Gurion, the man who had delayed Rabin's promotion to chief of staff, and the colleague of Dayan, who had also clashed with Rabin on numerous occasions. Rabin suspected Peres of being the author of numerous leaks to the press, including the transmission of transcripts of cabinet meetings during the shuttle negotiations to *Ha'Aretz* reporter Matti Golan. The book produced by Golan was highly embarrassing to both Kissinger and the Israeli government, and so Golan was forced to rewrite sections of it in order to get it past the Israeli censors, who had wide discretion on what could be banned on security grounds.[24]

In 1977 the Labor Party began to slowly disintegrate as numerous corruption scandals surfaced. On September 5, 1976, Rabin had nominated Asher Yadlin to serve as governor of the Bank of Israel, despite the fact that he had no banking experience. The following month the police opened an investigation against Yadlin, who was then director general of the Kupat Holim (the Israeli Labor Federation's health service), for fraud and bribery. Rabin was forced to withdraw the nomination. In February 1977 Yadlin was found guilty and sentenced to a five-year prison sentence.

On December 10, 1976, the first three F-15 Eagle fighters landed in Israel, and after they had performed some acrobatics a small ceremony was held in honor of the arrival of Israel's next generation of fighter aircraft. But because it was a Friday afternoon, some of the ministers had to violate the Jewish Sabbath by driving home after sunset. The opposition was eager to embarrass the government and so called a vote of no-confidence, which the government easily won. But the matter did not end here. Some of the ministers of the National Religious Party (NRP) abstained during the vote to protest the government's violation. Rabin decided to punish them by firing them from the government. This caused the NRP to withdraw from the coalition and forced Rabin to schedule new elections for May 1977.

On January 3, 1977, a former director of the Shikun Ovdim (a construction firm owned by the parastatal Histadrut Labor Federation), Avraham Ofer, committed suicide after he became depressed when word leaked that he was being investigated for corruption charges in connection with the role he played as a fund-raiser for the Labor Party. His death was announced dramatically on the evening news with the sentence "Avraham Ofer is no more."[25]

On February 23 the Labor Central Committee again held a leadership election. The two candidates were Rabin and Peres, as they had been three years before. This time the result was 1,445 votes for Rabin and 1,404 for Peres—a victory margin of 41 votes, three less than in 1974 in a much larger electorate.[26]

In early March 1977 Rabin went to Washington to meet with the new president, Jimmy Carter. The meeting did not go well, with Carter and his aides pushing Rabin for more territorial concessions to the Arabs. (At this time, Carter was starting the peace initiative that was the foreign policy-centerpiece of his administration.) But the visit proved even more unpleasant for Rabin. His wife Leah maintained a bank account in the U.S. from when Rabin was ambassador. For Israelis living in Israel, holding such accounts was illegal under Israeli law. Leah attempted to close out the account and receive the balance of $2,000 in traveler's checks. But she was rushed by American security personnel and so did not have time to complete the process. Two days later a bank employee mentioned her presence to an Israeli embassy employee visiting the bank. Eventually word leaked to *Ha'Aretz* Washington correspondent Dan Margolit, who, after verifying the story for himself, published it. Rabin felt that he must resign. But because the government was a caretaker government, he could not officially resign. Instead, he made Peres the acting prime minister. Peres would be at the helm during the elections.[27]

In 1976 former chief of staff General Yigael Yadin, who was a world-famous archaeologist for his excavations of Masada, the caves in the Judean Desert associated with the Bar Kochba Revolt, and Hatzor, formed a new reform party. The Democratic Movement for Change (DMC) was dedicated to electoral franchise reform and various other reforms. The corruption scandals in 1977 led many regular Labor voters to vote for the DMC as a protest vote in the May 1977 election. In addition, many voters, having more time to reflect than in December 1973, blamed Labor for the surprise in the Yom Kippur War. This allowed the Likud to win the election with 43 seats (four more than in 1973), compared to only 32 for the Labor Alignment (Labor plus Mapam) and 15 for the DMC. Menahem Begin, on his ninth try, was finally elected prime minister.[28]

Rabin was fined IL 15,000 (about $1,600) for his passive role in his wife's legal violation. Leah, however, was fined IL 250,000 (nearly $27,000) by the judge and had only 45 days to pay. She and her husband were forced to borrow the money from friends. During his time in the opposition Rabin became a regular member of the lecture circuit in the United States and Europe so that he could raise the money to repay his friends. He was criticized for this, but it did not affect either his popularity or his standing in the party.[29]

In late 1979 former foreign minister Yigal Allon announced his intention to run for the leadership of the Labor Party against party leader Peres. Rabin announced his support for Allon's leadership bid. But in February 1980 Allon suddenly died of a heart attack. His widow then urged Rabin to take up the leadership of her husband's supporters and challenge Peres. Rabin did so, but with little success, as Peres had more support in the Labor Party Central

Committee than Rabin did.[30] For the next decade Rabin would unsuccessfully contest the party leadership and feud with Peres. But in 1983 he went to Peres and made a deal that he would support Peres for the premiership if he was appointed defense minister. Peres agreed.[31]

Starting with President Sadat's visit to Jerusalem in 1977, Peres gradually began a conversion from hawk to dove, inspired by events in the Arab world, the views of his young advisors, his membership and contacts in Socialist International and his own background. This had the effect of making Rabin into more of a hawk. He was the candidate known for his security expertise, heroic past and analytical abilities, compared to Peres, who was noted for his visionary thinking.[32]

The result of the 1984 election was a deadlock that left neither of the main parties able to form a government. So the two parties entered into negotiations to form a government of national unity. Because Labor had more seats, Peres was given the premiership, but he was forced to cede it halfway through the period of the government's tenure—in October 1986—to Likud leader Yitzhak Shamir, who would be foreign minister under Peres. Rabin was appointed defense minister for the whole period of the government. A security cabinet of equal numbers of Labor and Likud ministers determined government policy.[33]

Rabin's role model for defense minister during his tenure could have been Dayan based on the way that he behaved. Rabin wanted to be Mr. Security. His main challenge was designing a plan to withdraw from Lebanon following the collapse of Sharon's grand design from the June 1982 invasion. Peres and the cabinet approved the plan on January 14, 1985, with the Likud ministers (except David Levy) voting against and Labor and the smaller coalition partners voting in favor. The IDF withdrew in stages, falling back behind natural defense lines based on the topography between February and June 1985. Most troops returned to their bases in Israel, while a small number remained in the southern security zone and worked alongside the South Lebanon Army, made up of Christians and Shi'ite Muslims.[34]

Peres then concentrated on getting inflation under control. He did this by developing a working knowledge of macroeconomics, which then became part of his portfolio along with security and foreign policy expertise. The rift between Rabin and Peres began to heal as a result of their cooperation to save Israel's economy. Rabin pledged himself to cutting Israel's defense budget by 20 percent. He was constantly on the phone with Peres, coordinating. This did not end the rivalry between the two for leadership of the party, but it began to cure Rabin of his poisonous hatred of Peres.[35]

Rabin became popular with Likud voters. It was said that Likud doves supported Yitzhak Shamir, and Likud hawks Yitzhak Rabin. This was because Rabin took a tough line against terrorism. This was demonstrated when the Intifada (or uprising) broke out in Gaza in December 1987. He used his new-found popularity to make compromises with the Likud. When Science and Technology Minister Ezer Weizman, who had joined Labor in 1986, met with Palestinian terrorist leaders, the Likud wanted him thrown out of the government. Instead, they compromised by stripping him of his ministry and making him a minister without portfolio and removing him from the security cabinet.[36]

From 1983 to 1986 King Hussein attempted a joint diplomatic initiative with the PLO. The idea was that Jordan would represent the Palestinians but negotiate on the basis of terms agreed to with the PLO. The precondition was that Arafat must get the PLO to support UN Security Council Resolution 242, which the PLO also objected to because it referred to the Palestinians only in terms of refugees and not in terms of national rights. Finally Hussein got tired of waiting and cancelled the initiative in a very critical speech on February 19, 1986.[37]

Peres attempted to negotiate a settlement on the basis of the Jordanian option with Hussein even before the latter broke the PLO connection. Peres favored calling an international peace conference to serve as a forum in which to negotiate a solution based on territorial compromises on the West Bank. Peres met with King Hussein at the latter's house in a London suburb on July 19, 1985, after receiving a memo from former general Avraham Tamir to the effect that the time was ripe for renewed diplomacy. It was their first meeting in a decade. Hussein proposed a settlement in stages, which was acceptable to Peres. But he wanted to include some PLO members in the Jordanian delegation, and this was not acceptable.

Peres passed on a message to Ambassador Dinitz saying that if Hussein included PLO members in his delegation, Israel would object publicly but live with it. But through special envoy Richard Murphy, the Reagan administration checked this out with Foreign Minister Shamir, who said that it was completely unacceptable. The issue went to Reagan to decide and he ruled in favor of Shamir.[38] The national unity government thus demonstrated that it was a government of national paralysis.

On May 20, 1985, Israel released 1,150 Palestinian prisoners held on terrorist offenses in exchange for just three Israeli soldiers who had been captured in Lebanon during the Lebanon War. The deal was arranged through Ahmed Jibril, leader of the PFLP-General Command, who was one of the most operationally competent Palestinian terrorist leaders. Rabin had softened over the years regarding Israeli casualties—probably a symptom of delayed guilt over all the men who died under his command in 1948.[39] In Israel, whenever a soldier is kidnapped the family and friends descend on the government and harass it to release prisoners in order to win the release of their loved one. The ethos of the Entebbe mission has been lost over the subsequent decades.

But Israel could still make war, and that was Rabin's responsibility. In September 1985, Force 17, Arafat's bodyguard security force, killed three Israelis who were suspected Mossad agents in the harbor at Larnaca, Cyprus. On October 1, 1985, Israel retaliated with a bombing raid on PLO headquarters in the Tunis suburb of Hamam al-Shaat carried out by eight F-16 fighter-bombers. The raid killed 56 Palestinians and 15 Tunisians, and wounded about a hundred more. This demonstrated Israel's long reach.[40]

The month following King Hussein's speech breaking the PLO connection, Rabin and Peres met near Strasbourg, France, to discuss developments on the West Bank. Rabin complained about increased PLO activity there. Hussein said he had no intention of allowing such an increase and promised to cooperate with Israel to end it. After Hussein returned to Jordan, he ordered the closing of the PLO's office in Amman and the expulsion of Arafat deputy Khalil al-Wazir (Abu Jihad).

Four months later Rabin, accompanied by Peres, again met with Hussein, this time at the king's holiday home in Akaba. They spent four hours discussing economic development on the West Bank as well as an international conference. Jordan wanted $1.5 billion in funding and Israel supported this, but Congress was only willing to allocate $90 million in funds for economic development on the West Bank.[41]

During the final months of Peres's premiership there was a flurry of diplomatic activity. Peres made an official state visit to Morocco on July 22, 1986—almost nine years after Morocco helped to facilitate the peace process between Egypt and Israel. Peres had twice visited Rabat as leader of the opposition, but this was the first open, official visit by an Israeli leader to Morocco. This was followed by a visit to Alexandria to see President Mubarak in September. Peres signed an agreement that allowed the Taba dispute over the location of the border between Israel and the Sinai near Eilat to go to arbitration. The arbitrator ruled in favor of Egypt. On October 20, 1986, Peres turned over power to Shamir and became foreign minister.[42]

In November 1985 a U.S. Naval Intelligence civilian employee named Jonathan Pollard was arrested outside the Israeli embassy in Washington while trying to get in. Pollard was an American Jew who had fantasized about working for the Mossad. He had approached an IAF pilot whom he knew and offered his services. The pilot was working for the Scientific Liaison

Bureau, a small intelligence organization run by Rafael "Stinkie" Eitan (not to be confused with the former chief of staff with the same name). Eitan used Pollard to collect American intelligence on Arab countries that the United States had chosen not to provide to Israel. Shamir, Rabin, and Peres worked together over the next year to convince Washington that none of them had known anything about Pollard and that he was the result of an overenthusiastic agent handler who had misinterpreted a directive forbidding espionage operations aimed at America. Pollard was sentenced to life imprisonment on the recommendation of Defense Secretary Caspar Weinberger, an anti-Zionist Jew, in the winter of 1987. Since then, Pollard has become a *cause célèbre* of the Israeli right and its American Jewish supporters.[43]

In April 1987 Peres met with Hussein in London again and the two agreed on a plan for an international peace conference on the Middle East. Peres then traveled to Washington and spoke with Secretary of State George Shultz, asking him to present the joint Peres-Hussein plan as an American plan to the Israeli government. But Shultz revealed the existence of the document to Shamir, who told him that to present the plan would amount to interfering with internal Israeli politics. Shultz dropped the matter and the initiative died. As a result, Hussein lost his faith in Peres and his ability to deliver on his promises.[44]

On December 8, 1987, a heavy Israeli truck with a container load and bad brakes slammed into a Palestinian car, killing four Palestinians and wounding several others. The rumor quickly spread that this was a revenge killing for the murder of an Israeli salesman in Gaza a few days before. This rumor resonated with the Arab culture of blood feuds and so was readily believed. In addition, two decades of Israeli occupation and the lack of diplomatic progress under successive Israeli governments made the situation ripe for rebellion. The accident occurred near the Erez Crossing on the Tel Aviv–Gaza highway. Soon youths began throwing stones at Israeli guards and roving Israeli patrols. Within days all of Gaza was in revolt, and then the uprising, or Intifada (Arabic for shaking off), as it became known, quickly spread to the West Bank.[45]

The day after the Intifada broke out, Rabin headed to Washington on a scheduled trip to discuss defense matters with the Reagan administration. Rabin's senior aides advised him to go through with the trip; after all, this was no different from many other outbreaks of violence that had occurred in the past and would soon be over, or so they thought. Rabin signed a memorandum on the purchase of 70 F-16 fighters with Defense Secretary Frank Carlucci. He also spoke before an Israel bonds convention in Florida. But as Israeli troops were shown on the American television news using live ammunition against rioters, the Intifada quickly became the leading topic of discussion in Washington. Rabin did not return to Israel until December 21.[46]

When asked about the Intifada, Rabin tended to blame it on either Iran or Syria or both. He personally had nothing but contempt for the military capabilities of the various Palestinian terror organizations. Therefore he had a tendency to blame those whom he did have respect for (at least in military terms) for anything that happened in the region. To Rabin, Iran and Syria (and Iraq before the Gulf War of 1991) were serious enemies that deserved respect. When he thought of a peace process, he thought in terms of one with Syria or with Jordan.[47]

Rabin's prescription for dealing with the Intifada was to use brute force. It is said that he issued an order to "break their bones," although no one can produce any evidence of this. Many believe that he may have said it but meant it figuratively rather than literally. But numerous soldiers did take it literally. Until the outbreak of the Intifada, Israeli troops were not trained in riot control. They were instead trained in conventional and counter-insurgency infantry tactics. The IDF did not have riot control equipment, such as riot batons, clear plastic shields and visored helmets, on hand to issue to Israeli troops in the field. So the troops—most of whom were teenaged conscripts—used live ammunition to defend themselves. As a result, seventeen Palestinians were killed and over a hundred wounded in the first two weeks of the Intifada.[48]

The outbreak of the Intifada caught the PLO in Tunis off guard. The outbreak was spontaneous, followed by a quick organizing effort by local Palestinian leaders from both the Fatah and the Muslim Brotherhood in Gaza, which in January 1988—if not sooner—became the Islamic Resistance Movement, or Hamas. The two movements began competing with each other for support in Gaza and the West Bank. In July 1988 King Hussein publicly disavowed any responsibility for the fate of the Palestinians in the territories and ended his financial subsidies to pay the salaries of former Jordanian government employees. The Jordanian option was over for Labor, but it took Labor several months to realize this.[49]

On November 1, 1988, a general election was held in Israel. The Likud won 40 seats and Labor won 39. The day before the election, Palestinian terrorists had tossed petrol bombs on an Israeli bus crossing through Jericho, killing five people aboard. Several people decided to vote for the political right at the last minute in an emotional reaction to this. But because there were more seats on the right than on the left, when the terms of the national unity government were negotiated, they did not include a rotation of the premiership. Shamir would remain as prime minister for the entire length of the government and Rabin as defense minister. Peres opted to become finance minister rather than foreign minister, probably because of his experience operating under Shamir as foreign minister from 1987 to 1988, and he became deputy premier as well.[50]

Chapter Seven

From Defense Minister to Martyr

The second consecutive national unity government of the 1980s lasted for just sixteen months, from December 1988 to March 1990. Defense Minister Rabin played one important role in it. In December 1988 the Palestine Liberation Organization (PLO) at last accepted the American conditions for a diplomatic role by recognizing UN Security Council Resoultion 242 and disavowing the use of terrorism. In one of his final acts in government, Secretary of State George Shultz recognized the PLO and opened a dialogue with it. Rabin realized that Israel could not remain passive, as it had since leaving Lebanon. He was also under pressure from the mainstream of Labor to take a more activist approach.

The new American administration of President George H.W. Bush wanted to do something in the Middle East conflict. Now entering his second term, Secretary of State James Baker wanted to make his mark after the relative passivity of the Reagan administration. Baker thus started the typical consultations. Rabin proposed to the government that it hold elections in the West Bank and Gaza for an assembly with which it would then negotiate. This Rabin Plan was accepted by Yitzhak Shamir and so became the Shamir Plan (or the Shamir-Rabin Plan).[1]

Within the Likud those politicians who wanted to attract a following began introducing conditions to the plan that they knew would be unacceptable to the PLO and thus deal breakers. The three ministers became known as the "constraints ministers": Ariel Sharon, Yitzhak Moda'I and David Levy. While Shamir defended his plan and presented it to the new administration, voting for it in the government, within the Likud he did nothing to defend it. He was happy to see the "constraints ministers" pass their deal-breaking conditions. The Shamir Plan in turn led President Mubarak of Egypt produce his own ten-point plan on behalf of the PLO. Then Baker came up with his five points in an attempt to reconcile the two proposals. The Israeli government voted not to accept the five points, however, and the initiative came to a halt by May. About the same time a small terrorist organization within the PLO, the Palestine Liberation Front (PLF), carried out an attack on a Tel Aviv beach, and Yasir Arafat refused to condemn the raid. This called the PLO's turn away from terrorism into question. Washington ended its dialogue with the PLO before it had proceeded very far. Baker addressed the America Israel Public Affairs Committee (AIPAC) and, giving the White House switchboard's number, said, "Call us when you are serious about peace."[2]

Rabin was content to continue presiding over the defense ministry and fight the Intifada once Israel was off the hook thanks to the PLF. Peres, however, wanted to leave the national unity government over Shamir's intransigence. He thought that he could either form his own coalition with the religious parties or bring down the government from the opposition benches and force new elections. Rabin was suspicious that Peres simply wanted power and he said as much in a speech on March 5, 1990. On March 11 Shamir said that he would not accept Palestinians from East Jerusalem in the Palestinian delegation to negotiate with Israel, nor would he accept the delegation consulting with the PLO.[3]

Shamir decided to preempt a Labor coup against the government by firing Peres as finance minister. This led all of the Labor ministers to walk out of the government. Rather than resign, Shamir went before the Knesset and became the first premier in Israeli history to lose a no-confidence vote (by a five-vote margin).

Peres then started holding consultations with the other parties about forming a coalition led by Labor. At one point he thought he had enough votes to form a government, but he fell victim to religious infighting. Rabbi Menachem Shneerson of Brooklyn, whose followers regarded him as a messiah, advised his Israeli supporters not to form a government with Peres, although the rabbi had never even been to Israel. Peres's razor-thin majority of 61 votes dropped to 59. Shamir went ahead and formed a government of the right, which included the same parties that had betrayed Peres. Rabin dubbed Peres's attempt to form a coalition the "stinking maneuver" (*hatargil hamasrekha*), as it had cost him his favorite job.[4]

Shamir's new government lasted for only two years. During that time Peres defeated another attempt by Rabin to wrest the party leadership from him in July 1990. The Gulf War took place in the winter of 1991, and afterward James Baker began organizing an international peace conference on the Middle East for the end of October. He had to twist the arms of both Shamir and

President Assad to get them to attend. The Madrid Conference, like Geneva eighteen years before, lasted for just two days, saw little agreement, and then served as the initiator for a separate series of talks. Peace talks involving Israel, the Palestinians, and the Jordanians began in Washington that fall.[5]

The Likud began to unravel in the fall of 1991, when the Bush administration denied Israel $10 billion in loan guarantees to help resettle Russian immigrants to Israel. This demonstrated to the Israeli public that Shamir, through his settlement activities, had lost Israel the support of its one reliable ally. In December the Tzomet Party of General Raphael "Raful" Eitan quit the government. Then, in mid–January, the Tehiya Party of Geula Cohen followed suit, along with the Moledet Party of General Rehavam "Gandhi" Ze'evi. Shamir easily won a no-confidence vote in late January, but he was inclined to agree to early elections with Labor before his situation deteriorated too far and the new Labor leader could properly organize.[6]

In February 1992 Labor held its first ever leadership primary in which ordinary party members could vote for the party leader as long as they were registered with the party. Peres was popular with the mainstream party activists, as he represented their views much better than Rabin did and was more inclined to consult with them. But Peres could not win the support of non-party members—the floating secular voters. He was considered too much of a dreamer, a schemer, and a politician. This was in comparison to Rabin's image of a patriotic war hero and security expert. So in the primary many of Peres's supporters voted for Rabin because of the electability issue. Two other candidates ran in the primary and took votes away from Peres. A minimum of 40 percent was needed for a winner to be declared, and Rabin won with 40.59 percent to Peres's 34.80 percent, 18.77 percent for Histadrut general secretary Israel Kessar and 5.44 percent for Ora Namir. This was the start of the Americanization of Israeli politics, with the Likud soon adopting the primary system as well.[7]

Rabin moved into Peres's old office the next day. As soon as an election date was agreed upon with the Likud, Rabin began campaigning full time from dawn until dusk and into the late hours of the evening. He had the stamina to go all day with just a sandwich and/or beer for lunch. Rabin had always been a high-energy person and a workaholic in his career in the military and as a minister in the government. He believed that he could win and that the time was ripe for peace with the Palestinians, and these two beliefs motivated him.[8]

Rabin and Labor had several things going for them in 1992. First, there had been some 420,000 new immigrants from the former Soviet Union who arrived in Israel between 1989 and 1992. They suffered greatly from adjusting to a country that was not ready to absorb them. The Russians (as other Israelis referred to all the former Soviet immigrants) were more naturally inclined toward the right than toward the left. But the election served as a good opportunity for them to protest their treatment by the government in a meaningful fashion. Russians voted nearly three to one in favor of Labor over the Likud. (This is ironic because Shamir had spent his entire career in politics as an advocate of the right of Soviet Jews to immigrate to Israel.)[9]

Second, many Mizrakhim, or Oriental Jews (those from Muslim countries), who served as the loyal base of the Likud felt forgotten by Shamir in his eagerness to settle the West Bank. State funding that the Mizrakhim thought should have gone to eliminate poverty, improve housing, and educate them instead went to settle mostly European Jews on the West Bank. Shamir was also much less adept at playing the ethnic card with Mizrakhim than his predecessor Menahem Begin had been. So on election day much of the Likud's base either stayed home or voted for Labor or for Shas, an ethnic religious party.[10]

Third, this was the election in which many settler leaders from the West Bank decided to head their own lists instead of merely appearing on the lists of the Likud or the National Religious Party. This tended to so disperse the settler vote that none of the new lists made the 1.5 percent entry barrier to the Knesset, and votes were wasted that otherwise would have resulted in a victory for the political right.[11]

When the final votes, including the soldiers' votes, were tallied after three days, Labor had won 44 seats, the Likud had won 32 (the same number as Labor in 1977), Meretz 12 seats, Tzomet 8 seats, the National Religious Party and Shas six each, United Torah Judaism four, Moledet three, and two Arab parties a combined total of five seats. This gave parties of the center-left 56 seats and a bare majority with the support of the Arab parties. Rabin could have quickly formed a coalition with just Meretz, but he wanted more support, so he also talked with both Tzomet and Shas. Tzomet wanted the education ministry for Eitan, but Meretz regarded him as too far to the right, and so insisted on this office for itself. Tzomet went into opposition and Shas took its place in the coalition.[12]

Rabin kept the defense ministry for himself, in imitation of Ben-Gurion and Eshkol. He also insisted that Peres, who became foreign minister, would have no control over relations with Washington or over the bilateral peace negotiations with the Arabs. Peres was instead in charge of foreign relations with Europe and the Third World, as well as the multilateral peace talks on topics such as arms control and the environment. Rabin had promised to make peace with the Palestinians within 18 months of taking power.

Rabin felt that the region was ripe for peace after the Gulf War. The PLO's support of Iraq during the war had resulted in a cutoff of subsidies from the Gulf States. This meant that the PLO was broke and could no longer afford to pay its employees. Jordan had also washed its hands of the West Bank. Rabin saw two main dangers on the horizon if peace was not made soon. First, Iran might acquire nuclear weapons and become more involved in the Israeli-Palestinian conflict in a bid for leadership in the Middle East. Second, fundamentalism might become the dominant belief system in the Arab world, and the conflict could become unresolvable as it turned into a religious fight and not a national one (this could already be seen with the Iranian Revolution and with the rise of Hamas and Hezbollah). Rabin wanted to free up the IDF to deal with the far dangers stemming from the Persian Gulf by making peace with the near dangers of the Palestinians and Syria. He also knew that once he had made peace with either of these, Jordan would likely follow in formalizing its peaceful relations with Israel. Rabin had by 1992 devoted over half a century to the cause of the security of Israel. This is what motivated him.[13]

Rabin spent his first year dealing with the security threat from Hamas terrorism and attempting to make progress in the Washington talks with the Palestinians. The local delegates from the Palestinian territories were initially taking their cues from the PLO in an effort to force Jerusalem to deal with the PLO. This was something that neither Peres nor Rabin wanted to do. Peres also dealt with Hamas by exiling over 400 Hamas activists to Lebanon. He got this past Meretz by winning a government decision to exile an unspecified number of Hamas leaders. And he got it past the Israeli Supreme Court by exiling each of them individually. This led the Palestinians to boycott the talks in solidarity and Peres was left without much. Beirut refused to admit the exiles into Lebanon, and so they remained in southern Lebanon in tents, where they met with local Hezbollah activists who trained them in various terrorist skills and networked with them. The exile ended up hurting Israel's image and its security.[14]

The first decision for Rabin, and for all subsequent Israeli leaders, was which track to give preference to: the Palestinian or the Syrian? After the initial paralysis in Washington, Rabin turned to Damascus. President Assad insisted on receiving the same treatment as Sadat—100 percent of the Golan back. Rabin wanted to know what type of peace would be the result before he would commit himself to this deal. He had run in the election on a platform of not leaving the Golan, and there were some 13,000 settlers on the Golan who were mostly Labor supporters. Finally, Rabin made a "deposit" with President Clinton of a verbal commitment to return all of the Golan if he was satisfied with the peace that Assad would offer. But his attempt to lease back the Golan from Syria was a non-starter with Assad.[15]

In January 1993 a couple of Israeli academics, Yair Hirshfeld and Ron Pundak, with ties to Yossi Beilin, who was Peres's top aide in the foreign ministry before leaving Labor to join Meretz and eventually become its leader, started secret negotiations with some PLO officials in Norway under the auspices of a nongovernmental organization supported by the Norwegian foreign ministry. They met outside of Oslo in a house owned by the Norwegian government, giving rise to the shorthand term "Oslo" or "Oslo process" for the peace process that resulted. Beilin informed Peres once the talks got going, and Peres in turn informed Rabin. The participants discussed what each side might be willing to concede for a peace agreement.[16]

Once the talks got serious, Peres brought Uri Savir, a foreign ministry professional, into the conversation. Rabin told his cabinet on April 18 that he no longer believed in the "Syria first" policy, but he resisted pressure to deal directly with Tunis. Then Rabin brought in his man: Yoel Singer, an Israeli lawyer practicing in Washington and a reserve colonel in the IDF's legal division. Rabin wanted him to conduct a systematic interrogation of the Palestinians regarding how the implementation of the peace process would work. This demonstrated that Rabin had bought into the process and was serious about it. In early July Histadrut Labor leader Haim Ramon approached Ahmed Tibi, an Arab member of the Knesset who sometimes advised Arafat about matters related to Israeli Arabs. Ramon wanted Tibi to clarify several issues related to Arab refugees, Israeli settlements, and the future of Jerusalem. Tibi went off to Tunis and got the answers from Mahmoud Abbas. After two months of questioning and consultations with their respective superiors, it was decided that the time had come to close the deal with an all-night negotiating session between Peres and Ahmed Qureia (a.k.a. Abu Ala) by phone. Peres was on business in Stockholm and conducted a series of calls through the night to PLO headquarters in Tunis to negotiate the final pieces of the deal.[17]

Initially, Peres offered Arafat a proposal of "Gaza first": an idea that had been in the Labor Party for over a decade (championed by Gad Ya'acovi, a Rafi colleague of Peres's) which involved implementing autonomy first in Gaza and then in the West Bank. Arafat countered with "Gaza and Jericho first." Arafat wanted a foothold in the West Bank, as he knew that Israel did not value Gaza but did value the West Bank for both religious/historical reasons and strategic value. He did not want it to be "Gaza first and last."[18]

In early July, 63 percent of Israelis had expressed dissatisfaction with the performance of the Rabin government in a poll. Rabin had turned 71 earlier that year. He wanted to make peace with the Palestinians and thereby demonstrate a major accomplishment and ensure his place in history. His first premiership had largely been a failure, and he felt that Dayan had unfairly gotten the credit for the victory in 1967 and that Begin had received credit for the peace treaty with Egypt, without him being really acknowledged for the role that the Sinai II interim agreement had played in building that peace. These legacy concerns, combined with his worries about Israel's long-range security, prompted him to forge ahead with the process.[19]

On August 24 Peres made a secret trip to Oslo, and he and Abbas (a.k.a. Abu Mazen) initialed the Declaration of Principles (DoP) agreement. Altogether, the Oslo agreements consisted of six documents: the DoP; an agreed memorandum clarifying some points in the DoP; and four appendices covering elections in the territories, the withdrawal of Israeli troops from Gaza and Jericho, Israeli-Palestinian economic cooperation, and regional economic development. For the initialing, the Norwegian hosts pulled out of storage a table on which the agreement giving Norway independence from Sweden had been signed.[20]

Peres then flew to Point Magoo Naval Air Station in California to personally brief Secretary of State Warren Christopher, who was vacationing there, about the agreements. Christopher wanted an American signing ceremony in Washington so that Clinton could take political credit for the agreement. Peres was happy to oblige. Originally the ceremony was to only involve Peres and Abu Mazen, but because of the nature of the PLO, Arafat insisted upon signing the agreement himself. So Rabin was also included. During the signing ceremony on September 15 on the White House lawn, Rabin made a very moving speech in which he declared "enough of blood and tears, enough." He called on the Palestinians to end the conflict with Israel.

During the ceremony, President Clinton nudged Rabin to move closer to Arafat. Arafat then stuck out his hand, waiting for Rabin to shake it. Rabin shook it with a grimace of distaste on his face—distaste caused either by the knowledge of how much Israeli blood Arafat had been responsible for shedding over nearly three decades or by the realization of what the photo of that handshake might cost him politically (probably both). Arafat then turned to Peres and Rabin mumbled to him, "Now it's your turn." He did not want his rival to benefit politically from his own handshake.[21]

In the months following the signing of the DoP in Washington, Hamas ramped up its terror campaign within Israel in an attempt to derail the peace process. Rabin declared (in a paraphrase of David Ben-Gurion's famous formula about the 1939 British White Paper on Palestine) that "we will fight terror as if there are no peace talks, and we will conduct peace talks as if there is no terror." (Ben-Gurion's formulation concerned fighting Nazi Germany on the British side during World War II.) Hamas initially targeted Israeli soldiers in a guerrilla campaign, but in the mid-1990s it turned to targeting Israeli civilians. Rabin's method of dealing with terrorist attacks was to close off the territories so that Palestinian laborers could not enter Israel, thus restraining potential terrorists. But the net effect of these actions was to actually help terrorism by increasing unemployment among Palestinians. Palestinians who suddenly found themselves unemployed and unable to feed their families would then volunteer for suicide missions, thereby increasing terrorism once the closure was finished. This approach also gave Hamas a veto over the peace process because Rabin would halt everything. Rabin never found a way out of this dilemma, and his successors continued it as well.

On February 25, 1994, a reserve doctor in the IDF, Baruch Goldstein, who was an American immigrant and disciple of the racist Rabbi Meir Kahane, entered the Makhpela Tomb of the Patriarchs mosque at Hebron during prayers. He leveled his army-issue M-16 rifle and began to systematically shoot the men at prayer. He fired for ten minutes, murdering thirty men before he was finally subdued while changing magazines and killed. It had been his aim to kill the peace process itself as well as the worshippers. Rabin reacted by applying a curfew to Hebron in a bid to keep Jews and Arabs apart.[22]

On May 4, 1994, Rabin traveled to Cairo to sign the Oslo I agreement giving control of Gaza and Jericho to Arafat. At the last minute Arafat refused to sign because he did not agree with the size of the Jericho district that was to be turned over to the PLO. Israel had interpreted the Jericho in the DoP as the municipality, whereas the Palestinians interpreted it to mean the district—a much larger area. Mubarak was furious with Arafat and began cursing him in Arabic. Rabin, however, agreed that the size of the Jericho enclave would not be limited to the 65-square-mile area shown on the map, but would be negotiated between the two sides. Rabin soon found that this was just the first of his problems with Arafat. But these types of stunts made Arafat popular with Palestinians, who believed that he was willing to defy the great powers on their behalf.[23]

Three weeks later, on May 25, Rabin stood side by side with King Hussein of Jordan as the two signed an agreement to end the state of war between their countries. Rabin excluded Peres from the peace process with Jordan—he wanted something all for himself. With the Palestinians it made good political sense to spread the risk around and implicate Peres in the process in case it failed. But the peace process with Jordan was low risk because the two countries had enjoyed de facto peace for decades, ever since the 1970 civil war. Hussein was happy to exclude Peres, whom he did not trust after the failure of the London agreement in 1987. So during the summer Rabin journeyed to King Hussein's palace in Amman, and the two of them and Crown Prince Hassan pored over maps and drafted a peace treaty. The treaty was then signed in a minefield in the Arava Desert that separated them in the south on October 26. This time Clinton was a guest rather than the host.[24]

At the end of 1993 *Time* magazine had named Rabin and Arafat, along with F.W. de Klerk and Nelson Mandela of South Africa, as its men of the year. In December 1994 it was announced that the Nobel Peace Prize would go to Rabin, Peres, and Arafat. By now the two quarreling Labor Party rivals had realized that peace was a big enough prize for both of them and that they were much better off cooperating and achieving this goal than they would be by fighting and missing it. The last two years of Rabin's life were spent in relative cooperation with his rival of three decades. The two became partners but never friends.[25]

Rabin trusted Peres enough to put him in charge of conducting the negotiations with the Palestinians for the Oslo II agreement, which involved the IDF withdrawing from the major cities and towns of the West Bank. After

Yasir Arafat (center) in conversation with Prime Minister Rabin (right) and Foreign Minister Peres at the Nobel Prize ceremony at Oslo, Norway, December 10, 1994. Photograph by Yaacov Saar, Israeli Government Press Office.

the Nobel Prize ceremony in Oslo in December 1994, Rabin began referring questions on the negotiations to Peres to answer. With only 37 percent of Israelis expressing support for the continuation of the peace process in early 1995 due to terrorism, which was at a much higher level than it had been before the process, neither Rabin nor Peres was willing to state publicly that they supported the establishment of a Palestinian state as the end goal of the process. Rabin's aides later said that he was willing to accept the existence of a Palestinian state in exchange for peace—he just did not see it as a positive gain. Rabin tended to stick to talking about Palestinian autonomy, and Peres would talk about regional economic cooperation in the New Middle East.[26]

After his failure in the 1992 election, Yitzhak Shamir had decided to retire from politics and write his memoirs. His anticipated successor for years had been former foreign minister and defense minister Moshe Arens. But Arens had expected Shamir to announce his retirement before the 1992 election. When he failed to do this, Arens decided to quit politics after the election. So the two leaders went out together. In the Likud, by far the largest faction in the early 1990s was the Shamir-Arens center faction, which also included a group of second-generation Likudniks known as "the princes." These were the sons and daughter of major figures in the Etzel underground and Herut Party, including: Benni Begin, Benjamin "Bibi" Netanyahu, Dan Meridor, Ronnie Milo, and Tzipi Livni, among others. Outside this group were the factions of Ariel Sharon and David Levy. Levy mostly had support among Moroccans and Sharon among settlers. On March 24, 1993, the Likud had held its first-ever primary for party leader. The candidates were Benjamin Netanyahu, Benni Begin, David Levy, and Moshe Katsav. Netanyahu won with 52 percent of the vote, with Levy trailing at 26 percent, Begin at 15 percent and Katsav at 7 percent.[27]

Netanyahu was the son of a former editor of the Revisionist Party newspaper in Palestine in the 1930s who had moved to the United States in the 1940s in pursuit of an academic position. Netanyahu grew up and attended high school in Philadelphia. After a stint in the IDF in the late 1960s and early 1970s, when he served as an officer in Sayeret Matkal under Ehud Barak, he returned to the United States to attend college. He worked as a furniture salesman, got his first political job working for the Israeli consulate and became the protégé of Moshe Arens. He also worked as a consultant with the Boston Group alongside Mitt Romney. He became a specialist in *hasbara*, or "explanation," and during the Gulf War he often appeared on ABC's *Nightline* to do interviews.[28]

The settlers saw the Oslo process as a mortal threat that might result in either their eviction from the West Bank or being forced to live in a Palestinian state under Palestinian law that might be enforced by former terrorists. So they organized in opposition to the peace process during the mid–1990s. With the demise of Tehiya in 1992, the Likud competed with the National Religious Party to be the party of the settlers. The champion of the settlers in the Likud was Sharon. On July 2, 1994, the day after Arafat publicly returned to Gaza after nearly three decades in exile, Sharon and Netanyahu reconciled.

In reaction to the Goldstein massacre in Hebron, Hamas began a series of bombings aimed at Jewish civilian targets that was masterminded by bomb maker Yahya Ayyash, known to both Jews and Arabs as "the engineer." These bombings destroyed public support for the Oslo process among Jews. After the Beit Lid bombing killed 21 (mostly soldiers waiting for rides), President Ezer Weizman in early 1995 made the first of many political remarks in his term as president and publicly called on Rabin to suspend the peace process. Rabin simply ignored him. The dove whom Rabin had saved from being fired by Shamir after Weizman had twice tried to keep him from winning the prime ministry by recalling the incident in May 1967 was demonstrating his enmity once again. Leah Rabin probably never forgave him.[29]

During 1995 both Sharon and Netanyahu appeared at several anti–Oslo rallies organized by settlers. These rallies were dominated by extremist elements who attempted to demonize both Rabin and Peres—especially Rabin, because of his greater public credibility. At these rallies they would carry posters with photos of Rabin in an SS uniform or wearing an Arab keffiyah like the one Arafat commonly wore. At none of these rallies did Sharon or Netanyahu ever distance themselves from those displaying these posters or from the religious rhetoric condemning Rabin as a traitor. Rabin was a hated figure among the settlers because, unlike Yigal Allon and Peres, he had never helped the settlers during the period of his first government, or even before that time. He also ridiculed them as "propeller heads" for the knit *kipot* skullcaps that they wore. At one raucous protest in Jerusalem in July 1995 the protesters went on a rampage against Arabs in the Old City and destroyed property.[30]

In the medieval period a prime fear of Jews living in the ghettoes of Europe had been that traitors within the community would betray them to Christian authorities. Jewish law, *halakha*, was adopted by outlawing certain types of activities and pronouncing death sentences on anyone who cooperated with outsiders against the community. Various rabbis in Israel during the 1990s cooperated with the settlers by issuing religious opinions that branded Rabin a *rodef* (a pursuer of Jews) or, alternatively, a *moser* (informant or seller of Jewish property). This gave Jewish extremists license to kill Rabin according to Jewish religious law. The assassin who would later kill Rabin shopped around before the murder, looking for a rabbi who would brand Rabin as a *moser* or a *rodef,* but he could not find one.[31]

Among Israel's many secular universities, there is a single religious university, Bar Ilan, which might be compared to Notre Dame University or Yeshiva University in the United States. One of the law students there was a young Yemenite student from Herzliya who had attended yeshiva before enrolling at the university to study law, computers, and theology. He was narcissistic and egotistical, and he tended to see issues in black and white. His name was Yigal Amir. He formed a secret organization, which he modeled on Yitzhak Shamir's Lehi, dedicated to assassinating political traitors. It was known as *Eyal,* or Jewish Fighting Organization. Among the members of Eyal was a Shabak informer, but he never notified his superiors of Amir's plans to murder Rabin.[32]

By the end of August Uri Savir had gotten as far as he could in the Oslo talks without the intervention of Peres. Peres thus spent September negotiating the final points of the Oslo II agreement with Ahmed Qurei (Abu Ala'a). The agreement divided the West Bank into three areas: Area A was under exclusive Arab control; Area B was under joint authority with Palestinian civil control and Israeli security control; and Area C remained under Israeli control. The agreement called for three major Israeli redeployments of unspecified size over a five-year period of autonomy before the final agreement would go into effect. In the first redeployment Israel would withdraw from seven major urban centers: Jenin, Nablus, Kalkilya, Tulkarem, Bethlehem, Ramallah, and Hebron. This in effect separated the Palestinian population from much of their land. Over 90 percent of the Palestinian population lived in Area A, but only a small fraction of the land on the West Bank. The IDF would withdraw from these areas and erect a large number of checkpoints to control Palestinian travel from Area A to Areas B and C. Area C consisted of a wide area to the west of the Jordan River encompassing the Jordan Valley and much of the land in the central region. The geography of the West Bank changed in 1995 and remains intact to this day. A current map of the West Bank resembles one of the KwaZulu homeland in Natal, South Africa, under apartheid.[33]

Rabin and Arafat signed the Oslo II agreement in the East Room of the White House on September 26. The agreement was then debated in the Knesset on October 5, 1995, and when it came to a vote it passed by a two-vote margin: 61 to 59. Had a single member from the winning side switched sides, it would have been a tie vote. Labor managed to induce a member of Raful Eitan's Tzomet Party to defect in exchange for a deputy minister's position in the government with a car and driver. Afterward the opposition taunted the government by saying that Oslo had passed thanks to "Alex Goldfarb's Mercedes." Three days after the debate, a huge rally was held outside Zion Gate in Jerusalem with some 30,000 settlers and rightists in attendance. Amir had organized a contingent of 150 students from Bar Ilan to attend the rally and had even arranged some of the speakers.[34]

Because of the many settler demonstrations against Oslo, the Peace Now organization, the main Israeli peace movement (created in March 1978), decided to hold a rally in support of the Oslo process. Both Peres and Rabin were lined up as speakers in order to ensure a good turnout. The rally was held in the Kikar Malkhei Israel (Kings of Israel Square) on the evening of November 4. This same square had been the site of a massive demonstration following the Sabra and Shatilla massacres in September 1982, calling for the resignation of Sharon. This rally was more modest in size but well publicized.

Amir took a bus and then walked the remaining distance to the Kings of Israel Square parking lot. He waited in the lot until after the rally had started, then made his way into the staging area that Rabin and Peres would exit into before leaving. He was carrying a 9 mm Baretta automatic pistol loaded with "dum-dum" bullets, which are illegal because of the massive wounds they cause. His plan was to wait until both Rabin and Peres had exited and then try to kill them both. Unlike friends of his who were afraid of being killed in the attempt, Amir was ready to die or risk life in prison in order to kill Rabin. If he could not get both, he would settle for Rabin alone.[35]

The rally ended with a rendition of "the song of peace," a song composed during the War of Attrition and banned from being sung by army entertainment troupes by then Chief of Staff Haim Bar-Lev, as he believed it was bad for morale. Peres sang off key and Rabin stood awkwardly and mumbled the words during the singing. He then folded the lyrics up and placed them in his pocket. The two exited the stage together. Amir waited for his opportunity. Then Rabin headed back to thank the organizers, and Peres got in his car and was driven away. When Rabin walked back, Amir came up behind him and extended his pistol nearly into Rabin's back before pulling the trigger three times. Two slugs ripped into Rabin's back and the third hit the arm of one of his bodyguards. Rabin was hustled into his car while Amir was disarmed by the other security men. As the driver drove off toward the hospital, Rabin was already dying from blood loss and shock. He was dead before they arrived at the hospital. He was 73 years old.[36]

Rabin paid the price for Shabak's tendency to see threats only in terms of Arabs. If someone spoke Hebrew without an Arab accent, he was not usually considered a threat. Karmi Gilon resigned after the murder in recognition of the failure of his organization. Amir, after proudly explaining why he had killed Rabin, was sentenced to life imprisonment. Like Baruch Goldstein before him, he became an icon among settlers and the religious Zionist right.[37]

Rabin, like John F. Kennedy, became a tabula rasa for the dreams of his various supporters. For the doves in Meretz and Labor who did not particularly like Rabin during his life, he became a posthumous peacenik and icon. Those in the Likud and Labor who had supported him when he was defense minister now felt like the political left had stolen their hero. They started the rumor that he was ready to end the peace process because of Palestinian violations when he was murdered. Those closest to Rabin, however, said that he had reconciled himself to the existence of a Palestinian state and was moving to conclude a final settlement with the Palestinians during his second term. He had also planned on negotiating a peace treaty with the Syrians when he was killed.[38]

Arafat was deliberately kept away from Rabin's funeral. A few weeks later his helicopter brought him to Rabin's house and he spent about 90 minutes paying his respects to Leah Rabin and the rest of the family. It was his first time inside Israel since the War of Independence. Arafat would now have to deal in rather quick succession with Peres, Netanyahu, Barak and Sharon.

Since his death, Rabin has gradually gone from Israel's Kennedy to Israel's Lincoln. First there were a number of conspiracy theories blaming Shabak for his murder, not through omission, but rather through active commission. Kings of Israel Square, where he was murdered, was renamed Rabin Square. The anniversary of his death became a major rallying date for the left—first, as a day on which to blame the right, and then, later, as a day on which to examine Rabin's complex legacy by inviting speakers who were not from the left. Rabin also occupies a major place in the Palmakh Museum in Tel Aviv.

In 1999 Uri Milstein, a military historian of the political right at Bar Ilan University and former instructor of Amir's, wrote a book on Rabin's military career that turned him into a draft dodger hiding away in the Palmakh rather than enlisting in the British army. He was also considered by Milstein to have been an incompetent commander in Jerusalem during the War of Independence.[39] In 2013, a book appeared on Rabin's youth and military career through the War of Independence that does for him what Carl Sandburg did for Lincoln.[40] Another study by Efraim Inbar examines his national security views from his period as chief of staff onward.[41] Maybe each new generation in Israel will see a new Rabin biography designed for its needs. Perhaps his major speeches at Hebrew University, at the White House lawn and at Rabin Square will produce in time their own detailed studies, like those of Lincoln's Coopers Union speech, Gettysburg Address, Pretoria speech, and so forth.

Most Israeli prime ministers, if they are important, are the subject of a number of books during their careers. So far only three have been the focus of sustained academic interest: David Ben-Gurion, Menahem Begin and Rabin.[42] Because some of the mythology surrounding Ben-Gurion has been discredited by historians, Rabin seems to be the model politician for the center-left, while Begin serves the same purpose for the right. Rabin is the guardian of the peace process, and Begin of *Eretz Israel haShlema*.

III. Ariel "Arik" Sharon, 1928–2014

Chapter Eight

General Sharon

Ariel Scheinerman was born on February 27, 1928, in the village of Kfar Malal in the coastal plain of Palestine known as the Sharon, from which he would later take his name. His father Samuil was an agronomist (a rare occupation in those days) who had arrived in Palestine from the city of Brest Litovsk on the Poland-Belarus border—the same city that Menahem Begin came from. He and his girlfriend Vera had gotten in trouble with the Bolshevik authorities in the Soviet Union and fled to Palestine in 1922. The year before they arrived, Kfar Malal had been destroyed in the Arab riots. Vera was not a Zionist and had planned on becoming a doctor, a plan she had to give up upon arriving in Palestine because of the lack of universities in the land.[1]

Kfar Malal was a *moshav*, or cooperative village, affiliated with the Mapai Party, but although Samuil was a registered member of Mapai, he was a contrarian and an individualist. He and his wife had very touchy relations with their neighbors because they dared to be different. Following the murder of Mapai figure Haim Arlozoroff in 1934, which was blamed on the Revisionist Party but was more likely perpetrated by Arab thieves,[2] Samuil expressed reservations about the general consensus. A decade later, when Ariel was in high school, his father made him promise to never betray Jews to Gentiles as the Hagana was doing to Etzel members during the *saison* in late 1944 and early 1945 following the assassination of Lord Moyne by the Lehi in Egypt. Scheinerman hinted that he did not want his son to join the Palmakh, which had carried out the saison, and Ariel honored his wishes.[3]

Ariel was indifferent to his studies in school, but he enjoyed the paramilitary training he received through the Hagana's youth organization, Gadna. Yosef Margalit, a friend of Sharon's from Kfar Malal, remembered, "From his first day in the Gadna, he changed. All of a sudden, with no warning at all, we discovered a totally different Arik." He excelled in all the tasks taught by the Gadna. His mother gave him a love of music, and he did attain something of a liberal education at home in spite of the worst of intentions by the local school. Upon his graduation from high school in 1945, he joined the Hagana and went through signal training.[4] Ariel Sharon (he did not change his name until 1953, but for simplicity's sake I will use this name throughout this chapter) was half a generation younger than Dayan and six years younger than Rabin, but that was enough for him to miss out on the pre-independence experiences of the Arab Revolt and the formation of the Palmakh.

Sharon ended up joining the Jewish Settlement Police, which Dayan had belonged to in the late 1930s. He also briefly served as an instructor in the Gadna. Throughout 1947 he was active patrolling by night with his local unit in the Sharon. He also developed a knack for reading the local terrain. On December 12, 1947, Sharon was mobilized into the Hagana as a full-time soldier to provide protection to his community in the coming War of Independence, which was in its very early stages. He became a platoon leader in the Alexandroni Brigade.[5]

He participated in the first Battle of Latrun, and on May 26, 1948, Sharon found himself in a survival situation. His unit had gone in at dawn to scout the battlefield and had been cut off and surrounded by troops of the Jordanian Arab Legion. The Legionnaires were on a hillside and Sharon's platoon was trapped in an open field. The men were low on both ammunition and water and suffering from the heat caused by the flames sparked by firing in the fields of grain. Sharon was shot through the abdomen and bleeding. Half of his men were already dead, and most of the rest were wounded. He gave the order to abandon the wounded and retreat. Sharon could not get up because of his wound and so had to crawl on all fours. During the retreat he ran into a new member of the unit, a sixteen-year-old boy who was missing part of his jaw. The boy helped Sharon over a wall and kept him moving. After a while the two ran into some more stragglers. One of the wounded helped Sharon, and the two staggered to the rear while leaning on each other. Sharon passed out just after they reached the rear and was taken away to an aid station.

An ambulance brought him to the Hadassah Hospital in Tel Aviv. He later found out that of the 35 men and boys in his platoon, fifteen were dead and eleven wounded—only nine survived the battle intact. The platoon was made up of men from three small villages and the surrounding farms. The news would hit them hard. While recovering in the hospital, Sharon often thought about what had gone wrong in the battle. He internalized the need for thorough preparation before battle and made it part of his military and political career.[6]

Sharon was released from the hospital in mid-July, just in time to rejoin his battalion for Operation Dani. Several weeks later he managed to roll the jeep he was driving with his company commander in it. He broke several ribs in the accident and was again hospitalized. Afterward, Sharon participated in the final offensives of the war as a battalion reconnaissance officer. His battalion fought first the Iraqis, then the Egyptians in October, and the Egyptians again in December.[7]

After the war ended Sharon decided to remain in the army. In September 1949 the Alexandroni Brigade was made a reserve unit, and he switched to the Golani Brigade as commander of its reconnaissance company. The Golani commander was Avraham Yoffe, Rabin's brother-in-law. In 1950 Sharon was promoted to captain and then went on a battalion commander's course. A friend of Yoffe's arranged for Sharon to be appointed the intelligence officer for the entire Central Command because of Sharon's reputation as a reliable recon officer.[8]

Sharon later contracted malaria, and by the end of 1951 he was quite weak from it. He took sick leave from the IDF and went to stay with relatives in Paris and then in New York. He toured the American South before returning to Israel in December 1951. Upon returning, he became the intelligence officer for the Northern Command under Moshe Dayan. He endeared himself to Dayan by taking the initiative in capturing a couple of Jordanian soldiers to trade for Israeli soldiers who had been captured after wandering across the border by mistake.[9]

In the fall of 1952 Sharon took study leave from the IDF to study Middle Eastern history at Hebrew University in Jerusalem. At the end of March 1953 he married his fiancée Margalit, who was a psychiatric nurse working in Jerusalem. In July 1953, while a major in the reserves, he was called in by his brigade commander, Michael Shaham, to recommend a method of dealing with the problem of Palestinian infiltration after a couple of people were murdered by a local Palestinian leader living in the village of Nebi Samuil. Sharon collected a few friends who were also released from the army and studying in Jerusalem, and they carried out an attack against the man's house in Nebi Samuil. The attack failed. Sharon then recommended a specialized unit of men who were adept at night operations. The person he wrote the report for subsequently recommended him for the job. This was to become the legendary Unit 101, which was only in existence for half a year before merging with a paratroop unit to become the paratroop battalion.[10]

At the end of July 1953, Chief of Staff Mordechai Makleff entrusted Sharon with the task of forming the unit he had recommended and carrying out reprisal raids whenever they were ordered by Makleff. This was the first of four major rounds of warfare Sharon would experience with the Palestinians, whether as a soldier in the IDF or as a politician. Sharon started looking for soldiers who had special skills but did not like the routine of a peacetime army. By September he had 20 men. In another month he had 45, which Sharon considered enough to carry out his mission. Sharon set up a base on a mountain near Jerusalem and began training his men with a rigorous regimen of physical conditioning, weapons training, hand-to-hand fighting, patrol techniques and night movement.[11]

In mid-October 1953, Unit 101 carried out its first reprisal raid, one that remains infamous to this day. They were ordered to infiltrate the village of Kibya and level all the houses in the village as a lesson to the Jordanians about the price of supporting infiltration into Israel. Each soldier carried ten kilos worth of dynamite in addition to his weapon and other equipment. Upon arriving at the village, they had a skirmish with the Jordanian Home Guard and killed ten of them. The villagers quickly exited the village or hid in their cellars. The Israeli soldiers went from house to house, firing a shot and calling for anyone inside to come out before throwing in a lit bundle of dynamite. Over 45 houses were dynamited.

After the raid, it was discovered that some 69 of the villagers had remained in their houses and been killed in the explosions. Most of these were women and children. Israel was condemned at the United Nations for this incident. Ben-Gurion had Israel's UN ambassador lie and blame the incident on civilians.[12] However, Sharon became very popular with his men because of his ability to plan and the esprit de corps that he created in the unit by denigrating his superiors, which made his men feel special. Dayan, who became chief of staff in December, appreciated that he had found an officer with initiative and skill who had his own sense of daring. Ben-Gurion also liked Sharon but did not appreciate his habit of lying to superiors.[13]

Sharon seemed to have a higher opinion of the fighting abilities of Arabs than did Dayan—probably as a result of his greater combat experience. Sharon considered them brave on the defense, as well as good marksmen, and he was aware that Arab armies knew how to use artillery. But he believed they lacked the ability to improvise and operate at night.[14] Sharon's military career in the IDF would last for 25 years—longer than either Dayan's or Rabin's. In that time he would serve in five wars, as well as the reprisal operations of the mid-1950s and a counter-insurgency campaign in Gaza in 1971.

In January 1954 Dayan began to merge Unit 101 with a parachute company to form the 890th Paratroop Battalion. Sharon split the Unit 101 core into several small groups and merged them with the paratroopers in smaller units for training. The idea was to train the Unit 101 fighters in parachuting, and the others in the skills that the Unit 101 men had mastered. Sharon supervised the training personally. He then used his free time to prepare contingency plans for carrying out reprisal raids in different situations. In order to overcome the resistance of many of the paratroopers toward merging with Unit 101, Sharon recruited attractive female conscripts as parachute packers and threw parties for the men after tough training to build espirit de corps.[15]

From 1954 through 1956 Sharon carried out some seventy reprisal actions, including the major raid against the police station in Gaza in February 1955, Operation Kinneret in December 1955, and others right up until the beginning of the Sinai War in late October 1956. (I have already related the details of these actions in the chapter on Dayan's military career.) As a result of the success of these raids (at least in the minds of Dayan and Ben-Gurion, if not quite in the minds of diplomats like Sharett and Eban), the paratroopers were expanded from a battalion to a brigade. Sharon's best officers, Mordechai "Motta" Gur and Rafael "Raful" Eitan, were made battalion commanders. Both would go on to serve as chiefs of staff, an honor that eluded Sharon. They also became bitter opponents of Sharon both while in uniform and afterward in their political careers. Gur had a short career as a politician in the Labor Party in the 1980s, and Eitan had a longer career in Tehiya, in his own Tzomet Party, and then in the Likud in the 1980s and 1990s.[16]

The Sinai War began with the IDF's first combat jump by Raful Eitan's paratroop battalion near the Parker Memorial at the eastern end of the Mitla Pass. Sharon led the rest of the brigade in an overland campaign across the Sinai from Nahal to Kuntila, and then on to Temed and Kilat Nahal, without encountering any serious opposition. Finally, after two days, Sharon's force rendezvoused with Eitan's force in the Mitla Pass. Sharon had counted on the war as his chance to achieve military glory and advancement within the IDF. He refused to accept that his part in the war was over within two days without having fought in a major battle. Sharon began bombarding IDF headquarters with requests to attack through the pass and on to the Suez Canal. But this was not part of Dayan's plan for the execution of the war. To make sure that Sharon understood the message, he had Central Command Chief of Staff Lt. Col. Rehavam Zeevi travel by light plane to Sharon's position.

When Zeevi landed and delivered his message, Sharon immediately began bargaining with him. He got Zeevi to allow a reconnaissance patrol to go into the pass, provided that it did not engage the enemy. Once Zeevi flew away, Sharon began organizing his "patrol" of two motorized companies, a tank platoon a brigade headquarters platoon, and a mortar battery. The force was led by Second Battalion Commander Gur, and the brigade deputy commander, Yitzhak Hofi, accompanied it.[17]

The Mitla Pass is essentially a long canyon. As the force went forward, the soldiers noticed men scrambling around on the canyon rim. After fifteen minutes an ambush was sprung against the lead vehicles—halftracks—by the Egyptians. Gur's force of about forty men was trapped in the halftracks and pinned down. Hofi's element successfully passed through them and continued onward under the mistaken impression that Gur was up ahead. The Third Battalion commander, Aharon Davidi, brought up the rear with the mortar battery. It was subsequently attacked by planes of the Egyptian air force, which used their trucks for target practice. The fighting continued for over seven hours until after eight in the evening. The paratroopers finally managed to withdraw with the bodies of 38 dead, and 120 wounded were taken to the rear. The Egyptians lost some three hundred in the fighting.[18]

Dayan was furious and ordered Major General Haim Laskov to investigate the incident. Sharon claimed in his defense that Zeevi had set no upper limit on the size of the patrol, and that he had sent the rest of the force into battle *only* to extricate Gur's men, who had become trapped. And he claimed that, in any case, his initial position at the end of the pass was not defensible. At the inquiry he was accused of being a coward and a glory hound who often did not share in the danger and who wrote reports to enlarge his own reputation. The war ended without Sharon being expelled from the army or having any formal punishment. But it was another seven years before he received a promotion. Gur and Eitan became alienated from him because of his lies at the inquiry, and Sharon became isolated within the IDF.[19]

Sharon suffered through a long period of professional and personal difficulty following the Sinai War. Two months after the war ended his father died. In 1957 he resigned as commander of the paratroopers due to the bad relations between himself and many of his subordinates. Afterward, he was sent to a staff officer's course in Kimberley, England. There he showed his independence by refusing to memorize his instructors' solutions to military problems, choosing instead to work out his own solutions. He was alienated by the patronizing attitude of many of the school staff to both Israelis and Arabs. At one point he took the initiative to drive to the country estate of military historian B.H. Liddel Hart and discuss with him the lessons of the British experience fighting Rommel in North Africa. He later mentioned Hart's opinions during discussion of a problem, and the staff reacted as if he had cheated by consulting an outside source. He replied that anyone else could have interviewed Hart or other military experts. The officers seemed to be convinced that Liddel Hart was Jewish and this was how Sharon had met him. The reaction only fed Sharon's sense of superiority.[20]

With Israel at peace over the next decade, Sharon had little opportunity to use his natural talent for planning and quick decision-making under fire. Instead, he had to content himself with a series of staff jobs. Major General Yosef Geva, commander of the training branch of the IDF, suspended Sharon after Sharon lied to him about his reasons for missing a meeting. After Ben-Gurion intervened, Geva appointed Sharon commander of the IDF infantry school. After a while Sharon grew bored and began taking night school classes in law at Tel Aviv University. Eventually he would complete a law degree in 1966, which was useful for his future political career.[21]

Sharon's frustration with his lack of action and the stalling of his career was evidenced by his insubordination and his fights with (and insults of) subordinates. After three years of command of the infantry school, Sharon took a special course and requalified as an armored commander. Sharon distinguished himself during the course through his original solutions to problems, the fruit of his analytical mind and his tutoring by Liddel Hart in Britain. But some of the staff considered his approach unnecessarily risky.[22]

In an after-action review of a reprisal raid, Sharon criticized the commander for exceeding his orders and taking unnecessary risks. At the end of the review Northern Commander Major General Meir Zorea started his summary by recounting the Greek myth of Narcissus. He then looked straight at Sharon and said, "You are Narcissus. You are incapable of accepting the fact that someone else has successfully led a military action." Possibly his Sinai experience explains Sharon's newfound worry about compliance with orders and not taking risks.[23]

On May 6, 1962, Sharon's wife Margalit was killed in a head-on collision with a truck when she recklessly swerved into the other lane. The police ruled the death an accident due to reckless driving. But there was some suspicion that it was a suicide caused by the belief that Sharon was having an affair with Margalit's younger sister Lilly. Sharon married Lilly a year later, after she had quit her job and taken over the care of his infant son, Gur. Margalit had confided her suspicions to a friend shortly before her death.[24]

After a year of marriage the new couple welcomed their son Omri, followed a year later by Gilad. Sharon now had three sons. He would remain married to Lilly until she died in 2000. She was his closest political advisor throughout his long career and the source of his personal stability. Although in many ways Sharon had a similar personality to Dayan, it did not extend to womanizing. This was partly because of his genuine love for Lilly (and probably for Margalit as well) and partly because he seemed to satisfy his carnal appetites through gluttony rather than sex. And because he did so, he would naturally be much less attractive to other women.[25]

When Rabin became chief of staff in December 1963, he finally decided to promote Sharon and made him the Northern Command chief of staff under Rabin's brother-in-law Avraham Yoffe, who had helped Sharon early on in his military career. Yoffe made it clear to Sharon that he would not be entitled to dismiss anyone without Yoffe's permission, and briefed his officers on this as well. Sharon got along well, but after a year Yoffe retired and was replaced by David Elazar. Sharon soon ran into problems and took a leave of absence to tour Africa with Yoffe, who had been appointed head of Israel's nature reserves. It seemed to have made a major impression on him, as he devoted most of a chapter in his memoirs to it.[26]

During 1964 and 1965 Israel was experiencing the problems mentioned earlier with Syria. Sharon took a very aggressive stance in regard to both defining Israel's northern border and defending it from Syria. Israel had a policy of working the land in the demilitarized zone that existed at the foot of the Golan Heights, and Damascus regarded this as a violation of the armistice agreement. As a result, there were several clashes between Israel and Syria in the zone. There was also the problem of Syrian attempts to divert the headwaters of the Jordan River that fed into Lake Kinnerett in order to prevent Israel from settling the Negev. This problem was solved by Israel using tanks to destroy the Syrian earth-moving equipment employed in the diversion.[27]

Sharon's critics in the IDF regarded him as nasty, egotistical, reckless, and an inveterate liar. His defenders regarded him as the IDF's most original military thinker, a great patriot, and a man of courage. As is sometimes the case in these situations, they were probably both right. Sharon, like Dayan, was definitely a highly original military thinker who liked to work outside of the box. He had proven his courage in the reprisal raids of the 1950s and would prove it again on many occasions. But he was a person who had problems seeing the point of view of others and accepting that he might not always be right. This may be why it took Rabin three months in the fall of 1965 to determine Sharon's future. During this time Sharon waited around at home nervous and morose. Finally, Rabin called him in for an interview. After a long recitation of Sharon's shortcomings, Rabin surprised him by announcing that he would promote him. Sharon was appointed head of the training branch of the IDF and commander of a reserve division and promoted to major general. This made him equal to all the other senior commanders of the IDF except for the chief of staff.[28]

In May 1967, when the crisis provoked by Nasser's expulsion of the UN peacekeepers from Sinai occurred, Sharon was serving as the commander of an armored division in the Southern Command. Sharon, along with Matti Peled, Israel Tal, and Ezer Weizman, was one of the commanders who was most confident about the upcoming confrontation with Egypt. This was because he thought that his men and commanders were well trained, and he had contingency plans ready for all imagined tasks. Sharon had been appointed a reserve army commander of armor after he graduated from the armor conversion course several years before. When the crisis began, he simply reverted from his permanent army training command to his reserve command. Dayan had enough confidence in Sharon that he both recommended to his daughter Yael that she accompany Sharon's division as a journalist and asked to serve in the division before he was appointed defense minister. When Levi Eshkol asked Sharon for his opinion about appointing Dayan as defense minister, Sharon replied honestly that it made no difference to him and his men who the defense minister was, but he respected Dayan's abilities.[29] He probably would have said the same thing about Yigal Allon if Eshkol had asked about him.

In June 1967 Israel had three armored divisions in Southern Command, led by Israel Tal in the north, by Yoffe in the center and by Sharon in the south—all of this in the northern half of the peninsula, which was the area most suitable for maneuver warfare, as the southern Sinai is full of mountains. Tal would attack across the northern coastal road from Rafah to El Arish, and then head south and continue through Abu Agheila west to the Suez Canal. Yoffe would capture the strategic Giddi and Mitla Passes, and Sharon would liberate Ras Sudar before heading south to liberate Sharm al-Sheikh, if the paratroopers had not already liberated it. Sharon executed a brilliant attack on Kusseima, conquering the base from the Egyptian forces who had been trained in Soviet defense-in-depth methodology.[30] If Dayan's role in Operation Dani was later studied in Israeli officer courses, Sharon's victories at Kusseima and elsewhere in 1967 were written about in Western military journals and studied throughout the West as a means of overcoming Soviet defensive doctrine.[31]

Sharon carried out his tasks brilliantly, fulfilling the hopes of his superiors, from Dayan to Rabin, who had overlooked his personal faults because of his dedication and original thinking. After two days the Egyptian army was in complete retreat and Sharm al-Sheikh was liberated, first by the Israeli navy, which found it deserted, and then by the paratroopers. On the third day the IDF reached the Suez Canal and set up a defensive line. And after four days the campaign in the Sinai was over.[32]

Sharon emerged as one of the heroes of the war. He was not yet at the level of popular recognition that Dayan and Rabin enjoyed. But he did well enough that he was on the track to promotion to regional command.

In October 1967, on the eve of the Jewish New Year, Rosh Hashana, a neighbor boy who was playing with Sharon's son Gur took an antique shotgun that had been given to Gur as a present and pointed it at Gur's head and fired. The boys had loaded the gun with gunpowder and scrap metal. Sharon ran outside to find Gur sprawled on the ground with a wound in his eye. His other son said that Gur had told the boy not to point it at him. Neighbors took Gur and Sharon to the hospital, but it was too late—the doctors could do nothing for him. This was the second death in his immediate family that Sharon had suffered in little over five years.[33]

Sharon refused to accept that the death was an accident and would yell "murderer" every time he drove by the boy. This continued until finally the boy's mother spoke to Chief of Staff Haim Bar-Lev about the problem. Bar-Lev spoke to Sharon and tried to reason with him, but Sharon refused to accept that the boy was too young to be responsible. Finally the other family moved out of the neighborhood after years of harassment by Sharon.[34]

Under Bar-Lev the reigning military strategy was defensive based upon the line of fortifications along the Suez Canal that bore his name. Sharon was derisive in his denunciations of this "Maginot Line mentality," as he termed it. So one day in early 1969 a general staff meeting was held with Defense Minister Dayan present, ostensibly to discuss the advantages and disadvantages of the Bar-Lev Line. But Southern Commander Yeshayahu Gavish and David Elazar soon launched personal attacks on Sharon for his criticism of Bar-Lev. Sharon angrily walked out of the meeting even after Dayan told him he could not do so.[35]

Shortly after this incident, Sharon was made aware that his term of service was coming to an end. He filed the necessary form for another extension, but Bar-Lev refused to approve it. So Sharon engaged in some psychological warfare and held conversations with Yosef Sapir, the head of the Liberal Party, and with Begin about joining one of their parties, which were united in the Gahal alliance, once he left the army. Pinchas Sapir (no relation to Yosef), a minister in the government from Mapai, got wind of this—he was an old friend of Sharon—and put pressure on Bar-Lev to allow Sharon to reenlist. Israeli newspapers also carried the headline "GENERAL SHARON JOINS GAHAL." Sharon had let everyone know that his position on the question of the future of the territories was much closer to that of the Gahal opposition than to that of the Alignment.[36]

In December 1969, at the height of the War of Attrition, Sharon replaced Gavish as Southern Commander. The War of Attrition was mainly fought by the Israeli air force and the Sayeret Matkal special forces. Sharon's chance to prove his abilities as a front commander came after the war was over. Gaza had been infiltrated by units of fedayeen from the Popular Front for the Liberation of Palestine (PFLP) of George Habash and Fatah. After an incident in which two children were killed when a grenade was thrown at their car, Sharon received permission to clean out the Gaza Strip. He began by dividing the region into squares and giving unit commanders responsibility for all the activity that took place within a particular square. Sharon then ordered the lower branches of all trees in orchards to be cut off so as to eliminate possible hiding places and to improve the army's field of vision. He also had caves and other natural hiding places sealed off. And undercover units of Arabic-speaking Jewish soldiers dressed as fedayeen were sent into the Strip to see where the terrorists were hiding by striking up conversations with the residents. Within seven months of starting this approach, he had virtually eliminated the problem. By the end of 1971 terrorism was no longer a problem in the Strip.[37]

It was alleged by some that Sharon was having captured fedayeen killed. Yitzhak Abadi, the senior field commander charged with implementing Sharon's policies, went to Dayan and requested a transfer. He explained to Dayan that he could no longer implement Sharon's cruel policies in good conscience. Sharon then called Abadi in and had him repeat what he had told Dayan. It was a very emotional meeting. Shortly after this, Dayan had the Gaza Strip removed administratively from the responsibility of the Southern Command and transferred to the responsibility of the Central Command.[38]

After three and a half years as Southern Commander, Sharon was finally forced to retire from the IDF in July 1973. Neither Dayan nor Prime Minister Meir was willing to intervene to extend his service by a year after Chief of Staff Elazar refused to allow him to reenlist. In his final conversation with Dayan while in uniform, Sharon warned Dayan that his replacement, Shmuel Gonen, was not ready for war. Dayan assured him that there would not be a war that year and Gonen would have plenty of time to get up to speed. Sharon also held a press conference and made it clear that he was being forced out of the army.[39]

With Ezer Weizman having served as transportation minister in the government for several months from late 1969 to August 1970, the Labor Party was no longer terrified of the prospect of a general joining the political right. It should have been. And no Labor politician was willing to do favors for Sharon after he had made it clear that he was a supporter of the right. If there had been plans to advance Sharon on to the next step as chief of operations or deputy chief of staff, he probably would have been rotated to one of the other two regional commands for a period so as to become intimately familiar with their problems. As the next chapter covers Sharon's early political career,

I will detail in it Sharon's creation of the Likud between July and September 1973.

During the summer of 1973, Sharon had retired to a routine of working his fields at his Sycamore Ranch near Beersheba in the morning and showering and eating before arranging afternoon political meetings in the afternoons. One Friday afternoon in early October, Sharon received a call at Likud headquarters in Tel Aviv as he was preparing to finish up campaign business for the weekend. He was told that the war he had feared was about to begin. After returning home to spend Yom Kippur with his family, he was ordered to report immediately to Southern Command headquarters. Sharon reverted to commander of his reserve armored division.

Ironically, after four wars of serving as a regular army officer—two as a general—in which military glory had eluded him, he was finally about to find it now that he had been forced out of the army. The day after the war started Sharon was at the Sinai headquarters in Bir Gafgafa in the northern part of the central Sinai.[40]

Sharon continually beseeched the Southern Command and IDF headquarters for permission to rescue the men trapped in the Bar-Lev Line with his tanks. He finally won permission from Gonen to attempt the rescue, only to have this permission rescinded when new intelligence arrived indicating that the Egyptian positions on the east bank of the Suez Canal had been reinforced. Regrettably, Sharon lacked respect for Gonen as an individual. He also regarded Chief of Staff David Elazar as an enemy who had kept him from becoming chief of staff by forcing him out of the army.

Relations between Sharon and Gonen deteriorated to the point that Gonen formally requested of Elazar that Sharon be relieved of command. Dayan refused to allow this, and Elazar refused to acquiesce to Gonen's replacement by Sharon, so the final compromise solution was that Bar-Lev was called away from IDF headquarters and employed as an additional level of command between Gonen and Elazar to approve Gonen's plans.[41] It was similar to the situation that General Ulysses S. Grant was in during the final year of the American Civil War, when he was both the supreme Union commander and stationed with the Army of the Potomac, thus overseeing General George Meade's plans. It was also the only time in the IDF's history when it had two lieutenant generals (*rav alufim*) on active duty at the same time.

Sharon vindicated his account of the war of the generals by successfully managing the crossing of the Suez Canal and establishing a bridgehead on the canal's west bank. Sharon crossed at night on October 15 in the "joint" between the Second and Third Egyptian armies. This allowed him to sneak through under the cover of darkness. This was the day after a major Egyptian

Eight. General Sharon

Southern Commander Ariel Sharon briefing former prime minister David Ben-Gurion along Suez Canal, January 27, 1971. Photograph by IDF spokesperson.

defeat at the hands of Israeli armor at the Battle of Chinese Farm. During an artillery bombardment of the unit, Sharon banged his head against the inside of his command armored personnel carrier and had to be bandaged. Photographs of Sharon directing his men with a bandaged head became iconic Israeli memories of the war. Sharon wanted to attack Ismailia as well, but both Dayan and Elazar were opposed to this. Sharon had a hard time accepting this denial and was insubordinate.[42]

Sharon did not return to Israel proper until January 20, 1974, despite a ceasefire on October 24 that ended the war. On December 31, 1973, Sharon was elected to the Knesset with Yitzhak Rabin and several others. His life was about to change dramatically. Sharon emerged as the leading Israeli war hero of the Yom Kippur War of October 1973, as most of his superiors were somewhat diminished by the Agranat Commission report. His friend, journalist Uri Dan, who had known Sharon since the mid–1950s, when Dan was a beginning journalist for the army magazine and Sharon was a commando leader, wrote the bestseller *Sharon's Bridgehead* about Sharon's crossing of the Suez Canal and wartime experiences. It appeared in Hebrew in 1974 and in English translation a year later.[43]

After 1967 and 1973, it became common to hear Sharon compared to

General George S. Patton from World War II. But I would argue that Sharon was much more like General Erwin Rommel, Patton's opponent in early 1943 and mid-1944. This is because Rommel, like Sharon, started out as an infantry officer and received Germany's highest military decoration, the *pour le merit*, for capturing a large number of Italian infantrymen during World War I. Rommel only converted to armor after the Polish campaign of September 1939. Likewise, Sharon spent his first two decades in the military in specialized infantry units, whereas Patton spent his entire military career as a cavalry and armor officer—the natural progression. Also, Israeli armored tactics were much more like the German *blitzkrieg* tactics of 1939–1942—their ultimate refinement between 1956 and 1973—than like the Allied combined arms tactics of 1943–1945. The IDF, like the Germans, also relied on close air support by tactical aircraft, whereas the Americans used much more strategic airpower and aerial interdiction of roads and railroad lines and centers. But the Patton comparison is correct in the sense that Sharon was Israel's most talented armor field commander.

Chapter Nine

Sharon Charges into Politics

After the press conference following his departure from the army in 1973, Sharon started the task of adjusting to civilian life. He borrowed $200,000 from Israeli casino mogul Meshulam Riklis in the form of a no-interest loan conditional only on his remaining involved in public life. He used this as leverage to arrange a loan from a commercial bank in Chicago for the other two-thirds of the $600,000 price of his Sycamore Ranch near Beersheba, one of the largest farms in Israel. After purchasing the place, he immediately set to work moving in, restoring the property and working the land.[1]

In the afternoons, after having worked the fields in the morning, showering and eating lunch, he drove to Tel Aviv or Jerusalem to meet with members of the different parties of the right that he was attempting to join into a superparty: Herut, the Liberals, the State Party (the remnant of Rafi after most of Rafi joined the Labor Party and Ben-Gurion retired from politics in 1970), the Free Center Party (a splinter group from Herut led by attorney Shmuel Tamir, a former Etzel commander in Jerusalem), and the Land of Israel Movement (Tenuat Eretz Israel), a collection of hawkish figures from the socialist left before 1967. The core of this proposed new list, to be known as the Likud (union) were Herut and the Liberals, already joined since 1965 in Gahal (Herut-Liberals Bloc). Sharon categorically refused to simply join Gahal and said he would stay out of politics if the parties could not agree and form a bloc. To increase his leverage, he got Ezer Weizman, Herut's only general, to back him up on this point. Weizman was frustrated with Begin's leadership and relished the chance to shake up the party.

At issue was not really the platform or ideology of the party—all were agreed on decreasing government regulation, freeing up the economy and retaining all of the territories conquered in 1967. What was at issue was the spoils: the number of seats granted to the three smaller parties and to the existing Gahal list, and in which position these seats would be. Free Center's Tamir wanted four seats for his party (and the State List as a combined faction) in the top 32 positions. Begin would only agree to three. At this point, Sharon and Weizman issued their joint ultimatum. Initially Gahal voted to reject the ultimatum, but eventually the two leaders compromised, with the Free Center getting three seats within the 32, plus the 36 spot. On September 14, 1973, the agreement was signed and the Likud was in existence—forever changing Israeli politics. It was the equivalent of the formation of the Labor Party and Alignment in 1968-1969. Sharon had accomplished this in seven weeks of hard negotiating.[2]

Sharon began organizing for the election scheduled for October 30, 1973—he was the designated campaign manager for the new list. But then, as mentioned in the previous chapter, he was called away by war and did not return to Israel on a permanent basis until after the election. The new list won 39 seats, compared to only 28 for the component parties in 1969. Sharon had chosen to join the Liberal Party, so as to not compete directly with Weizman in Herut, although he could have joined in the new La'am faction, made up of the State List and the Free Center. He then converted his influential role in the party into a seat on the prestigious Knesset Foreign Affairs and Defense Committee, where he was put in charge of overseeing the defense budget.[3]

Sharon was still set on being chief of staff someday, and he was using his political career as a means of fulfilling that dream. He kept his reserve commission as commander of an armored division and actually spent more time seeing to his duties as commander than fulfilling his political duties. This caused a number of deputies from the Labor Party to pass a bill prohibiting any Knesset member from serving as a commander at that rank. As Sharon was the only person affected, it was dubbed the "anti-Sharon bill." Sharon ended up resigning his Knesset seat in December 1974, less than a year after having been elected. However, Sharon was quite happy with the bill because it gave him a handy excuse to give up his boring political duties while claiming that he was being persecuted by the left.[4]

Sharon's next political venture was to get himself appointed a special advisor to Prime Minister Rabin on terrorism. Rabin and Sharon, although not personal friends, respected one another, and Sharon remembered that it was Rabin who had given him his final promotion. Sharon was hoping that this would be another stepping-stone in his journey to be chief of staff. Rabin wanted someone who could give him legitimacy with the right and contribute to a more centrist personal image for himself. Rabin was also experiencing problems with the Gush Emunim settlers and needed someone who could talk to them. Sharon had helped to facilitate negotiations between the government and the settlers at Sebastia in November 1974 before he left the Knesset.

Sharon started as an advisor to Rabin in July 1975. Rabin would solicit his opinion on issues relating to terrorism and defense (although Peres had agreed to the appointment with the understanding that Sharon would not be advising on defense matters) and Sharon would oblige. Earlier Sharon had objected to Kissinger's two separation-of-forces agreements and was opposed to giving up more territory in the peninsula without a peace treaty with Egypt. Rabin's appointment temporarily neutralized Sharon. After nine months, however, Sharon realized that Rabin had no intention of creating political problems for himself by appointing Sharon chief of staff. So in March 1976 he resigned as Rabin's advisor, having served a valuable apprenticeship in the halls of power.[5] Four months later came the biggest terrorism incident of Rabin's first government and Sharon missed it.

At this point Sharon wanted back in the Likud that he had created three years earlier, but its leader Simcha Erlich wanted nothing to do with him. Sharon thus formed his own list, the first of the general's lists that would become a standard feature of Israeli politics. He named it *Shlomzion*, meaning the "peace (or wellbeing) of Zion," which was the title of one of the last Hasmonean monarchs in ancient Israel. Although the list initially did quite well in political opinion polls—as such parties tend to do at first—it quickly lost support as Yigael Yadin formed his rival Democratic Movement for Change three weeks later. Politically Shlomzion was all over the map, with leftist as well as rightist positions on issues, and it called for electoral reform. Sharon held extensive merger talks with first Yadin's party and then the veteran Independent Liberals, a party that had split off from the General Zionists a decade before and appealed to German-speaking Israelis. But both rejected Sharon as an opportunist likely to hurt their images. Sharon lambasted the Likud as being no better than the Labor establishment, and he promised that he would never go back to it and would stay true to his announced mission even if he failed at the polls.

Sharon, like Ross Perot in the 1990s, preferred to surround himself with sycophants and admirers rather than with professional political organizers who knew what they were doing. His wife Lilly determined who had Sharon's ear in the party and so tended to pick flatterers. Once, Sharon flew to Los Angeles to meet with an American supporter who had written that he wanted to make a contribution. He collected a check in an envelope, but when he later opened it he discovered that it was only for $25.

When Sharon failed to attract support on the left, he went for expansionist nationalism. A couple of months before the election, when Shlomzion was polling only 1 percent in the polls, Sharon conducted talks with Begin about joining Herut. But Yitzhak Shamir could not be located in time to finalize the merger and Sharon was forced to compete as an independent. Shlomzion won only two seats—just over the 1 percent barrier for getting into the Knesset.[6]

After the election a relieved Sharon joined the Likud as leader of his own faction, before merging it quickly with Herut. Begin wanted to make Sharon defense minister, but most of those in the Likud objected, as Weizman had been in the party since 1969 and had served as the Likud's successful campaign manager in the 1977 election. So instead Sharon became minister of agriculture—an advantageous position, as Dayan and two other agriculture ministers had gone on to serve as defense ministers.[7] Sharon was also appointed to head the party's committee on settlement. This was the start of an alliance between Sharon and the settlers that would last for nearly three decades. Sharon now had the second main group in his political following along with his war groupies.

Sharon spent the first Begin government mostly working on settlement issues. Within a month of being appointed head of the settlement committee, Sharon had a plan for settling Eretz Israel. In mid-September 1977 Sharon presented his plan, largely based on proposals that he had seen while Rabin's advisor and written by Professor Avraham Wachmann, an architect. The plan had three concentrations of settlements: one in the central mountain ridgeline of Samaria, another in the Jordan Valley, and the third around Jerusalem. The settlements had three main strategic goals: first, to protect Israel from the Eastern Front of Jordan, Iraq, and Syria; second, to prevent a division of Jerusalem that would allow East Jerusalem to become either the capital of a Palestinian state or a major city within Jordan; third, to divide the West Bank and deal with the demographic problem by planting modern Orthodox religious Zionists from Israel and abroad with high birthrates among the Arabs.[8] Nearly thirty years later Sharon would recognize that this attempt had at least partially failed when he moved to divest Israel of Gaza for demographic reasons.

Begin's main emphases in his first government were settling the West Bank and making peace with Egypt. The first task he delegated to Sharon and the second to Dayan—thus his two most important tasks were not entrusted to members of the "fighting family" made up of underground veterans. At Camp David, Weizman came up with the idea of contacting Sharon to get his permission to evacuate the settlements in the Rafiah area in the northeastern corner of the Sinai. Sharon agreed to support Weizman on the evacuation. In 1981 he razed the city of Yamit in the settlement out of concern that it could cause future security problems for Israel if President Sadat populated it with Egyptians who would then infiltrate Israel to look for work.[9]

In May 1980 Ezer Weizman quit as defense minister over policy differences with Begin regarding the implementation of the peace settlement with Egypt. Rather than appoint Sharon to the position, as he had appointed Shamir to replace Dayan as foreign minister following the latter's resignation in 1979, Begin assumed the position himself in imitation of David Ben-Gurion and Levy Eshkol. This irritated Sharon, who made his feelings plain. But Begin simply joked with reporters that if he did do this, he might find the government buildings surrounded by tanks one day. Begin probably did not seriously believe that Sharon would carry out a coup d'etat, but Sharon's rude conduct during cabinet meetings, in which he insulted those with other viewpoints, had left him feeling uncomfortable about letting Sharon have the sensitive position of defense minister.[10]

The position of the Likud in the polls deteriorated throughout 1980 and 1981. Sharon was worried about reports from the Mossad regarding progress on the Osirak nuclear reactor in Baghdad. Israel had had a nuclear monopoly in the region since the late 1960s and was wary of losing that monopoly to

Ariel Sharon at Moshe Dayan's funeral, October 18, 1981. Photograph by Herman Chanania, Israeli Government Press Office.

any Muslim country, particularly a radical nationalist government like the Ba'athist regime of Saddam Hussein in Iraq (or the Ba'athist Assad regime in Syria or the Islamic Republic of Iran). Sharon repeatedly urged Begin to react and use the IAF to bomb the reactor. On June 7, 1981, Israeli F-16 fighter bombers destroyed the nuclear reactor before it went active and less than a month before scheduled elections. Three weeks later the Likud won 48 seats, one more than Labor's 47 seats and enough to win the Likud a four-year extension in the government (with Sharon gaining the ministry of defense). Labor had recovered the fifteen seats that it lost to the reformist Democratic Movement for Change four years before, but the Likud attracted enough support from smaller parties to be able to win. Sharon's pushing Begin to act was partly responsible for this victory, as well as his settlement activities. The Likud gained three seats since 1977, as well as Tehiya, a splinter party from the Likud. In addition, the National Religious Party had its total representation cut in half from 12 to six, with three going to Tehiya and three to the Likud.[11]

On August 5, 1981, the new Likud government was sworn in and Sharon obtained his consolation prize of becoming defense minister after he was denied the senior position in the IDF. Since 1969 the Palestine Liberation Organization (PLO) had operated from a protected position in southern Lebanon that allowed it to mount terrorist and guerrilla attacks on Israel. After 1971 this became the main Palestinian front with Israel. On July 24, 1981, American envoy Philip Habib negotiated a ceasefire between the PLO and Israel. The PLO claimed that the ceasefire only governed actions taking place across the border, whereas Israel claimed that it was a general ceasefire. Israel also held the PLO responsible for all Palestinian terrorist attacks, whether committed by factions belonging to the PLO or not.[12]

When Sharon ran for the Knesset in 1977, his platform called for making Jordan a Palestinian state. Because Palestinians are a majority within Jordan—on the East Bank as well as the West Bank, the Jordanian Option of the Israeli right was to either directly or indirectly get rid of the Hashemite monarchy and turn Jordan into a Palestinian state. This meant, for Sharon, that the PLO had to be disabused of the notion that it could make Israel a Palestinian state. The way to do this was to destroy its enclave of Fatahland in southern Lebanon, which functioned as a state within a state. Israel had been cooperating with the Phalangist Maronite Christian militia within Lebanon since the mid-1970s, shortly after the Lebanese civil war began in April 1975. Sharon's plan was to smash the PLO in both Fatahland and Beirut and install Israel's Maronite Christian allies in the presidential palace in Beirut.[13]

Shortly after taking over as defense minister, Sharon set to work on contingency plans for an invasion of Lebanon based on existing plans that Ezer Weizman and Raful Eitan had worked up previously. Sharon then came up with two versions: Little Pines and Big Pines. Little Pines was for an operation similar to Operation Litani, the March 1978 invasion of southern Lebanon that drove up to the Litani River, but with blocking groups to prevent the fedayeen fighters from escaping ahead of the invading Israeli soldiers. The second, Big Pines, had Israel driving up to Beirut along the coast and in the interior west of the Syrian army. Sharon traveled to Washington and met with Secretary of State Alexander Haig, a former general himself, and won what he thought was a green light to invade. The Reagan administration saw the world in bipolar Cold War terms: American allies were the good guys, whether democracies or not, and Soviet allies were the bad guys. When the ally in question was Israel and the enemy was a terrorist organization, there was no question for Washington regarding who was in the right. Sharon also paid a secret visit to Lebanon on January 12, 1982, and met with Phalange leader Bashir Gemayel in Beirut and was given a tour of the Christian enclave on the coast.[14]

Sharon's plans were well publicized by both Israeli and American media as a form of psychological warfare on his part, and also by his opponents in the media in an attempt to prevent it. The al-Fatah Revolutionary Cells, better known as the Abu Nidal Organization, was interested in provoking an Israeli invasion that would weaken or eliminate its rivals in Fatah. Its leader had broken away from the mainstream Fatah in 1974 and since been supported by Iraq (and later by Syria and Libya). On June 3, 1982, an Abu Nidal assassin shot Israeli Ambassador Shlomo Argov in the head as he prepared to enter his vehicle outside a London hotel. The shooting was not fatal, but it left the ambassador severely handicapped. This was the incident that Sharon was waiting for. The IAF bombed two PLO targets in Beirut, and the PLO responded with a bombardment of northern Israel that lasted two days. The ceasefire was in tatters.[15]

Sharon went before the cabinet and presented a plan that was like Little Pines: he promised that the IDF would go no farther than 40 kilometers (24 miles) from Israel's border. After winning approval, he then instructed Eitan to implement Big Pines. A major problem with the invasion, however, was that Aman, the intelligence branch of the IDF, lacked sufficient up-to-date information about Lebanon because it had never been a priority. The IDF knew the area between the border and the Litani River from Operation Litani in 1978. And it knew Beirut from Operation Spring of Youth, when hit teams went in to take out three top Fatah terrorists in April 1973, and from the earlier attack on Beirut International Airport in December 1968. But it did not really know the area between the Litani River and the capital. As a result, in the planning more divisions were assigned to the invasion than the roads could support, leading to traffic jams that made the soldiers targets for brave Palestinians with RPG-7 anti-tank rocket launchers. And "fuel convoys could not get through, the wounded could not be evacuated, and commanders who went forward to observe ... were unable to return to headquarters," according to military historian Professor Martin van Creveld.[16] Operation Peace for Galilee, as the Lebanon War was officially known, involved four independent divisions, an amphibious brigade, a two-division corps and a reserve corps. Altogether it was about twice as many troops as had fought on the Southern Front in 1973.[17]

Sharon also assured both Washington and the Israeli cabinet that Syria would be left out of the war. On June 8 Begin told the Knesset that Jerusalem was not interested in a war with Syria and called upon Damascus to refrain from any offensive action. But that same day the IDF attacked a Syrian unit around the town of Jezzine and dragged Syria into the war. The war with Syria lasted for four days, until a ceasefire went into effect on June 11. The IAF destroyed the Syrian air force in the skies over Lebanon on June 9–10 by jamming the fire control radars for the Syrian surface-to-air missiles and then shooting down 90 Syrian combat aircraft without a single Israeli loss. It was an unparalleled feat in the history of aerial warfare in the 66 years since aerial warfare became a major activity in 1916. Sharon wanted to teach Damascus a lesson that it would not forget and he did.[18]

By the time of the ceasefire on June 11, the IDF had driven the Palestinian artillery north and out of range of Israel. The ostensible goal of the war had been achieved. But fighting broke out again on June 12, after Israel continued its aerial bombardment of the Palestinians. Early on, Begin told the Knesset that Israeli troops would not be involved in urban warfare and would stay out of major Arab cities, which in turn encouraged Arafat to declare that he would transform Beirut into Israel's Stalingrad. By June 12, six days after the start of the war, the IDF was on the outskirts of Beirut. From this point on, it was a matter of Israel putting pressure on the PLO to evacuate Beirut by cutting off the water to the Palestinian quarter of the city while continuing to shell it. Beginning June 14, some four hundred Israeli tanks and a thousand artillery pieces began shelling Palestinian positions within Beirut; this continued for two months. Israeli navy gunboats also shelled Palestinian positions, while the IAF systematically bombed all known Palestinian buildings in West Beirut. Slowly the city was put under siege. On June 25 a number of villages east of Beirut were occupied by the IDF. And on August 4, the IDF took control of Beirut International Airport.[19]

At this point President Reagan sent Philip Habib back into the field to arrange for a PLO evacuation from Lebanon in exchange for an end to the siege. The problem was that after the PLO had tried to take over first Jordan and then Lebanon, no Arab country wanted to accept large numbers of armed Palestinian fighters in its territory. Reagan began "arm twisting" with pro-American regimes, and finally a plan was agreed upon to send PLO fighters to Tunisia, Yemen, South Yemen, Syria, Algeria, Sudan, and Jordan. On August 21 international peacekeepers from France, Italy, and the United States arrived and Palestinians began evacuating from Beirut, firing thousands of shots in the air to celebrate their "victory" over Israel. The evacuation was completed with 9,000 leaving, and the peacekeepers withdrew after about two weeks.[20]

On August 23, Bashir Gemayel was elected president by the Lebanese parliament, with Israeli officers advising Shi'ite deputies in southern Lebanon to vote in the election. Three weeks later, on September 14, Gemayel was assassinated by a bomb placed in the building where he gave a weekly lecture to a Maronite women's group. The bomb was planted by a Christian mercenary in the pay of Syria.[21] The next day Sharon ordered Eitan to let Phalangist militiamen into Palestinian refugee camps in West Beirut in order to clean out any terrorists who may have remained behind after the evacuation. Afterward Israeli intelligence officers monitoring what was going on in the camps from nearby rooftops heard radio traffic indicating that something had gone wrong. Following several hours of confusion, Northern Commander Major General Amir Drori ordered the Phalangists removed from the two camps, Sabra and Shatila. But the camps were never sealed off and new militiamen entered on September 17. Foreign Minister Yitzhak Shamir was informed of the possible massacres by concerned Israeli journalists and did nothing. Sharon finally entered the camps on the morning of September 18, after the Phalangists had been in the camps for three nights and two days. He ordered the last of the militiamen removed and the camps sealed off. By then several hundred (and possibly more than a thousand) Palestinians had been killed.[22]

On September 20 the three countries that made up the international peacekeeping force said their men would return to Lebanon in about a week to deal with the aftermath of the massacres and protect the Palestinian refugees. The following day Bashir Gemayel's younger brother Amin was elected president to replace his dead brother. On September 24, four hundred thousand Israelis—about a tenth of Israel's entire population at the time—attended a Peace Now demonstration in Tel Aviv and demanded an investigation into the massacres. Peace Now had been founded in March 1978 by reserve officers who thought that Begin's coalition had been slow in taking advantage of Sadat's trip to Jerusalem. After the Camp David summit, the organization went into decline until the start of the Lebanon War, when it revived with a major rally in July. Although the Likud mounted a counterrally with twice as many attending soon afterwards, the government could not overlook a demonstration of this size.[23]

A deeply shaken Begin appointed a three-man investigative committee on September 28. Its head was Supreme Court President Yitzhak Kahan, and its other two members were Supreme Court justice Aharon Barak, who had served as Begin's legal advisor at Camp David and would be a future Supreme Court president, and retired major general Yona Efrat.[24]

Sharon's grand strategy for remaking the politics of the region slowly disappeared over the next two years. Already during the war the Phalange and other militias refused to participate in attacks in conjunction with the IDF. Amin Gemayel had much less support among the Maronites than his brother and was more inclined to coordinate with Sunni Arabs and other Christian denominations than Bashir had been. In December he announced that Lebanon was not prepared to enter into a peace treaty or private deals with Israel that would cause dissension or isolate Lebanon in the wider Arab world. After months of negotiations, an agreement was signed with Israel in May 1983 that declared that Lebanon was no longer at war with Israel and called for Syria to withdraw its troops from Lebanon. However, President Assad declared that he had no intention of withdrawing from Lebanon. In March 1984 Gemayel was pressured by Damascus into declaring the May 1983 agreement void.[25]

The Kahan Commission issued its report on February 10, 1983, which held that the IDF bore indirect responsibility for what had occurred. But the report held Sharon *directly responsible* for the massacres. The report called for the removal of Defense Minister Sharon from his ministry, the prompt retirement of Chief of Staff Eitan, it also recommended and the removal of Aman chief Major General Yehoshua Saguy from his post, and that Brigadier General Amos Yaron not receive a field command for at least three years. The cabinet voted sixteen to one to accept the Kahan Commission report. Sharon was the only dissenting vote. Sharon later spoke to Begin and accused him of handing him over to his enemies, just as the Hagana had handed over Jews to the British in 1944–1945.[26]

Sharon became a minister without portfolio in the government. Media commentators considered him politically dead—after all, he had voluntarily quit the Knesset in 1974. Uri Dan wrote, "Those who did not want him as chief of staff got him as defense minister. Those who don't want Sharon as defense minister, will get him as prime minister." The prediction was ridiculed at the time. In August 1983 Begin announced to his cabinet that "I cannot go on." He had suffered from depression throughout his life, although this was carefully kept secret. The death of his beloved wife Aliza in November 1982 and the continuing deaths of Israeli soldiers from injuries incurred in the war finally broke Begin, and he never recovered. He officially retired as prime minister in September 1983 and went into a seclusion from which he never emerged. The Likud elected Foreign Minister Yitzhak Shamir as his successor, and he became prime minister until elections the following year.[27]

The Lebanon War produced a major shakeup in Israeli politics and in Jewish politics in the United States. Colonel Eli Geva, the youngest colonel in the IDF and the son of Sharon's old superior Yosef Geva, requested during the war to be relieved of his command and made an ordinary tanker because he was opposed to ordering his unit into Beirut for fear of large civilian casualties. He was relieved of command and sent home, ending his military career. This was the first time such a mutiny had occurred since 1948. Several young conscripts produced novels or movies about their Lebanon experiences decades later in the 2000s. In addition, Peace Now came into its own as the mainstream peace party. In the United States many mainstream American Jews from Reform or Conservative denominations who had dutifully supported the Likud governments of Begin in 1977 and 1981 began questioning Israel's desire for peace. This was the source of the Brit Tzedek vaShalom and J Street movements two decades later. In the meantime, they stopped giving donations to the United Jewish Appeal and started donating to groups like Americans for Peace Now and the New Israel Fund.[28]

Sharon went into a period of slow recovery that lasted fifteen years, finally ending in October 1998. Until then he held second-rank ministries in Likud governments. This "exile" was not as severe as Dayan's reduced status in the Labor Party from June 1974 to June 1977 or after October 1979 but more like his status under Levy Eshkol from 1964 to 1967 (or Barak's status from 2001 to 2007). Or, for Americans, it can be compared to Richard Nixon's status between November 1960 and 1968 rather than to his status after August 1974.

The recovery began when Sharon challenged Shamir for the leadership of the Likud in 1983 and received 42 percent of the vote to Shamir's 56.5 percent. David Levy dropped out of the race to give Sharon a clear shot, and this was the start of a de facto alliance between the two. In June 1984, when Labor received 44 seats to the Likud's 41, neither was able to form a partisan ideological coalition. So Sharon conducted talks with Labor leader Shimon Peres about forming a government of national unity. After several weeks, they had agreed on a ten-member inner cabinet with five seats each for both parties, a rotating premiership, and a platform. During the talks Sharon made sure that the religious parties refused to enter into talks with Labor. For his reward, Shamir gave Sharon the ministry of trade and industry and a seat in the inner cabinet.[29]

During the negotiations Sharon was commuting on a regular basis to New York to participate in a libel trial. On February 14, 1983, *Time* had published an article claiming that Sharon had met with Phalange leaders following the assassination of Gemayel and agreed on the need for revenge. The author, an Israeli journalist, claimed that this information was contained in a secret Appendix B of the Kahan Commission report. Sharon promptly filed suit for libel in both New York, *Time*'s headquarters, and Tel Aviv. Attorney Milton Gould offered to defend Sharon pro bono. In January 1985 the New York jury ruled that the charge was both false and defamatory, but that *Time* had not acted with actual malice, which is necessary to prove libel in America. With the verdict in New York obtained, Sharon easily won in Tel Aviv, where, as in most of Western Europe, it is not necessary to prove malice in order to prove libel. Sharon's friend Uri Dan wrote a book, *Blood Libel*, about the case. Sharon used the verdict within Israel to create the feeling that he had been wronged by the left.[30]

Under Shamir, the Likud was divided into three main factions or camps. The main group was the Shamir-Arens faction, which included the "fighting family" of Etzel and Lehi veterans of the Herut and their children, the "princes." It also included those from La'am, which later that decade ceased to be a separate faction within the Likud. Over the next decade Shamir served as foreign minister and then prime minister in two consecutive governments of national unity, and Moshe Arens served as both foreign minister and defense minister. A second Likud faction was headed by David Levy and consisted of Moroccan Jews and other mizrakhim who were more interested in the social and economic progress of mizrakhim toward equality with Ashkenazi Jews than in foreign policy. And then there was a faction headed by Sharon, consisting of his personal followers.[31] In 1983–1984 the rehabilitation within Likud of Sharon seemed as likely as the rehabilitation of Robert McFarlane or Oliver North within the Republican Party after the Iran-Contra affair. Begin, like Reagan among movement conservatives in the United States, was regarded by Likudniks as their ideological figurehead and standard bearer. Sharon was held responsible for Begin's retirement due to depression by son Benny Begin and others. Shamir was elected his successor, as he was seen as largely a Begin copy.

Sharon could take credit for expelling the PLO from Lebanon. Although Arafat and many of his followers sneaked back into Lebanon over the course of the next year, Assad conspired with dissidents within Fatah to provoke a revolt against Arafat that led to Arafat's final expulsion from Lebanon in November 1983 in two stages: first from the Beka'a Valley and then from Tripoli in the north.[32] Arafat spent the next decade in exile until the Oslo peace process led to his return to Mandatory Palestine in May 1994. From Tunis Arafat had no chance of conduct a real armed struggle against Israel and was forced to finally sue for peace. Over the next two decades Sharon would remind audiences of his role in humbling Arafat while ignoring his grandiose plans of 1981–1982.

Sharon in his first decade in politics had bounced from side to side across the political landscape like a bumper car in an amusement park ride. His fortunes had gone drastically up and down in a roller-coaster fashion. This, surprisingly, is not unusual for former generals when they enter into politics in Israel. Rabin experienced the same phenomenon from 1974 to 1984, as did Ezer Weizman between 1969 and 1979 (and even until 1985) and Barak from 1995 to 2007. I believe this is because these generals rely on their instincts in this new environment in which they have not yet gained the knowledge to act instinctively. They receive too much power too quickly and make major mistakes in the full glare of the public spotlight. This is why only in dictatorships are civilians made overnight into generals.

Sharon had a somewhat smoother journey during his second decade in politics. Although he was twice forced to issue letters of apology to Peres for defamatory public statements that he had made, he remained as Shamir's minister of industry and trade for six years. Sharon had claimed that Peres had conspired with Saddam Hussein to hold an international conference on Israel. On July 23, 1988, he told *Ha'Aretz* that the Intifada would never have broken out if he had been defense minister instead of Rabin.[33]

Lilly and his two sons became Sharon's principal political advisors, and together they decided whom to support and whom to oppose in the party. Sometimes Lilly and Sharon would talk all night about party politics. In March 1987 Sharon beat Levy's candidate, Ovadia Eli, for the position of chairman of the Likud Central Committee by a margin of 66 percent to 34 percent. Only a year before, Benny Begin had gone on the political talkshow *Moked* and claimed that there was no Sharon camp in the Likud. But after the November 1988 election gave the Likud 40 seats, the Sharon camp was represented in the Knesset only by Sharon and two other MKs.[34]

In May 1988 Sharon's mother, Vera Scheinerman, died at the age of 88. She had seen her son rise to the top of the defense establishment—and then self-destruct. She would not witness his ultimate triumph. Sharon spoke to the press of the favorable influence that she had on his development as a child. He had first his father as a role model, and then his mother. After Sharon's second marriage, his source of psychological support became his wife Lilly. Once she was gone, he would be profoundly lonely.[35]

In August 1988 the Likud was transformed from a joint list similar to its Gahal predecessor to a united party. No longer would each faction within the two component parties appoint its own representatives to agreed-upon positions on a common list; instead, a 3,000-member Central Committee dominated by the members of the Shamir-Arens faction and the Liberals would decide upon the composition of the Likud's election list. Sharon decided to get the press to attack him in order to boost his prestige within the party, and said that he would annex parts of the West Bank to deal with the Intifada. Labor publicized this in its election campaign.[36]

In 1990 Sharon used his rabbinical connections to help oppose the formation of a Labor government by Peres. Shamir appointed him minister of housing when the Likud-led coalition was sworn in. This was just in time for a major exodus of Jews from the former Soviet Union as emigration was allowed freely for the first time in decades. Sharon presided over the commencement of the construction of over 170,000 housing units and hundreds of thousands of apartments to house all the new immigrants as they arrived in the biggest aliyah since Israel's first decade. In the meantime, Sharon made sure that trailers were available to house the immigrants until their apartments were built.[37]

In March 1993 the Likud held a leadership election to choose a replacement for Shamir. With Moshe Arens having retired at the same time as Shamir, the leadership was being passed to the next generation. The three candidates were Benjamin "Bibi" Netanyahu, a protégé of Arens who had served in the Sayeret Matkal and was the brother of slain Sayeret Matkal commander Yonatan Netanyahu, and a successful *hasbaran* (spokesman); Benny Begin, geologist son of the former Etzel commander and Herut and Likud leader; and David Levy. Netanyahu won with 52 percent, more than twice that of his nearest rival, Levy. From the start Sharon and Netanyahu formed a rivalry and mutual antipathy reminiscent of that between Rabin and Peres. Sharon considered Netanyahu a lightweight with no real accomplishments, and a liar to boot. Netanyahu considered Sharon a has-been and a loose cannon.[38]

After Rabin signed the Oslo agreement with Arafat on the White House lawn in September 1993, the Likud came out in bitter opposition to the new arrangement. Sharon met with Rabin on several occasions and warned him that Arafat could not be trusted to keep his word. Despite Sharon's outbursts during the national unity governments when Rabin was defense minister and the debacle in Lebanon, Rabin still had respect for Sharon's opinions. But Rabin pressed ahead and Netanyahu and Sharon, despite their mutual antipathy, found themselves sharing the speaker's platform at many anti–Oslo rallies in 1994 and 1995, at which settlers appeared with posters portraying Rabin in an SS uniform or dressed in a keffiya like Arafat.[39]

During the election campaign of 1996, Netanyahu promised Sharon one of the top three positions if the Likud won (although Sharon did not believe that he would follow through on this promise). Sharon worked hard campaigning for the ticket and induced both Raful Eitan of Tzomet and David Levy of Gesher to run as part of the Likud. After Netanyahu narrowly nosed out Peres in May, he decided not to give Sharon a ministry at all in the new government. But Levy announced to reporters the promises that Netanyahu had made to Sharon and not fulfilled. Levy threatened to leave the coalition with his faction if Sharon were not given a ministry. A ministry of national infrastructure was custom built for Sharon by stripping functions from several other ministries.[40]

In the summer of 1997, Netanyahu pushed out Finance Minister Dan Meridor, another leading prince, whom Netanyahu probably viewed as both too dangerous and too liberal. Netanyahu then turned to Sharon and asked him if he would take the ministry, and Sharon agreed. But Sharon never got the office. Netanyahu's *modus operandi* was to promise the same office to several people and then give it to whoever provided the most benefit for himself. When Netanyahu called Sharon to his office, Sharon stood in the doorway and said, "A liar you were and a liar you have remained."[41]

In January 1998 Foreign Minister David Levy quit the coalition over the budget, which he claimed slighted the disenfranchised. This left Sharon as the second most important person in Netanyahu's coalition. Netanyahu kept the foreign ministry for himself while Sharon bided his time. In October 1998 Netanyahu was scheduled to attend a summit in the United States to decide upon territorial concessions as part of a scheduled Israeli redeployment under the Oslo accords. On October 13 Netanyahu appointed Sharon as his new foreign minister on the eve of departing for the summit in exchange for Sharon's support for whatever concessions were necessary to make at the summit.[42] This was Sharon's first chance at the limelight in fifteen years.

Chapter Ten

Prime Minister Sharon

After being appointed as foreign minister, Sharon flew to Minnesota from Israel to visit King Hussein of Jordan, who was being treated for cancer at the Mayo Clinic in Rochester. This signaled Sharon's acceptance of the Hashemite monarchy and likewise Hussein's acceptance of Sharon's new role in the government. Sharon then spent the weekend in New York before traveling on to the Wye River Conference in Maryland, which was already in progress.

At the Wye summit, Sharon sat directly opposite Arafat but never acknowledged his presence directly and always referred to him in the third person. Arafat was not upset by this treatment—Sharon was as much a devil for the Palestinians as Arafat was for the Israelis. During the conference several Clinton administration senior officials, including Secretary of State Madeleine Albright, National Security Advisor Sandy Berger and CIA Director George Tenet, worked to draft compromises in which the Palestinians would agree to specific security arrangements in exchange for Israel giving up territory on the West Bank. A very ill and pale King Hussein flew down from the Mayo Clinic to urge everyone involved to make the necessary sacrifices for peace. Less than four months later he was dead. Prime Minister Netanyahu agreed to transfer 41 percent of the West Bank over the next three months from Area C—under total Israeli control—to Areas A and B: under total Palestinian control in Area A and under Palestinian civil control and Israeli military control in Area B. The 13 percent being transferred directly to Area A included the city of Hebron with its Jewish enclave. The agreement was signed on October 23, 1998, after nine days of talks at Wye and a year and a half of negotiations with the Clinton administration. The Knesset ratified the Wye agreement the following month, with Labor and Meretz supporting as the former had done with Camp David.[1]

In January 1999 Sharon made official visits to the United States, France,

Germany and Russia. In Russia, Moscow proved eager for new relations with the Jewish state and Prime Minister Yevgeny Primakov, an Arabist by training, laid out the red carpet for Sharon.

After the death of King Hussein in Jordan in February 1999, Sharon attended the funeral as a representative of Israel. At the funeral President Ezer Weizman shook hands with terrorist leader Nayef Hawatme, for which he was soundly criticized at home. He defended himself by arguing that Arafat was also a terrorist.[2]

Netanyahu's coalition was in a state of collapse. Right-wing ministers were upset over the territorial concessions at Wye. On December 21, the Knesset voted for new elections in May 1999. Defense Minister Yitzhak Mordechai resigned from the government to join the new Center Party being formed by former chief of state Amnon Lipkin-Shahak and Ron Milo, a Likud prince, in January. Mordechai, a mizrakhi, soon took over as the party leader, as polls showed him to be more popular than either Lipkin-Shahak or Milo. Netanyahu replaced Mordechai with Moshe Arens as defense minister.

In April 1999 Sharon made his third visit as foreign minister to Russia. He was trying to prevent Moscow from selling anti-aircraft missiles to Tehran, which could complicate an Israeli strike against Iranian nuclear facilities. While there Sharon came out against independence for Kosovo, both in order to appease the Russians and because he feared that it could serve as a precedent for a future Palestinian state.[3]

The May 1999 election resulted in a majority for the center-left. The Labor Party, campaigning as One Israel, received 26 seats, with former chief of staff Ehud Barak imitating Rabin by running a personalized campaign. Barak formed a wide cabinet with the religious parties as well as Meretz and the Center Party. David Levy had reformed his Gesher Party and joined as part of the One Israel coalition. He was then appointed by Barak as foreign minister.

Netanyahu quit as party leader and retired—temporarily—from politics. Sharon was elected as the Likud leader on September 2, 1999, with 53 percent compared to 24 percent for Ehud Olmert and 22 percent for Meir Shitreet—by then all his serious opponents had left either the party or politics in general: Levy had defected to Labor; Netanyahu had retired; Benny Begin had formed his own Herut Party. The Likud had been left with only 19 seats and no one seemed to want the task of rebuilding the party except Sharon.[4]

But Sharon was faced with several personal tragedies. First his wife Lilly was diagnosed with lung cancer, and Sharon spent much of his time caring for her. Then in December 1999 a short-circuit in some wiring caused a fire that burned down his home at the ranch. Lost in the fire were many personal

Ariel Sharon at David Ben-Gurion's grave in Negev, December 3, 2000. Photograph by Yaacov Gefen, Israeli Government Press Office.

records, notes and photographs. In January Lilly was hospitalized in poor condition. She died on March 25, 2000, in a Tel Aviv hospital leaving Sharon alone after 37 years of marriage. Now he had only his two adult sons, Omri and Gilad, to rely on for advice about politics and government, and when they disagreed he would have to decide for himself. So they made a division of tasks: Gilad advised his father on economics, strategy, and ideology, and Omri on party politics.[5]

Barak's attempts to negotiate a peace treaty with Syria collapsed in Geneva in March 2000, causing him to turn to the Palestinian track. On the eve of the Camp David summit in July 2000, Barak lost his majority in parliament. In the aftermath of the failed summit Barak was vulnerable. Polls showed that Netanyahu would beat Barak in an election. In June 2000, Sharon had met with professional political advisor Arthur Finkelstein, who told him to concentrate on a single campaign theme. Sharon chose a united Jerusalem and accused Barak of wanting to divide the city.[6]

After getting permission to do so from Barak, Sharon decided to visit the Temple Mount to demonstrate that the site remained under Jewish control. Barak gave Sharon permission because he feared being attacked politically by Sharon if he did not. Both Arafat and Abu Ala'a (one of Arafat's top advisors and later his prime minister) urged Barak to cancel permission for the visit. Arafat said that it would "destroy everything." "You know it's very dangerous, it might result in bloodshed," said Abu Ala'a to Gilead Sher, the chief Israeli negotiator with the Palestinians. Interior Minister Shlomo Ben-Ami informed Palestinian security chief Jabril Rajoub, who said it would be okay as long as Sharon made no attempt to enter either of the two mosques on the Mount. He later denied saying this.[7] Rajoub may have been disingenuous, as he realized that this would give Arafat a perfect rallying cause to spark a new Intifada—the Al-Aksa Intifada. As the whole area of the Noble Sanctuary (Temple Mount) is considered one giant mosque, having a large number of booted security guards and politicians would definitely be considered a serious violation.[8]

Sharon entered the Temple Mount at 7:55 a.m. on the morning of September 28, accompanied by five Likud MKs and dozens of elite police officers with over a thousand police on standby in the Old City in case they were needed. The visit lasted only forty-five minutes and resulted in Sharon helping to set off a new wave of unrest. Palestinian protesters attempted to claw their way through the police escort to get at Sharon, who sweated in his bulletproof vest. Former chief of staff Amnon Lipkin-Shahak, who was a minister in Barak's government, claimed that Sharon made the visit to punish Barak for having made concessions regarding Jerusalem.[9]

Within a day seven Palestinians had been killed in riots. Arafat went on the radio to call for all Palestinians to defend the Al-Aksa Mosque. With negotiations deadlocked, he fancied that violence was more likely to advance his cause than continuing talks. And with living standards falling due to a stalled economy, the Palestinian territories were ripe for a new Intifada. By October the Intifada was in full gear.[10]

Barak resigned as prime minister by calling for new elections on December 9, 2000. Because the double-voting system was still in effect, Barak could either have his entire government resign or just resign personally. He decided to resign personally, bringing about the only election in Israeli history for just the prime minister in February 2001. Likud MKs introduced a special bill to allow a non-MK—that is, Netanyahu—to compete for the premiership. It seemed likely to pass. But then Netanyahu announced that unless Barak would call for a full election—for the Knesset as well—he would stay in retirement and not run. The Knesset passed the Netanyahu law on December 18, 2000, but refused to call for a general election. The way was clear for Sharon.[11]

Based on a scale devised by Arthur Finkelstein, Sharon's campaign manager Reuven Adler measured Sharon's rating on the Arab question as 4.7, where 5 was the extreme right and Meretz was 1. Adler's pollster determined that the general Israeli public was between 2.6 and 3.2 on the scale. Adler decided that Sharon needed to be perceived as about 2.7 in order to win. So he came up with the slogan "Only Sharon Will Bring Peace."

By early January 2001 Sharon led by twenty points in the polls. Late in the campaign the Sharon team switched the slogan to "I Have Confidence in Sharon's Peace." This depended on the deliberate double meaning of the word *bitakhon*, which means both confidence and security in Hebrew. In January 2001 Barak went into final negotiations with the Palestinians at Taba in Sinai, but the move smacked of desperation. Even though he broke off the negotiations a week before the election, it did not help him. Sharon concentrated on mobilizing three groups of voters for the election: settlers, the ultra-Orthodox, and Russian immigrants. With only Sharon and Barak in the race, the Likud did not have to worry about these groups voting for other parties like Shas and the National Religious Party. On February 6, 2001, Sharon beat Barak by a margin of 62 to 38 percent, or 24 points—even more than Barak had beaten Netanyahu by in 1999.[12]

Now Sharon would have to govern for another two years with a parliamentary minority for his party. First he formed a government of national unity with Labor (26), Shas (17), Israel B'Aliya (6) and the Likud (19). He offered the defense ministry to Labor. Initially, Barak seemed inclined to take it, but after his party revolted he was forced to surrender it to former brigadier general Benjamin "Fuad" Ben-Eliezer. Sharon made Peres his foreign minister and Eli Yishai of Shas his interior minister. By adding the National Union, he soon had a coalition of 68 votes, and the National Religious Party, the Center Party, and Gesher were all ready to serve in the coalition if necessary.[13]

Sharon's government took office in early March 2001. Its first goal was to end the Intifada on terms favorable to Israel. There was an unprecedented wave of terror attacks during Sharon's first hundred days in office, more intense even than the wave in 1996 that helped to elect Netanyahu. But this worked to Sharon's advantage when the September 11 terrorist attacks occurred in the United States. President George W. Bush, who had been Sharon's guest on a guided tour of Israel in 1999 when he was governor of Texas, was receptive to the message that Arafat was just a local version of Al Qaeda leader Osama bin Laden. In March Sharon had traveled to Washington to meet with Bush and spread the word that he was ready for peace and compromise but would not negotiate under fire.[14]

On September 23, 2001, Sharon became the first Likud leader in history to say he was ready for a Palestinian state in a speech at Latrun. But Sharon's state comprised only about 42 percent of the West Bank and resembled more a South African homeland like KwaZulu than the map of the state that the Palestinians had in mind. Nevertheless, many Likud Central Committee members regarded it as a betrayal of principle, just as many Palestinians had regarded the Oslo agreement as a betrayal. On October 13, 2001, National Union leader Rehavam Ze'evi and Israel Beitenu leader Avigdor Lieberman resigned from the government. But before their resignations could take effect officially, Ze'evi was assassinated by terrorists from the Popular Front for the Liberation of Palestine at his home in the Old City of Jerusalem. Netanyahu called for an all-out war against the Palestinian Authority and the exile or killing of Arafat.[15]

Sharon sent troops into the six main Palestinian towns in an attempt to root out terrorism. Bush was preparing to wage a coalition war in Afghanistan and so could not risk condoning Sharon's moves openly, although Sharon was warned to have his troops out of the towns before coming to Washington on a scheduled visit. In November Sharon rescheduled the visit rather than prematurely pull his troops out.

In January 2002 Israeli naval commandos captured the Palestinian arms ship *Karin A* on its way from Iran to Gaza. It was boarded in the Red Sea. Arafat denied any knowledge of the ship, but documents from the ship that refuted this story were produced and shown to several Western leaders. On January 14 Sharon said that Arafat would not be allowed to leave Ramallah until he arrested Ze'evi's killers and those responsible for the *Karin A*. That same day Sharon signed a death order for Ra'ad Karmi, a Palestinian terrorist from Tulkarem who belonged to Arafat's Fatah movement. Sharon was reviving a policy first used when Peres was prime minister in 1996 of "targeted killings," or assassinations of terrorist leaders who were operationally involved in terrorism rather than merely endorsing its use. The idea was to retard the enemy's capability of carrying out terrorism by depriving it of the experience of veteran operatives.[16]

In order for targeted killings to work, Israeli intelligence (usually Shabak) had to have information about the location and movements of the target and be able to transmit this information and get a decision to kill back in time to execute the attack, usually by helicopter or fighter jet. This meant taking into account any possible collateral damage—innocent civilians killed or injured in the attack. As several former heads of Shabak later admitted in the film *The Gatekeepers*, the targeted killings were a tactic intended as a stopgap measure in order to buy the government time to come up with a permanent (that is, political) solution. But Sharon never really envisaged a political solution with the Palestinians. He thought wholly in terms of whatever Bush would allow him to do.

On July 23, 2002, the IAF bombed the house of Salah Schade. He was the leader in Gaza of Hamas's military wing, the Izz al-Din al-Kassem Brigades, named after a resistance leader killed fighting the British in late 1935, when Sharon was seven years old. (Ironically, Kassem was a hero of Arafat.) The house had been bombed with a one-ton bomb that killed twelve people in addition to Schade. On March 22, 2004, Sheikh Ahmed Yassin, the spiritual leader and ideologue behind Hamas, was killed by Israeli rockets fired from a plane as he left his mosque after mourning prayers. This was a departure from the previous policy of only hitting operational leaders, and it served as an Israeli declaration of war on Hamas. Less than a month later, Yassin's successor, Abdel Assis al-Rantissi, was also killed by the IAF in a targeted air strike on April 17. These two would be the first of many senior Hamas members to be killed, resulting in Hamas not publicly identifying its leaders. In June 2004 the U.S. House of Representatives passed a resolution by a vote of 397 to 5 supporting Israel's right to use targeted killings to defend itself.[17]

In March 2002 a suicide bomber blew himself up in a hall in Netanya where a Passover seder was taking place. He killed 29 people and injured 140, twenty of them seriously. The killer was from Hamas and his name was on a list of known terrorists given several times to Arafat for apprehension. Sharon reacted by ordering an invasion of the West Bank cities evacuated under the Oslo II agreement in late 1995. Israeli tanks poured into the cities and Israeli soldiers made their way from house to house checking for terrorists. In Jenin there was a very destructive battle, as several houses had to be destroyed to protect the troops going in. The Palestinians claimed that 500 people had been killed. It later turned out that the figure was about 50 Palestinians, roughly double the number of Israeli soldiers killed. In all, Operation Defensive Shield—as the invasion was officially called—lasted for forty days; 29 Israeli soldiers were killed and about a hundred were wounded.[18]

In October 2002 Ben-Eliezer pulled Labor out of the coalition in order to put distance between it and the Likud before the general election. Ostensibly the pullout was caused by the Likud allocating too much of the budget to settlements at the expense of the poor, but it was really a political decision driven by polls indicating that Labor might disappear if it remained in the coalition. Labor chose Avram Mitzna, a former major general in charge of Central Command during the first Intifada and later mayor of Haifa, as its candidate for prime minister. Sharon easily won the Likud primary for the leadership and named Netanyahu to replace Peres as foreign minister and former chief of staff Shaul Mofaz as defense minister to replace Ben-Eliezer. Mofaz, a hardliner, became Sharon's protégé.[19]

Sharon ran on his record of combatting terrorism and used the terms "peace" and "security" almost interchangeably in his election campaign. Mitzna was too much of a dove in the new Israel that had emerged as a result of the failure of Camp David and the start of the Al-Aksa Intifada. Because the Sharon "brand" was much stronger than the party brand, the Likud ended up running a personalized campaign much like Rabin ran in 1992 and Barak ran in 1999. On January 28, 2003, Sharon was reelected prime minister. The Likud doubled its number of seats from 19 to 38, while Labor lost seven seats (leaving it with only 19); Yosef "Tommy" Lapid's Shinui Party gained nine seats for a total of 15, Shas lost six seats (ending up with 11), and the dovish Meretz had its seats halved to six.[20]

Sharon formed a coalition with 68 seats made up of the Likud (40), Shinui (15), National Union (7), and National Religious Party (6) on February 28, two days after his seventy-fifth birthday. Sharon, now that he had his coalition of the right, was much more interested in implementing a strategy than he had been before. For the remainder of his time in office, Sharon concentrated on two main projects: the building of the Separation Barrier—a combination of fences and walls that separated Jews from Arabs and ran inside the West Bank so that the main settlements were included behind it— and the disengagement from Gaza. The barrier was authorized by the government in June 2002. Later the Israeli Supreme Court made the government modify the route of the barrier to minimize the nuisance to Palestinians along the route. The International Court at the Hague ruled the whole barrier—which it called a wall—illegal because it was built on Palestinian territory.[21]

During the spring of 2003 Sharon also had to contend with the Road Map. This was an attempt by the Bush administration to revive the Israeli-Palestinian peace process through the Quartet (the United States, Russia, the European Union, and the United Nations) by creating a "road map" for what needed to be done to ensure both security and compliance under the Oslo agreement. The problem was that neither side trusted the other, and neither was really interested in a negotiated peace. But Bush was under pressure from British Prime Minister Tony Blair to revive the peace process as a condition of British participation in the invasion of Iraq in March 2003. On May 23, 2003, the Israeli government officially agreed to the Road Map "in principle," but with so many qualifications as to mean a rejection in practice. The Bush administration forced Arafat to appoint Mahmoud Abbas as his prime minister. Arafat was a ruler who did not really want to share power—this was not the Arab model. So he used his control over his security chiefs to frustrate Abbas until he finally resigned in August. Arafat then appointed Ahmed Qurei (also known as Abu Ala'a) as the new prime minister.[22]

The Bush administration indicated repeatedly that Arafat was off limits to Israel—he could not be killed or forced into exile. So Sharon kept him under siege in his compound in Ramallah, known as the Mukata. Sharon was itching to have Arafat killed, but he gave his word to Bush that he would not do so. But Arafat was politically dead or irrelevant as far as both Sharon and Bush were concerned, as the latter indicated in his speech on the Middle East on June 24, 2002, which called on the Palestinians to choose a new leader untainted by a connection with terrorism.[23]

In his final months in 2004, however, Arafat was back in his element, as if he were back in Beirut under siege by Sharon in 1982. This was Sharon's fourth and final round of confrontation with the Palestinians. The first was on the West Bank and in Gaza from September 1953 to October 1956, the second was in Gaza in 1971–1972, and the third was in Lebanon in 1982–1983. The only other native-fighter politician to have such a long confrontation with his enemy was Andrew Jackson, who fought Indians off and on from 1788 to 1837, when he resigned as president. Besides their lengthy careers, the two men had many other personality traits in common. But Sharon, unlike Jackson, could not intimidate rivals by challenging them to a duel or simply shooting them; he had to stick to lawsuits and bullying.[24]

Sharon, according to his confidante and attorney, Dov Weisglass, had thought that upon taking office he could negotiate a 25-year truce with the

Palestinians. Then he concluded that he had to eradicate terrorism first and wait for a successor to Arafat. But in the meantime, the opposition was busy attempting various peace initiatives with moderate Palestinians. Ami Ayalon, a former head of both the Israeli navy and Shabak, got together with former Intifada organizer Sari Nusseibeh to mount a petition drive. More serious was a negotiation between elements in Labor and Meretz, on one hand, and members of the Palestinian Authority, on the other, to continue the negotiations where they had left off at Taba in January 2001 in an attempt to reach a peace agreement. The Swiss government underwrote this initiative financially, and the final agreement was signed in Geneva in August 2003. An infrastructure was appointed to publicize the venture among Israelis and Palestinians and took the name of the Geneva Initiative.[25]

This was in concept very similar to an initiative carried out by the parliamentary opposition in apartheid South Africa in the mid-1980s known as KwaZulu/Natal Indaba, or simply the Indaba for short. This was a negotiation between the former provincial government of Natal (before it was abolished by the government's constitutional reforms) and the government of the KwaZulu homeland and numerous third-party groups. The Indaba was rejected by the National Party government as being a form of majority rule—though it was actually power sharing—but it caused a number of independent candidates to challenge the National Party in the next election. One of these was elected and a second lost by only 39 votes to a senior government minister. This in turn influenced President F.W. de Klerk to institute major reforms once he took power in 1989. A similar dynamic operated in Israel with the Geneva Initiative.[26]

Sharon in 2003 saw himself under pressure from Washington to do something. National Security Advisor Uzi Dayan, a former deputy chief of staff and nephew of Moshe Dayan, briefed Sharon about the demographic challenge to Israel presented by the combination of the higher Arab birthrate and the occupation. Sharon decided to partially alleviate this problem by withdrawing from Gaza.[27] Settlers later charged that Sharon was merely trying to solve his legal problems by withdrawing from Gaza so that the liberal legal establishment would quash the investigations against him because he supported their political agenda. All those who knew Sharon refute this allegation.

There were three separate corruption investigations pursued against Sharon and his family in the early 2000s. The first was the Annex Research affair, involving illegal campaign contributions to the Sharon campaign by international corporations during 1999 and 2000. Eventually his son Omri was indicted and convicted for receiving illegal campaign contributions, and he served some six months in a minimum-security prison.[28] The case against Ariel Sharon was closed by the prosecutor for lack of evidence. The second was the Cyril Kern affair. Kern was an old friend of Sharon's who had helped to save his life by rushing him to the hospital after he was wounded in the Battle of Latrun. Kern then became a financier and made his fortune in casinos in the homelands of South Africa, which became a playground for South African whites under apartheid. Kern had made a loan to Gilad Sharon to finance Sharon's leadership bid in the 1999 Likud contest. Sharon claimed that it was a loan with interest and was paid back in full, including interest. The third scandal was known as the Greek Island affair and involved David Appel paying Gilad Sharon a major fee ($400,000) and an annual $20,000 salary to promote his investments on the Greek island of Patroklos and in the city of Lod in Israel. The police thought that this was an influence-peddling scheme whereby the investor, Appel, was paying for Sharon's influence through his son. In April 2005 the charges in the Greek Island affair were dropped because of insufficient evidence—a weak case. It would seem that the Gaza disengagement did not prevent Omri from serving time in prison and that the other matters were dropped due to a lack of evidence.[29]

On October 16, 2003, Gilad Sharon wrote a position paper for his father in which he expounded on the principle of unilateral action as a means of dealing with Israel's security problems. He did not mention anything in particular—only the principle. With this in mind, Sharon went to Italy for three days on a secret trip on November 17. There he met with Assistant Secretary of State for Near Eastern Affairs Elliot Abrams at his hotel. This was the first occasion on which Sharon spoke of the possibility of a withdrawal from Gaza. A week later his personal attorney, Dov Weisglass, met with Elliot Abrams and National Security Advisor Condoleeza Rice in Washington. Weisglass briefed Sharon back in Israel on November 26. The Americans were concerned that the disengagement might clash with the Road Map and they did not want anything to interfere with that—even though Arafat had declared the Road Map dead on September 2. They later decided, however, that this unilateral move would not interfere with the Road Map.[30]

Three government ministers, including Finance Minister Benjamin Netanyahu and Foreign Minister Silvan Shalom, publicly opposed the disengagement plan and led the movement to defeat it. On November 21, 2003, Israel's Channel 2 announced in its newscast that Sharon intended to carry out his disengagement from Gaza by the end of the summer of 2004. On December 18, 2003, at the Dan Hotel in Herzliya, Sharon made a speech on disengagement in which he defended it as a means of reducing both terrorism and friction with the Palestinians. He started out by speaking in favor of the

Ten. Prime Minister Sharon

Road Map plan, but stated that if the Palestinians did not soon endorse the Road Map and began to implement it, he would be forced to act unilaterally.[31]

The settlers took Sharon at his word from the moment he made the speech. On January 12, 2004, some 120,000 settlers and their supporters demonstrated in Rabin Square in Tel Aviv (where Rabin was assassinated in 1995) against the disengagement plan under the slogan "Arik Don't Fold." The demonstration was organized by the Yesha Settlement Council, the governing body for the settlements.

In February 2004 Sharon had breakfast with *Ha'Aretz* reporter Yoel Marcus. Because *Ha'Aretz* was the newspaper of the political and business establishment in Israel—the equivalent of the *New York Times*, the *London Times* or *Le Monde*—Sharon figured it would be the ideal vehicle to announce his plan to withdraw from 17 settlements in Gaza and four on the West Bank. The media soon got behind Sharon's initiative, but he had problems with his own party. Sharon met with Bush at the White House on April 14, 2004, and got his support for the Gaza disengagement. Bush also handed Sharon an official letter in which he made three crucial recognitions of Likud positions:

- no return of Palestinian refugees to Israel;
- a de facto recognition of the legitimacy of the settlement blocs; and
- no return to the 1949 armistice lines.

On May 4, the Quartet met in New York and endorsed the idea of the disengagement as being consistent with the Road Map.[32]

Sharon's son Gilad later wrote that the disengagement was the main order of business for the Israeli government from its announcement in December 2003 until its execution in late August 2005—and even afterward until the election of March 2006.[33] The next major step was getting an endorsement from the Likud. Sharon decided to conduct a referendum on the disengagement open to all party members. Sharon knew that he could never win support for the plan from the party's Central Committee. But he figured that with his personal reputation and speaking ability, he could sway ordinary Likud members. A referendum was scheduled for May 4, 2004. Ten days before the referendum Netanyahu, and then Shalom, came out in favor of the disengagement. But then the tide of opinion began to shift. Three days before the referendum, polls showed the opposition ahead by 3–9 percent. On May 4 party members were asked a single simple question: "Are you for or against Ariel Sharon's political plan?" Sharon was trounced by a 59.5 percent to 39.7 percent margin—almost exactly a 3:2 ratio. Sharon decided he had to bypass the party and win support in the government and the Knesset for the disengagement.[34]

On May 15 a pro-disengagement rally was held in Rabin Square and attracted 150,000 people. The next day President Moshe Katsav admitted that there was a national majority in favor of withdrawal. Sharon decided to hold a vote on the disengagement plan at the regular weekly cabinet meeting at the beginning of June. First, he decided to improve the odds by firing two ministers, Benny Elon and Avigdor Lieberman, both members of the National Union who were opposed to the disengagement. The two decided to stay away but were found and served with legal papers announcing their dismissal. The government voted 14–7 to authorize disengagement, but not evacuation of the settlements—they would do that on another occasion.[35]

On October 25, 2004, the Knesset voted 67–44 in favor of the disengagement plan, with all of the political left voting in favor of the plan. The political atmosphere in Israel was eerily similar to that of nine years before. There were terror attacks by Hamas and Islamic Jihad, with Israeli targeted killings in response. The settlers held mass demonstrations in opposition to the disengagement plan and demonized Sharon as they had, with his support, once demonized Rabin and Peres. There were counter-demonstrations in favor of the disengagement plan. The day before the vote, Arafat had been flown by air ambulance to a Paris hospital, gravely ill. Arafat died on November 11 in Paris of undisclosed causes. Palestinians claimed that he had been poisoned by Israel, and Israelis countered that he had died of AIDS as a known bisexual. Mahmoud Abbas asked for permission to bury Arafat in Jerusalem, but this was refused. However, Israel allowed him to be buried in the Mukata in Ramallah, where he had spent the last years of his life. After an emotional and raucous funeral procession in which the shrouded body was carried by the crowd, he was interred there.[36]

The settlers took Arafat's death as a sign of divine intervention. Sharon, a shellfish-eating agnostic, laughed at this theory. A budget was created that included funding for compensation payments for evacuated settlers. On January 10 Labor entered the government in order to help it carry out the disengagement and was given seven ministries. Three weeks later the government voted 17–5 to approve the government's final disengagement plan. This was after a dispute with Shinui over the proposed budget led Sharon to side with the ultra-Orthodox parties and Shinui to quit the government in November. Labor leader Shimon Peres announced that Labor's presence was purely ad hoc in order to carry out the disengagement. Sharon was essentially left with a choice of a coalition composed of the Likud, Labor and Shinui, or one composed of the Likud, Labor and the religious parties. Sharon opted for the latter, as he would then be in the center of the coalition and have more flexibility than if he were the most conservative party. He fired the five Shinui ministers immediately after the vote.[37]

On January 15, 2005, Mahmoud Abbas was sworn in as the new Palestinian Authority chairman and president of the PLO. His only opposition in the election was Mustafa Barghouti, a cousin of imprisoned Fatah leader Marwan Barghouti. Abbas, also known as Abu Mazen, was opposed to the armed struggle as a failed strategy, but he still publicly supported the right of return for Palestinian refugees. Abbas, the Bush administration and Meretz all pleaded with Sharon to coordinate his disengagement with the Palestinians, but Sharon refused to do this. His advisor, Dov Weisglass, said, "The Palestinians are not a partner; they're a problem to be dealt with." This had the net result of allowing Hamas to take credit for the disengagement rather than Abbas, with banners that read, "Four years of resistance beat ten years of negotiations." Sharon and Abbas met at a summit at Sharm al-Sheikh on February 8 hosted by President Mubarak of Egypt and King Abdullah of Jordan.[38]

In February Defense Minister Shaul Mofaz announced that Chief of Staff Moshe "Boogie" Ya'alon's term would not be extended for the customary fourth year. Ya'alon was known as both a bit of a loose cannon and mistrustful of the Palestinians. Sharon did not want him in charge when the disengagement took place. Sharon pulled strings behind the scenes to pick Dan Halutz as the IDF's next chief of staff and the first to come up through the IAF instead of the ground forces. He also ended Shabak director Avi Dichter's term in May and replaced him with Yuval Diskin. Sharon thought highly of Dichter as a professional, but Dichter was not in complete agreement with the disengagement.[39]

At midnight on August 15, 2005, the IDF closed the borders of Gaza and began the evacuation of settlers from the Gush Katif settlement bloc in southern Gaza. The entire evacuation from the seventeen settlements took a total of six days and was really only met with violence on one day at a single settlement, Kfar Darom, on August 15. Most of the resistance came from West Bank settlers who wanted to make the evacuation as difficult as possible in order to forestall a future possible evacuation of settlements in the main blocs of the West Bank. Hundreds of settlers gathered on the roof of the synagogue of the settlement and threw lightbulbs filled with blue paint at the soldiers and pushed off their ladders. Finally the IDF used a crane to put a shipping container filled with police on the roof of the synagogue, and the settlers were forced off. Despite settler rabbis having issued religious opinions (*pskei din*—the Jewish equivalent of Muslim *fatwas*) for months forbidding the evacuation and urging soldiers not to obey their orders, problems were avoided by simply giving the job to secular units (the majority of the IDF) and allowing anyone who felt strongly opposed to the disengagement to opt out of the evacuation operation.[40]

James Wolfensohn, the former head of the World Bank, raised private funds to buy out the settlement greenhouses so that they could be used by the Palestinians. But they were soon vandalized by Palestinian mobs when the settlement bloc was turned over to the Palestinian Authority.[41]

Ever since Sharon publicly announced the disengagement, Labor MK Haim Ramon had been pushing the idea—it was not really developed enough to be called a theory—of the "big bang." The "big bang" was a shake-up of Israeli party politics by creating a new party of centrists from the existing three major parties: the Likud, Labor, and Shinui. His idea was to promote a centrist ideology of privatization of state enterprises, a mixed economy, and the abandonment of both the Oslo process and the idea of Greater Israel (*Eretz Israel haShlema*) in favor of unilateralism on Israel's part in order to safeguard its future by withdrawing to safer, more defensible borders. Ramon talked about his idea with both Sharon and Shinui leader Tommy Lapid.[42]

Two months after the disengagement Sharon suddenly decided that he would implement the "big bang" by quitting the Likud with his followers and forming a new party, known as Kadima. Likud rebels loyal to Netanyahu had scheduled a party primary for April 2006. Sharon had big plans to implement an agenda of domestic reforms: electoral reform, reform of the education system, and several others. He needed a party that would back him in order to forge ahead with these plans. He had taken discreet soundings within the Likud and found thirteen Knesset members who were prepared to follow him into a new party. This was enough to have the new party officially recognized in the Knesset.[43] He knew that in Labor at least Haim Ramon and Shimon Peres would follow him—Ramon because it was his idea, and Peres because he wanted the presidency to end his long political career.

On Saturday, November 12, the ranch forum, or septet (*sheviya* in Hebrew), Sharon's closest political advisors, met at the Sycamore Ranch for a marathon session to discuss whether Sharon should quit the Likud. Nearly all of them were in favor. Only Uri Dan, Sharon's longtime reporter friend, was opposed to the plan. Three days later Omri Sharon pleaded guilty to an amended indictment for keeping false financial records, perjury, and violating campaign finance laws. Sharon knew that his son's political career was over. On November 19 Sharon met with Amir Peretz, the new leader of the Labor Party, who had just beaten Peres in the leadership contest. The two agreed to hold new elections on March 28, 2006. The next day Sharon thought about his decision for hours. The day after that he awakened with his mind made up and called a press conference for that evening. Then Sharon announced to the nation that he was leaving the party that he had formed 32 years earlier, along with thirteen MKs, in order to form a new party.[44]

Polls quickly predicted thirty to forty seats for the new party. Peres, Ramon and Telecommunications Minister Dalia Itzik announced in the next few days that they were quitting Labor to join the new party. At first Defense Minister Shaul Mofaz announced that he was staying with his political home, the Likud. But the next day, after a plea from Sharon, he changed his mind and followed Sharon into the political wilderness. A few mayors also announced that they were joining the new party.[45]

On the evening of December 18, 2005, Sharon suffered a mild stroke that left his mental faculties unimpaired. The doctors gave him a clean bill of health, but prescribed a blood-thinner medicine and told Sharon to work no more than four hours per day. For a man used to fifteen-hour workdays, this was impossible to follow. He was also put on a whole-grain, nuts and fruit diet in order to deal with his obesity. But it was far too late in his life for this. Less than three weeks later, on the evening of January 3, 2006—the evening before he was to go to the hospital for heart surgery—Sharon felt a severe chest pain and his personal physician recommended immediate hospitalization. On the ambulance ride to the hospital Sharon suffered a severe stroke, and subsequently went into a coma from which he never emerged.[46]

In January 2006, the Palestinian elections that Washington had pushed for resulted in a Hamas victory. On March 28, Kadima emerged as the largest party, with 29 seats under the leadership of Ehud Olmert, who had started his career in the Free Center Party. Olmert formed a coalition with the Labor Party, Shas, and the Pensioneers' Party. In late 2008, however, Olmert was forced to resign due to corruption charges. Foreign Minister Tzipi Livni became the new party leader and prime minister, but was forced to call new elections when she was unable to form a new coalition. In 2013 Kadima emerged with only two seats under the leadership of Mofaz. Sharon's final party survived him by only a few years.[47]

Sharon died of massive organ failure on January 11, 2014, just over eight years after his stroke.[48] Even if he had revived from the coma, his political career would have been effectively over due to the combination of his advanced age and worry about his cognitive abilities. It would have taken him months to recover basic functions after such a massive stroke—if he were not already a vegetable beyond recovery.

IV. Ehud Barak, 1942–?

Chapter Eleven

Barak: Israel's Most Decorated Soldier

Ehud Brog was born on February 12, 1942, on Kibbutz Mishmar haSharon, located northeast of Netanya on the coastal plain of Israel known as the Sharon. The kibbutz had been founded in that location eight years before in 1934, after having moved from the Galilee, where its members, mostly from Poland, had gone for training. Ehud's father, Yisrael Mendel Brog, was born in Lithuania in 1910 and had later immigrated to Palestine. Yisrael's parents were murdered by thieves in 1912 in his small village. His older brother Meir made aliyah (immigrated) to Palestine in 1923 and Yisrael followed in 1930. He studied poetry and Hebrew literature at the Hebrew University in Jerusalem. As a student Yisrael became acquainted and friendly with Ben Zion Netanyahu, starting a link between the two families that would extend over three-quarters of a century. Due to peer pressure, Yisrael joined a settlement group named *Mishmar* (Guardian), based on Lithuanian Jews. He then quit his studies and began training to settle the land. Mishmar joined with Young Gordania, a settlement group of Polish Jews, in 1933, and the two groups became one and founded Kibbutz Mishmar haSharon in 1934.

Ehud's mother Esther Godin was born in Warsaw in 1915, the daughter of an Orthodox Jew active in the Habad movement. She made aliyah to Palestine in July 1936 and went directly to the new kibbutz upon landing in Haifa, where she was quickly assimilated. Yisrael and Esther were married in 1940 in Netanya. After the UN partition resolution decision was announced, kibbutz members danced around a large bonfire for several hours in celebration. Because the kibbutz was located in the heart of Jewish settlement during the Yishuv period and not on the frontiers, it was not threatened during the Arab invasion in May 1948 and did not see heavy fighting like the Negev, Galilee, and Jezreel Valley experienced during the civil war phase of Israel's War of

Independence from January to May 1948. The Brogs would have been part of the Alexandroni Brigade, the brigade that Sharon served in during 1948. But with two small children—Ehud, age six, and Avinoam, age four—Esther would have been restricted to the part of the kibbutz defense force to be used only if the kibbutz were directly attacked.[1]

Ehud was a precocious child who loved to play the piano, and would take apart locks, watches and clocks to learn how they worked. Had he been born a generation or two earlier in Europe, he probably would have become a watchmaker. Instead, he became Israel's most decorated soldier. The children on the kibbutz were raised communally, spending only a few hours a day at their parents' home. Ehud was the youngest and smallest of about a dozen children on the kibbutz at the time—the entire population was just a few dozen. His parents lived in a small shack that was furnished only with a simple bed, a dining table, a large stool, and many books that Yisrael had brought with him from Lithuania. Due to a prank, Ehud was expelled from school and did not graduate before being drafted into the IDF at age 17 in 1959.[2]

Ehud wanted to be a pilot and read everything he could get his hands on about aviation and aircraft. But when he appeared before the medical board of the IAF in August 1959, he was rejected due to a throat condition. He then went into the infantry. Because of his motivation, he was invited to try out for a rather secretive new unit in 1960.[3]

This new unit Ehud was encouraged to join had been founded two years before—*Sayeret Matkal*, or Headquarters Reconnaissance. The unit, established by Brigadier General Avraham Arnan, was in many ways a successor unit to Sharon's Unit 101, tasked with providing strategic reconnaissance to the IDF general staff. Arnan, who had served under Rabin in the Harel Brigade during the War of Independence, modeled it after British officer David Sterling's Long Range Desert Patrol Group, the forerunner of the Special Air Service.[4]

During his national service Barak (he changed his name in 1972) made up his high school education and earned the Israeli equivalent of the GED. In 1962 he went to an officer's course and began his climb to the top of the IDF. Observing him, Yitzhak Rabin, who himself was not yet chief of staff, remarked that "something is wrong with the system if he does not end up as chief of staff one day."[5]

Barak spent his first sixteen years in the IDF in the Sayeret Matkal, known simply as the Unit because of the prestige and secrecy surrounding it. His two brothers also joined the Unit and the Brogs became the first family in IDF history to have three sons in it. (The second family to achieve this feat was the Netanyahus.) By the time his younger brother Avinoam joined the unit in 1963, Barak was already a senior officer.[6]

The Unit came into its own during the War of Attrition following the Six-Day War of June 1967. Barak spent that war attached to Israel Tal's armored brigade, crossing the Sinai with part of the Unit. On the fifth day he was transferred to the Golan and took part in the capture of the plateau. He had been promoted to captain a few months before the war.[7]

In 1968–1969 the IDF set up ambushes along the Jordan Valley to kill and capture infiltrating Fatah and other fedayeen. From March 1969 to August 1970, the War of Attrition raged along the Suez Canal and was fought mainly by the IAF in its deep penetration raids into Egypt and by various Israeli special forces units raiding along the canal. Barak took part in planning a mission that attempted to capture Egyptian soldiers along the canal in early 1969. After the mission he came in for criticism from Brigadier General Raful Eitan, who wanted a monopoly on commando operations for the units he commanded. After the War of Attrition, the Unit became an anti-terrorist hostage rescue force like the Special Air Service in Britain, the GS-9 in Germany and Delta Force in the United States. This was the period when Barak was commander of the Unit, from 1971 to 1975.

As soon as Barak decided to make the IDF his professional career, he began planning for his position after he became the Unit's commander. After doing a basic armored course in 1968 and finishing up his BA in physics at Hebrew University, he spent much of the latter part of 1969 and early part of 1970 in a six-month-long armored officer's course, so that he could eventually command a unit during conventional wars. Barak was praised for his technical ability and comprehensive knowledge. He spent extra time in his tank learning the systems after the day's training was finished. At the end of 1969 he was promoted to major and then, after finishing the course, he became a platoon commander in the 401 Armored Battalion on the banks of the Suez Canal during the final days of the War of Attrition.[8]

Barak is best known for three events that occurred while he was commander of the Sayeret Matkal. The first was the rescue of Sabena Airlines flight 571 on May 8, 1972. The flight was a regularly scheduled run from Vienna to Lod Airport in Israel. The plane was boarded by four terrorists from Black September, the Palestinian terrorist organization that was a cover name for radical elements within Fatah and cooperated with the Popular Front for the Liberation of Palestine (PFLP). The four took over the aircraft and had it fly to its destination, where they demanded the release of 315 Palestinian prisoners held in Israeli prisons. They threatened to blow up the aircraft with its passengers if their demands were not met. Defense Minister Dayan stalled and seemed to go along with the hijackers' demands while actually ordering the preparation of a hostage rescue effort. At 4:24 p.m. sixteen commandos from the Unit disguised as aircraft maintenance personnel stormed the aircraft. Firing continued for ten minutes, until the two male hijackers were dead and the two women were captured. During the capture of one of the women, Captain Benjamin Netanyahu was wounded in the arm by friendly fire as one of his fellow rescuers struck the woman with a pistol and it accidentally discharged. Three passengers were wounded in the rescue, with one later dying from her wounds. The two women hijackers were eventually freed in a prisoner exchange over a decade later.[9] The operation was studied by other Western anti-terrorist units and may have served as the basis for the planning of a Lufthansa hijacking in Mogadishu in 1977.

The second incident was Operation Spring of Youth on April 9, 1973.[10] Following the murder of eleven Israeli athletes at the Munich Olympic Games in September 1972 by Black September during a botched rescue attempt, Prime Minister Golda Meir ordered that all those from the organization involved in the planning and execution of the massacre be pursued by the Mossad and, if possible, killed. Mossad assassination squads were sent into Europe to pursue the terrorists and kill them on their home ground.

In early 1973 Barak got wind of planning by the IDF for an operation inside Beirut. He sent an aide, Major Biran, to find out more about the operation. Biran came back with the location of the homes of the three targets of the operation within Beirut. In early February Barak called a planning meeting of his senior staff within the Unit. Two targets were assigned: the apartments of three senior terrorist figures in a building on Verdun Street and the headquarters of the Democratic Front for the Liberation of Palestine (DFLP) on Khartoum Street. The three targets on Verdun Street were Muhammed Yussef Najar, the number two man in Fatah at the time and a lawyer by training; Kamal Adwan, the commander of the Western Wing, charged with planning attacks inside Israel; and Kamal Nasser, the PLO's chief spokesman. The first two had been involved in terrorist operations since 1968 and may have been involved in the Munich operation. But, in any case, the operation was intended to be more preventative than vengeful. Adwan lived on the second floor of the building, Nasser on the third floor, and Najar was on the sixth floor.[11]

Western terrorist groups all had cells in Beirut, which they used to liaise with Palestinian and other Third World terrorist groups. The Mossad sent a team of undercover agents into Beirut disguised as Western terrorists during the first week of April 1973. Each team member arrived individually and was assigned a target to survey and monitor. The members all took long walks that allowed them to pass by the targets. Each member learned the layout of every building: the dimensions of the lobby, the number of steps on each flight of stairs, the entrances and exits, and the likely police response to firing.[12]

The previous month, the police were called in Tel Aviv as paratroopers practiced assaulting an unfinished apartment building. The responding policeman arrested the commander of the paratroopers, but upon calling his superiors the policeman was told not to interfere with the operation. Chief of Staff David Elazar even took part in the training at night to get a feel for what he would be asking his men to do. This was after his usual day of work in the IDF headquarters in Tel Aviv.[13]

On the evening of the mission on April 9, Chief of Staff Elazar and Aman head Eli Zeira bid farewell to a 16-man squad from the Unit as the men boarded the missile boats that would take them to Beirut. Elazar told them to kill rather than capture their targets. Killing them would be less dangerous to the valuable commandos and there was the danger that the men might be released in a prisoner for hostage exchange in the future. The missile boats headed into the eastern Mediterranean Sea towards Cyprus, before they eventually veered back towards the coast of Lebanon. This longer route was taken in order to increase the odds of escaping premature discovery. Each commando carried four small photos: one of each of the targets and one of Ali Hassan Salame, who had organized the Munich massacre and might be found in the building by chance. The commandos were organized into three teams— one for each intended target—and each team had one member disguised as a woman. Barak himself was one of these "cross dressers"—he wore a brunette wig, carried a handbag crammed with explosives and had two grenades stuffed into his bra to complete the effect. Each commando sat with his boots covered with ponchos to keep them dry during the final transit to the shore on inflatable rubber assault boats. They also wore ponchos over their jackets and wigs—no one wanted to be betrayed by dripping water in an emergency.[14]

At about 1:30 a.m. Barak's teams arrived at their targets by rental cars, which had been waiting for them on the beach, along with drivers who had memorized the route to the target, The commandos got out of their cars, entered the building and proceeded up the stairs. When all three teams were in place, they blew open their respective apartment doors with explosives, entered and, upon sighting their targets, opened fire. One commando was wounded by his target before one of his team members dispatched the man. In another apartment, the target's wife threw herself in front of her husband and was killed along with him. The entire operation at Verdun Street took only four minutes.[15]

At the start of the operation a Mossad agent had phoned the chief of the municipal police force and reported that the fedayeen were having an interfactional battle. This was enough to keep the police from intervening. One police vehicle that was on patrol did pull up and was dispatched by a grenade tossed onto its canvas roof by one of the men of the Unit. However, the paratroopers at Khartoum Street, commanded by Lieutenant Colonel Amnon Lipkin-Shahak, had a worse time of it—two men were killed and one seriously wounded by unseen guards huddled in the shadows of the building. The dead and wounded were taken with the rest of the men back to the beach and from there evacuated by helicopter. The rental cars were left on the beach with the keys in the ignition.[16]

Operation Spring of Youth had a major deterrent effect in the Arab world. Lebanese newspapers carried stories of two beautiful women keeping the police and army at bay with automatic weapons. This operation, along with the Mossad assassination teams in Western Europe, made it clear to the intellectuals within the fedayeen movement that they faced a personal threat if they got involved with planning, executing or justifying terrorist operations. Numerous journalists wrote about the assassinations in Europe and Beirut, and in 1984 Hungarian-born Canadian writer George Jonas wrote a fictionalized account of one Mossad team in Europe entitled *Vengeance*. Two years later Home Box Office made a movie, *Sword of Gideon*, based on it. When the book was used as the basis for the movie *Munich* (2005), by directed Stephen Spielberg, a scene was inserted in which the army leader of the Mossad team talks his way into going along on Operation Spring of Youth and appears next to an actor playing Barak.[17]

The third incident for which Barak is well known was a more secretive operation in which a team from the Unit, led by Yonaton Netanyahu and Uzi Dayan, stopped a car filled with five senior Syrian officers in southern Lebanon and kidnapped them. They were spirited away to Israel and quietly exchanged for three Israeli pilots who had been shot down and were in Syrian captivity.[18]

In June 1973 Barak turned over command of the Unit to Giora Zorea. The IDF wanted to send him to the United States for a special combat command course with the U.S. Marine Corps that they sent their high flyers on, but Barak wanted to get an MA in engineering economic systems at Stanford University instead. It was then IDF policy not to allow officers to earn advanced degrees abroad, but Barak threatened to take his terminal leave and quit the army. So he set a new precedent. Before leaving with his family for Stanford in August 1973, he officially changed his last name from Brog to Barak, meaning "lightning," which was the name of one of the biblical judges who ruled in ancient Israel before the monarchy. None of Barak's siblings adopted the new name.[19]

Upon hearing of the outbreak of the Yom Kippur War, Barak phoned the Israeli embassy in Washington and spoke to the military liaison, Motta Gur, who promised to reserve him a seat on the first plane back to Israel after urging him to wait a day or two for more news. Barak flew back on the first flight from Kennedy Airport, along with Benjamin Netanyahu and many others. Upon landing in Israel he caught a ride to the Kirya with Uzi Dayan, another Unit member. At IDF headquarters he spoke briefly with Chief of Staff Elazar, who urged him to see Brigadier General "Motka" Tzippori, who was forming an armored battalion out of reservists. After three days without sleep, Barak arrived at the new unit's base in the Sinai, where he was given two companies of M-60 Pattons, the American tank he was familiar with from his commander's course, and a company of British Centurion tanks. His men were all volunteers who were eager to get to the front, but Barak insisted on putting them through a few days of maneuvers so that he could see how they performed.

On October 17, Yitzhak Mordechai's 890 Paratroop Bn. got into trouble when it was surrounded by Egyptian infantry equipped with Soviet Sagger anti-tank missiles and pinned down by accurate artillery fire. Barak's battalion was sent in to save them. As the rescuers approached the paratroopers' position, morning fog obscured the view of the tanks. The Egyptians were briefly surprised by their appearance but quickly recovered, and several of the first tanks were hit by Saggers and went up in flames. Barak ordered his tanks to take up defensive positions, and then he was hit in the neck by an Egyptian bullet fired from close range. After several hours his battalion was relieved by another armored battalion. Mordechai in later years sounded ungrateful and complained that the tanks had arrived too late. Among his men, between 40 and 70 were killed and a hundred wounded. Barak, for his part, only claimed that his own force as well as the paratroopers needed to be rescued because of their heavy losses. This was part of the Battle of Chinese Farm, which was the largest tank battle fought since World War II. After his battalion reached the canal, Barak went to sleep under his tank, and even the sound of Egyptian shelling could not wake him from two hours of deep sleep after two nights without any. After two hours he was woken up by an officer who said they had orders to attack an Egyptian SAM missile battery. During the mission the battalion was strafed by an Israeli Skyhawk attack jet by mistake, but no one was hurt.

After returning to base, the battalion swapped out its tanks for fresh ones and some crews were replaced. One armored personnel carrier was discovered to be missing and so Barak, knowing that his men lacked infantry skills, decided to go alone to search for the crew when efforts to contact them by radio failed. After half an hour of running among the burnt-out hulks of destroyed armored vehicles, Barak discovered two of the men and brought them back. The rest of the crew had been killed.

Barak spent the remainder of the war fighting around Suez City on the African bank of the canal. He captured some 200 Egyptian prisoners but could not spare anyone to guard them. So he ordered them in Arabic not to move. In the morning many of the Israelis were surprised to see the prisoners still waiting for them when they returned.[20]

After the conclusion of the Egyptian separation-of-forces agreement in January 1974, Barak returned to Palo Alto, California, to close out his accounts and pay his bills. He flew back with his family to Israel because the IDF needed experienced officers. During the war he had kept in touch with his parents on the kibbutz, and they called back to assure his wife Nava that Barak was okay. Shortly before leaving office, Dayan met with Barak and promoted him to colonel. Barak was assigned to the Operations Branch of the IDF, where he was in charge of planning for special missions.[21]

In mid-1975 Zorea handed over control of the Unit to Yonaton Netanyahu.[22] On June 29, 1976, Prime Minister Rabin summoned Chief of Staff Motta Gur to a cabinet meeting and asked him if a rescue of the Israeli hostages being held at Entebbe Airport in Uganda was possible. Gur replied that in theory it was possible, but that he had not thoroughly researched the situation yet. Major General Benny Peled of the IAF advised both Gur and Peres against giving in to the terrorists once he was informed that the IAF's Hercules Squadron could fly to Entebbe with more than a thousand men. Barak was on loan from the Operations Branch for the length of the crisis. He served as the liaison officer between the Unit and the IAF during the planning for the mission. Although Rabin dismissed all of the early plans for a rescue as simply not feasible, Barak was in favor of the operation. Peres likewise believed that a rescue was essential and he was very impressed by Netanyahu's quiet confidence that his men could pull off the mission.[23]

Barak was one of seven officers involved in the initial rescue planning: these consisted of five generals and two flag officers. Barak and Muki Betzer were the Unit's representatives in the planning stage. When the plan was complete, Barak was one of three officers (the others were Dan Shomron and Major Iddo Embar of the Hercules Squadron) who briefed Chief of Staff Gur, who then briefed Rabin on the plan. Dan Shomron, who was the overall operation commander, initially appointed Barak to lead the hostage rescue force because Shomron knew Barak's skills. But Netanyahu later got the decision reversed because he was itching to prove himself and felt that, as the commander of the Unit, he should be leading the rescue. At that point it was decided to send Barak to coordinate with the Kenyan armed forces to refuel the aircraft in Kenya after the rescue.[24]

During the rescue many of the future commanders who worked with Barak as prime minister played key roles. Major Shaul Mofaz was in charge of a close security force consisting of four armored personnel carriers that was in charge of protecting the rescue force from any possible interference by the Ugandan army. Colonel Matan Vilnai led the paratroopers in the backup force.[25] Barak phoned General Gur from Kenya after the rescue and informed him that Yoni Netanyahu had been killed by a Ugandan soldier located in the control tower outside of the old terminal where the hostages were being held. After he returned from Kenya, he personally went to see Benjamin Netanyahu and inform him of his brother's death.[26]

On January 12, 1981, Barak was promoted to the rank of major general (*aluf*) and appointed head of the IDF planning branch. Chief of Staff Eitan did not like planning and so was content to leave strategic planning for the IDF to Barak, who did not wait to be assigned tasks but created them for himself. In the event of war, Barak was slated to serve as deputy commander of the Armor Corps under Amos "Yanosh" Ben Gal.[27]

For the first three days of the Lebanon War in June 1982, the Corps had little role to play as brigades led by Yitzhak Mordechai, Avigdor Kahalani, Emanuel Sekel and Menahem Einan crossed the border and moved north. On the fifth day the sector heated up, and Sharon ordered it to attack any Syrian unit that looked as if it were preparing to intervene on the side of the Palestinians. The Corps was ordered to capture the Beirut-Damascus highway. Barak prevented a potentially disastrous incident when he countermanded an order to open fire until the targets were rechecked. They turned out to be friendly forces. Many of the units did not know their real locations during the night-time movement north.[28] In the end, Barak managed to survive the Kahan Commission's report with his reputation intact.

In April 1983 Barak was appointed head of the IDF's intelligence branch, Aman, as the next step in his preparation to be chief of staff. In January 1986 he was made commander of Central Command, the only one of the three geographic commands that he held during his military career. In May 1987 he was appointed deputy chief of staff, signaling that he was next in line to become chief of staff. In December the Intifada broke out, and Barak was tasked with finding solutions to the special problems posed by this conflict. He ordered the use of plastic bullets to replace live ammo in confronting unarmed demonstrators. Barak also pushed to use elite reconnaissance units from the paratroopers, Golani and Givati to relieve the special undercover army units "Cherries" and "Samson," in which IDF soldiers who spoke Arabic posed as fedayeen.[29]

On April 16, 1988, Fatah chief of operations Khalil al-Wazir (a.k.a. Abu Jihad) was assassinated at his home in the suburb of Tunis by Israeli commandos who were ferried to shore from Israel by the Israeli navy. The operation was a joint effort of the IDF and Mossad, and Barak was said to have been involved in planning it, according to the BBC. After the assassination, *Washington Post* reporter Glenn Frankel wrote a long feature on the assassination. He claimed that it was motivated by an attack waged by Fatah terrorists on a bus full of nuclear plant workers in Dimona about a month prior. The terrorists had entered Israel from the Sinai and managed to kill three workers before they were killed by an anti-terrorist unit that took control of the bus. Before the final clash one of the terrorists yelled, "Abu Jihad sent us."

At the beginning of April Prime Minister Yitzhak Shamir raised the possibility of eliminating Abu Jihad. Three Labor ministers (Foreign Minister Peres, Education Minister Yitzhak Navon, Minister Without Portfolio Ezer Weizman) objected, but the rest of the Labor ministers and all the Likud ministers were in favor. The decision was taken on April 6, 1988, at a special cabinet meeting. Shamir then had Deputy Chief of Staff Barak form a planning committee with Barak as its head. With Barak on the committee were Aman chief Amnon Lipkin-Shahak, the head of Mossad, and select IDF officers. At the committee's first meeting Barak determined that Aman would be responsible for providing operational intelligence, the Mossad for on-site preparations, the IAF for providing air cover, the navy for transporting the teams to Tunis and back (with the naval commandos providing security on the beach), and Sayeret Matkal for carrying out the actual hit.

The intelligence file on Abu Jihad was rather bare except for his name and position and a few basic facts, so a Mossad team was sent to Tunis to gather intelligence. It came back with several photos of both the interior and exterior of the house, as well as Jihad's daily routine. They also bugged his phone. Barak appointed Lieutenant Colonel Moshe "Boogie" Ya'alon, the Sayeret Matkal commander and a later chief of staff who would follow Barak as defense minister in 2013, as the commander on the ground during the mission. Ya'alon already had his men practicing landings, movement, house takeover and withdrawal at a beach in southern Israel. At the next regular cabinet meeting, Shamir announced that Abu Jihad would soon be dead. "It is the only thing they understand," he said.

On April 13, 1988, a number of missile boats left Haifa equipped with special military equipment: a field hospital, electronic communications systems, and a rescue helicopter. On board were the naval commandos, the Sayeret Matkal team of about 20 men, and Barak, who accompanied the mission to Tunis. During the passage to the target they received an intelligence report that Abu Jihad was at home and following his normal routine. The Mossad also reported that several other key PLO officials, including Arafat, were in the area. Barak was tempted to carry out a decapitation of the organization as at Beirut fifteen years before, but after conferring with Chief of Staff Shomron they decided to stick to the original mission.

Barak gave Ya'alon a big hug before the men boarded the rubber boats and headed for shore. At about 2 a.m. Abu Jihad's personal bodyguard, Abu Suleiman, answered a knock at the door by carefully opening it and peering out—he was hit on the head and knocked unconscious. Abu Jihad exited his study on the second floor armed with a pistol and saw several strangers in olive drab uniforms crossing quickly in front of him. He was then hit with a burst of bullets and collapsed at the top of the stairs. His wife, Um Jihad, was escorted into a room and told in Arabic to remain quiet. She stayed there with her son while the commandos gathered up anything of apparent intelligence value from Abu Jihad's study and headed out of the office. After a few minutes she began screaming, "They have killed Abu Jihad!" Arafat's security men were called and went to the house. By then the assassins were long gone. In the morning they found two minivans and a car on the beach. Only 72 hours later the boats were again at anchor in Israel.[30]

Barak influenced the IDF to treat the first Intifada as a popular war rather than simply a series of riots. It was easier to deal with the Palestinians as enemy combatants than as a population in rebellion, because the former was more familiar territory for the IDF. This was crucial foreshadowing for how Prime Minister Barak would deal with the outbreak of the Al-Aksa Intifada in October 2000.[31]

Finally, in April 1991, Barak was appointed the fourteenth chief of the general staff, or chief of staff at the rank of lieutenant general (*rav aluf*). He served in this role for almost four years, until January 1, 1995. During his term as chief of staff Barak oversaw the redeployment of the IDF away from the Gaza Strip and Jericho in accordance with the Oslo I agreement. He also played a central role in finalizing the military aspects of the Israel-Jordanian peace treaty in 1994. And he met with his Syrian counterpart as part of the Israeli-Syrian negotiations on the Golan, which, however, did not advance very far. During his 35 years of military service, Barak was awarded the Distinguished Service Medal and four times chief of staff citations, which tied him with one other person as the most decorated soldier in IDF history.[32]

Barak was considered to have been the most political chief of staff in

IV: Ehud Barak, 1942–?

Chief of Staff Ehud Barak shaking hands with the Jordanian chief of staff, October 26, 1994. Photograph by Avi Ohayon, Israeli Government Press Office.

IDF history. He knew many politicians from both Labor and the Likud and was familiar with the corridors of power. He was open minded and enjoyed long political discussions. Members of the government would often call him up and ask for background or his opinion on security matters.[33]

Barak earned a reputation as a territorial hawk while chief of staff by making a number of statements about the importance of the Golan Heights to Israel's security. On August 17, 1994, Lieutenant General Barak told the American secretary of defense that "even in peace we need a presence on the Golan." Two weeks later he told Yediot Ahranot, "From a purely professional military viewpoint it is important to remain deployed along the Golan even with a peace agreement." On March 7, 1995, retired General Barak told the *Washington Post* that an Israeli presence on the Golan was also important in peacetime. And in 1996 Foreign Minister Barak said, "I don't think we will arrive at any situation where the Syrians will wade in the Kinneret." Some have claimed that General Barak was opposed to the Oslo agreement. But Yossi Beilin claimed in his memoirs that he put the question directly to Barak, and Barak answered that he would reluctantly support the agreement because it was something historic, but "not with an easy heart."[34]

For his mandatory cooling-off period before serving in the government,

Barak went to the Center for Strategic and International Studies think tank at Georgetown University as a visiting fellow to get some exposure to Washington and America in general before entering politics. He was doing what Yitzhak Rabin had done in the late 1960s, except that he would spend only months rather than years in Washington.

Like Rabin before him, Barak was parachuted into the Labor Party as minister of the interior from July to November 1995. Then, following Rabin's assassination, acting Prime Minister Peres appointed him as foreign minister, in which office he served until June 1996. His period as foreign minister can be divided into roughly two periods: before Peres decided to call for early elections in April 1996 and afterward. On November 23, 1995, Barak handed over the keys of the interior ministry to Haim Ramon and took over the foreign ministry from Peres. Before Barak four foreign ministers (Sharett, Meir, Shamir, and Peres) had gone on to serve as prime minister—so it was definitely considered a major step up for Barak.[35]

Barak's first big challenge was the Barcelona Conference of foreign ministers from Mediterranean countries. Israel was the only country represented in this group that was neither European nor Arab, and hence very isolated.

Interior Minister Barak greeting Prime Minister Rabin after the latter's return from Morocco, October 1, 1995. Photograph by Yaacov Saar, Israeli Government Press Office.

It was at the Barcelona Conference that Arafat and Barak first met. They came together in an empty palace to which they had both been invited and conversed for about twenty minutes in Arabic and English. Others arrived, ending the conversation, but it was later resumed in Arafat's hotel room in the middle of the night and lasted for three hours.

The major challenge at the conference was negotiating the joint final declaration. The Syrians wanted to include language that equated terrorism with the struggle for national liberation. Barak successfully resisted this attempt. But his direct appeal to the Syrians in his conference speech, "Israel offers you a hand in peace," fell flat, and the Syrians responded with boilerplate rhetoric.[36]

In December 1995, during an official visit to Budapest, Barak met with Tunisian Foreign Minister Habib Ben-Yekhiya at his (Barak's) hotel suite. The following month American Secretary of State Warren Christopher hosted both Barak and Ben-Yekhiya at a luncheon at which an agreement on establishing diplomatic relations was supposed to be signed. But Ben-Yekhiya tried to gain last-minute concessions through blackmail. Middle East envoy Dennis Ross mediated between the two, and it was announced that the offices would be opened by April 15, 1996. The office in Israel was in fact opened a month late, only days before the May 1996 election.[37]

On May 8, Barak hosted Omani Foreign Minister Yusuf Ben-Alwayi at his suite in the Mayflower Hotel in Washington. Ben-Alwayi was very interested in opening trade relations with Israel. Oman and Qatar established overt relations with Israel under Rabin, while Kuwait and Bahrain preferred to maintain secret relations. At the end of December 1995 Barak visited Egypt. The Egyptian media was very hostile and termed him an "expert in murder" and spoke of his bloody deeds. Foreign Minister Amr Musa reported later that Barak spoke fluent Arabic and knew the songs of the popular Egyptian singer Um Kalthum. On January 19, 1996, Barak made an official visit to Morocco on his way to Washington. The visit went very well despite a potentially embarrassing situation in which Barak arrived needing to urinate because the small executive jet he flew on had lacked an onboard toilet. An honor guard had to be hastily cancelled to accommodate this need.[38]

Barak's final visit to Washington as foreign minister was in May 1996. The purpose was to brief Secretary of State Christopher on Operation Grapes of Wrath, which had taken place the previous month, to coordinate counter-terrorism actions, and to help Peres's election campaign. During the trip Barak caused a major security snafu when he visited some stores near Kennedy Airport while he was killing time due to problems caused by an airport workers strike in Israel. Actor Mel Gibson, who was shooting a film in the next street over, entered the store to chat with Barak. Barak said hello and then ignored Gibson, as he was busy receiving a report on the first election broadcasts from Foreign Ministry Director Uri Savir and looking at a disassembled watch. His aides later had to explain to him who Gibson was.[39]

Barak attempted to actively help in Peres's reelection campaign by giving advice. Many recommended that Peres appoint Barak as defense minister following the first major terror bombing on February 25, 1996, in order to restore public confidence in the government. But Peres refused, as he thought he was just as capable as Rabin of serving as his own defense minister. Following the bombing Barak advised Peres to freeze negotiations. "Don't talk about peace when there are bombings like this," he advised Peres. But Peres ignored the advice and pressed on. Barak chaired a meeting to consider solutions to the terrorism problem. The participants recommended a separation strategy. Peres accepted the recommendations and announced them in a press conference.[40]

Exactly one week after the first bombing, the No. 18 line was hit again. This time Peres understood that he was involved in a war against the terror organizations. As a result of these bombings, Peres quickly lost his status as Rabin's successor and the old image of Peres the loser returned. Later that spring there were rumors that Barak, Haim Ramon and Yossi Beilin were preparing a "coup" to force Peres to name Barak as his defense minister. Barak refused to deny the rumors publicly for a long time, merely telling members of Labor that they were not true and that whoever spread them should deny them. Finally, however, he was forced to deny the rumors publicly to the media.[41]

In May Barak briefed Peres on a series of measures that should be taken in the event of another terrorist attack to deal with the consequences. Peres immediately adopted the plan. Barak's pollster had advised him that if there wasn't another major bombing before the election, Peres would win, but if there were another bombing, he would lose. Barak recruited a friend of his, French millionaire Jean Friedman, to finance a series of polls from Panorama Marketing, which turned up more pessimistic results than those of Peres's team, although not stark enough to shock them into making changes. Ramon, who was emerging as Barak's main rival to head the post–Peres Labor Party, rejected every attempt by Barak to alter the campaign strategy that he had decided upon. Barak told Peres that he was living in a bubble and that the real information on how things were going was not reaching him.

A week before the election, Barak wanted to concentrate on preparation for the final debate between Peres and Netanyahu. Barak wished to send a message that would reassure hawkish voters (Rabin supporters): "no concessions to the Arabs, smash terror and bring peace." This was much like Netanyahu's own campaign message of "peace with security." Barak said that Peres must look into the camera and project decisiveness and security. Instead, the debate was a catastrophe for Peres—he stuttered, hesitated and projected fatigue, age, and lack of self-confidence. American election consultants prepared a report for Barak on the debate, and their conclusion was pessimistic.[42]

Barak watched the election results in his hotel room with a few aides. He spoke with Peres and advised him not to turn up at the Labor Party headquarters too early, but to wait until the results were known. Reports from friends on opinions in reserve units led Barak to believe that Netanyahu would close the gap and win the election.

The next day Barak breakfasted with Beiga Shohat and Fuad Ben-Eliezer. They told him that the time had arrived to make his move: "You must take the matter into your hands; Shimon is finished. It won't occur without struggles. But it must occur. Everything is flowing toward you and you must take the initiative." They also advised him to check out the possibility of a national unity government with the Likud. Shohat and Ben-Eliezer were Barak's first two open allies in the struggle to take over the party.[43]

In the election that brought Netanyahu to power, Barak was elected to the Knesset for the first time.[44] So Barak had slightly more ministerial experience than Rabin did when he became prime minister. But because he inherited two separate peace tracks—the Palestinian and the Syrian—Barak faced a tougher set of challenges than Rabin had in 1974.

Barak had spent his time in the government in 1995–1996 carefully studying what his superiors did. He came away very impressed by Rabin's thoroughness and analytical abilities. He had become Rabin's protégé while serving as chief of staff under Defense Minister Rabin during Rabin's second term as prime minister. Even then Rabin was grooming Barak and Barak's successor as chief of staff, Amnon Lipkin-Shahak, to be his successors as leaders of the Labor Party.

Before the internal election, Barak began meeting his main rival, Haim Ramon, at the house of a mutual friend. Ramon advised him to support "open primaries"—open to anyone who registered as a party member—in order to make his victory appear more dramatic. On September 9, 1996, Barak publicly announced his candidacy for the Labor Party leadership. Ramon decided not to run. Nine days later Peres announced that he would not contest the leadership. Barak went abroad and returned with a full campaign chest as Peres began a whisper campaign against Barak. "That gunfighter will destroy our party," he predicted. When Peres attempted to delay the leadership contest in a bid to hang on to power, Barak declared, "The party has a constitution and we will operate according to it. We don't have extra time." The date for the primary was fixed for June 3, 1997, and the date for which Peres would have any say over joining a government of national unity was set as September 15, 1997. Barak was elected on June 3 with slightly over 50 percent of the vote. Beilin came in second, followed by Shlomo Ben-Ami and then Ephraim Sneh. This was the first of two times that Peres would be replaced as party leader following Rabin's assassination. Polls gave Barak a big lead over Netanyahu in a national election.[45]

Barak basically copied Rabin's playbook from 1992 in running for the premiership seven years later. He ran as head of One Israel, a joint list with David Levy's Gesher and the dovish religious party Meimad, in a bid to look more centrist and thus attract votes from mizrakhi voters. He also used polling extensively, having hired Clinton pollster Stanley Greenberg and his associate James "Ragin' Cajun" Carville at the suggestion of President Bill Clinton, who wanted to replace Netanyahu and the Likud with a Labor coalition.[46]

Netanyahu was advised by Arthur Finkelstein, another professional American political consultant. The use of American political consultants in Israel dated back to the 1981 election. Netanyahu's first government was characterized by the special-interest politics of the ultra–Orthodox parties and the settlers; when Netanyahu no longer pleased the latter, his coalition collapsed.

Three weeks after he became head of the Labor Party, Barak flew to London to meet with British Labour Party leader Tony Blair and his entourage. Barak was shown Blair's "war room," which was a replica of Clinton's "war room" from the 1992 election. Greenberg conducted a seminar in London on Clinton's 1992 campaign and he showed the documentary film *The War Room* about that campaign. Greenberg took away from that first meeting the impression that Barak was "brilliant, analytical, arrogant and dictatorial"—a perfectionist with a "famous memory for details" who was either lecturing or educating. Barak did not respect politicians, and the feeling was mutual. He was only interested in battles for big goals.[47]

Netanyahu's government voted on December 20, 1998, to suspend the withdrawal agreed to at the Wye River plantation until the Palestinians met certain conditions. The next day Netanyahu entered a bill for new elections. Two days later the Knesset voted 80–30 to dissolve itself, and elections were set for May 17, 1999.[48] The representatives of the settlers in Netanyahu's coalition voted against the government and he lost his majority. It was part of a process that had been going on for over a decade—as soon as a government tried to advance a solution to the Israeli-Palestinian conflict, it lost its majority and collapsed.[49] This would not be the last time this occurred.

The 1999 election campaign took place during a relatively secure time in Israeli history. The focus of the campaign between the two main blocs was on how to make peace more than on questions of security. Greenberg found out that Labor had no economic strategy in 1999 until Barak finally hired a team of economists to come up with one. Getting the country unstuck became the main theme of Barak's campaign. Thirty-one different lists competed in the 1999 election. Barak committed himself to keeping Jerusalem intact in the campaign by running an ad in which Ehud Olmert said that Barak was for a united Jerusalem.

Unlike in 1996, the political right was bitterly divided in 1999. Three former senior ministers from Netanyahu's government defected to Barak: Justice Minister Dan Meridor and Defense Minister Yad Mordechai through the Center Party and Foreign Minister David Levy through Gesher. Originally there were three other candidates in the direct election for prime minister: Benny Begin of Herut, Azmi Bishara of Balad, and Yitzhak Mordechai of the Center Party. All these candidates eventually dropped out so that there could be a straight contest between the candidates of the two main parties. Greenberg later determined that Barak won the election because of peace, the economy and social issues, which combined to create a majority in favor of change. But Labor, Meretz and the Center Party added up to only 41 seats in 1999, meaning that in order to obtain a majority Barak would have to rely on the same parties that had supported Netanyahu. The Likud won 19 seats and Shas 17, so these two parties actually had the same number of seats as Labor and Meretz combined. The Knesset ended up with fifteen parties represented, making it the most fractious in Israeli history.[50]

Barak had the fastest political rise in Israeli history. Rabin won his second election as prime minister after 18 years in politics—he replaced Meir over six years after leaving the army. Peres ran five times for the premiership without ever receiving a clear mandate. Shamir became prime minister seven years after entering politics, and Netanyahu eight years after serving as UN ambassador. Barak was elected prime minister in little over half that time.[51] This election, however, would turn out to be the high point of his political career.

Chapter Twelve

Barak Attempts Peace

Barak was elected prime minister on May 17. After the victory party he immediately faced two important decisions. First, should he form a narrow ideological government like his mentor Rabin did, or should he form a wide nonideological government? The former would be easier to work with and cause less headaches than the latter. But with the Labor Party having only 26 seats and Meretz another ten, he was forced to seek allies elsewhere in order to win a majority in the Knesset. He faced a choice of forming a government with the Likud, which virtually precluded attempting to make peace with the Palestinians, and probably with Syria as well, or forming one with Shas (17 seats) and the other religious parties. On July 4, 1999, Barak presented a coalition consisting of Labor, Gesher, Meretz, Shas, the Center Party and other parties that gave him 73 votes—a comfortable majority of twelve over the minimum.[1]

Next, Barak, having campaigned on making peace with the Arabs, had to make a decision on which track to proceed with first: the Palestinian track or the Syrian track. It was in many ways the same choice that had faced Rabin in both of his governments and that faced Peres after Rabin was murdered. Because Israel is incapable of voluntarily giving up territory on two fronts at the same time, a choice of a particular track based on which front peace is more achievable or on which one it is more important. In military terms, which tend to carry more weight with a general than with a civilian leader, Syria was more important because it constituted a greater security threat. The Syrian military was the last of Israel's neighbors to present a real threat to Israel even if it by no means balanced Israel militarily. The Palestinians were more of a threat to individual Israelis—especially settlers in the West Bank—but not to the state as a whole. The Palestinian issue was the core of the conflict, and if peace could be made with the PLO, it would be recognized by most Arab countries. Syria as a state rather than a liberation movement, was also easier to deal with than the PLO, especially for a former general like Barak, who could negotiate with President Hafiz al-Assad as a fellow former general—rather than with Arafat, a terrorist who played at being a soldier.[2]

Barak, like his mentor Rabin in 1974, and unlike the same mentor in 1992, opted to negotiate with the state rather than with the liberation movement. But he had a basic problem: Assad had always played hard to get. Like a "proper girl," he did not want to appear too eager for peace and his attitude was that he could always live without peace. In fact, many questioned whether he could really live with it. With his regime based on the small heterodox Alawite clan that Sunni Muslims did not even consider a true branch of Islam, Assad had a problem of legitimizing his rule within Syria—a country whose population is 60 percent Sunni. He based it on the Ba'athist form of Arab nationalism that presented Syria as the true champion of the Arabs when less pure regimes (like those in Egypt and Jordan) were settling for peace with Israel.[3] Assad's model was Salah al-Din (Saladin), the medieval Kurdish ruler who had unified Syria and Egypt to defeat the first Crusader kingdom in 1187 and then fought Richard the Lionheart to a standstill during the Third Crusade.[4]

Assad took power in a coup in November 1970, two months after his decision not to intervene with the Syrian air force had led to a Syrian defeat in Black September. After consolidating his power, he gladly participated in Sadat's Ramadan War against Israel in October 1973 in an attempt to recover the Golan for Syria. He succeeded—but only for a week. Afterward he had refused to show up for the Geneva Peace Conference alongside Egypt and Jordan in December 1973 when the peace process started. But on May 31, 1974, he signed a separation-of-forces agreement with Israel and recovered Kuneitra. He thereafter maintained a ceasefire with Israel even when Israel attacked his forces in Lebanon in June 1982. Assad refused to recognize UN Security Council Resolution 242, with its land-for-peace formula, until the PLO did. Throughout the 1970s and 1980s his professed goal was parity of forces with Israel, which he pursued by "buying" Soviet arms on the basis of long-term loans that he pretended that he would someday repay.[5]

When the Cold War ended in the late 1980s, and along with it Syria's supply of arms on generous terms, Assad needed to make peace with Washington. The 1991 Gulf War presented a good opportunity to do just that when he joined the alliance against Saddam Hussein, his old Ba'athist foe. (The Syrian and Iraqi Ba'athist parties represented two rival versions of Ba'athist ideology, much like the Soviet Union and China during the Cold War.) Assad's foreign minister attended the Madrid Peace Conference in October 1991 and presented as convincing a pro-peace demeanor as Prime Minister Yitzhak Shamir of Israel did.[6]

In the bilateral Israeli-Syrian negotiations in Washington in the early 1990s, Damascus had managed to extract the "deposit" from Rabin of a promise of a complete return of the Golan if Israel was satisfied with the terms of peace that Syria was offering. Receiving little in reply from Assad, Rabin dropped the Syrian track and opted for the Oslo agreement with the Palestinians in the late summer of 1993. During Clinton's first term, Washington had favored the Syrian track over the Palestinian track simply because the American diplomats believed that a peace with Damascus was more feasible than one with Ramallah— although Assad did his best to disabuse both Washington and Jerusalem of that notion by keeping Secretary of State Warren Christopher waiting for hours in Damascus for a meeting, and also by allowing Palestinian terrorist groups headquartered in Damascus to operate during negotiations, which led Prime Minister Shimon Peres to break off peace talks with Syria in the spring of 1996.[7]

On the American side, many NSC and State Department officials favored the Palestinian track over the Syrian track, possibly due to memories of Assad's conduct during Clinton's first term. But special envoy Dennis Ross and Martin Indyk (who was twice American ambassador to Israel during the Clinton administration, and also assistant secretary of state for Near East affairs before and between those two periods) both favored the Syrian track because of its perceived simplicity and Barak's view, and they convinced Clinton to favor this opinion. So the Palestinian track was put on hold, with the Palestinians openly referring to Assad as "the other woman."[8]

The main issues at stake were the location of the June 4, 1967, border and the amount of normalization that Syria would agree to. The Egyptian peace treaty of 1979 could be interpreted as a precedent for either returning to the June 4, 1967, line or returning to the international boundary, which in the case of Syria were two different things. Because of the demilitarized zones along the 1949 armistice lines and Syrian capture and occupation of part of one of the zones, the lines were different from the international border between British Mandatory Palestine and French Mandatory Syria that had been agreed to in 1923. Assad argued rather illogically that the principle of not rewarding aggression applied to Israel in 1967, but not to Syrian forces in 1948 and afterward. Israel also claimed that the waterline of the Kinneret (Sea of Galilee) had changed over the years due to drought in the 1990s (the Arabs would say it was due to Israeli overuse of the water), which justified the border being advanced to the eastern shoreline rather than ten meters away, as had been the case from 1949 to 1967. In reality, this argument worked in Israel's favor and justified moving the border back from the lake.[9]

Barak had previously been opposed to the deposit—he thought it was a mistake on Rabin's part. As a result, he refused to commit Israel to a withdrawal to the June 4, 1967, lines throughout 1999. He was also cautious because most of the cabinet favored a Palestine-first approach rather than a Syria-first approach (due largely to the Oslo process). Most Israelis also preferred peace with the Palestinians over peace with Syria, because the conflict with the former touched their lives much more directly than their conflict with the latter. In October 1999 Barak approved new settlements for the Golan as a way of both pressuring Assad to negotiate and assuring the Israeli right that he would not abandon the Golan. Quiet diplomacy between Israel and Syria in Washington and the Middle East, conducted through American mediation, resulted in the announcement of the resumption of formal peace talks in December 1999 in Washington and Shepherdstown, West Virginia. Barak's demands tended to expand as he became more nervous about a lack of support in Israel.[10]

Barak ran his government by polls. He had two individuals doing polls for him: Dafna Goldberg, formerly with Gallup and who had worked for Netanyahu in 1996, operated inside the Prime Minister's Office as his personal pollster, and Stanley Greenberg, who had worked for Barak during the campaign, did polls for him on a bi-monthly basis. (Greenberg was a former professor of political science who gave him political analysis as well.) Barak conducted more than a hundred polls in his 20 months in office and had at least one or two polls per week. Barak received the poll results no matter what the time of day, and Goldberg was considered a very influential advisor. Barak paid Greenberg about $1.5 million for his polling and analysis during his time in office, including special polling for the Shepherdstown summit, for Camp David, and for the 2001 election. Danny Abraham of Slimfast paid for Greenberg's polling for Barak.[11]

Two negotiating sessions were held in December and January. The Israeli team consisted of Prime Minister Barak, Foreign Minister David Levy, Tourism Minister and former Chief of Staff Amnon Lipkin-Shahak, Attorney General Elyakim Rubinstein, and Major General (Res.) Uri Saguy. The Syrian team included Foreign Minister Faruq al-Shara, who for the first time in his career had some real power thanks to Assad's weakening health due to cancer; Deputy Foreign Minister Majid Abu Saleh; General Ibrahim Omar, head of Syrian military intelligence; former Syrian army commander General Youssef Shakkour; international lawyer Riad Daoudi, the legal advisor; former ambassador to Washington Walid Moallem; Mikhael Wahbah, the Syrian UN ambassador; Majed Daoud, former head of the international water department; and Suleiman Serra, a member of the embassy staff in Geneva. The delegates discussed four separate issue areas: borders, water, normalization of relations, and security.[12]

Barak obliquely conceded the principle of a return to the June 4, 1967 line that he had resisted throughout the fall, but otherwise he was not very forthcoming. During the session there was a demonstration in Tel Aviv by 100,000 Israelis protesting against giving up the Golan. During the conference Barak was supposed to speak by phone with people and officials, so as to give the impression that he was concerned about economic and social matters that concerned the people most. He also announced the appointment of a new comptroller for the Bank of Israel. The conclusion at the end of the Shepherdstown sessions was that there would have to be a high-level meeting involving Assad in order to make a breakthrough. Shara enunciated the principle that the land was Syria's, but the water was Israel's, meaning that Syrian claims would not extend into the lake itself.[13]

Before Barak left for Shepherdstown, he had some negative polling. Ten days before the conference Greenberg wrote to tell him that 47 percent of the public thought he was moving way too fast and 59 percent thought that he was moving too fast, to some degree in the negotiations. Greenberg split his polling of Israelis into three groups: veteran Israeli Jews, Russian Jews, and Israeli Arabs. Of just the former, 45–46 percent opposed peace with Syria. "We clearly find ourselves at a dangerous point if you plan to bring the state into a new era," wrote Greenberg. "This clearly leaves us distant from a Jewish majority in a referendum or apparently even without a majority among all the electorate." Greenberg advised Barak to present any agreement as the culmination of a national project rather than a personal achievement. "It is clear that there will be moments that the process will appear at a halt," Greenberg went on. "These moments will serve you well. The public wants to see tough negotiations and caution in regard to these critical matters." Avrum Burg of the Labor Party also sent Barak a memo on the Russian Jews. He said they could not understand giving up territory to a weak state like Syria, and he advised a special treatment for the Russians in the referendum campaign. The next day Greenberg sent a memo on "the collapse in the Russian sector." Barak had gone down 11 percentage points compared to Sharon in a single week. Barak took the polls and analysis with him on the long flight from Israel to Washington for the peace conference.[14]

Barak was also paranoid about possible Israeli leaks of any concessions he might make. The draft peace treaty appeared in the newspaper *Ha'Aretz* on January 13, apparently the result of an Israeli supporter of the peace process, Nimrod Novick, who had interviewed the Israeli delegation. One member shared the draft with him and he shared it with his network back in Israel, and someone leaked it to the paper. This made Barak cagey. He insisted on working from a photo-map from 1967, refusing to use one from the 1990s, despite the difference in the position of the shoreline due to a drought. The leak infuriated Assad, who was sure that it came from Barak in order to point out Syrian concessions. Assad thus cut off all contact with the Israelis. Martin Indyk termed it "the most damaging leak in the history of the peace process." Dennis Ross said, "It hit hard at the possibility of arriving at an agreement between Israel and Syria." As a result of the leak, Barak had Shabak head Ami Ayalon open up an official investigation into the source of the leak. This was unprecedented in Israel.[15]

On February 13, 2000, Shara appeared before the members of the Arab Writers' Union in Damascus to defend and explain the government's position regarding Israel in response to an attack on the policy by a union member. Because he was attempting to sell the policy to different constituencies, he did not present a coherent, logical defense, but rather a mix of statements.[16]

Two weeks later U.S. negotiator Dennis Ross met with Barak at the latter's home and they went over maps together. Barak said he would have to have a 600-meter-wide strip off the northeast shore of Lake Kinneret in order to sell the deal to the Israeli public. Ross thought that his actual bottom line was much less but that Barak was keeping it guarded so he could make a final concession to Assad in the negotiation process. The strip was also problematic because Barak was using a 1967 photo-map, so that, in reality, the strip would be about a kilometer wide off the 2000 shoreline. In exchange, Barak would return an Arab village to Syria that was part of Palestine by the 1923 international border. In essence Barak was proposing a land swap that would give Syria slightly more territory (about five percent) than before 1967, but it would be *different territory*. Assad had always argued in favor of recovering 100 percent of the lost territory as a point of honor rather than real estate.[17]

Barak suddenly wanted to have a major summit with Clinton and Assad and could not understand that Clinton had other commitments—in this case, a trip to South Asia that would start on March 18. Clinton wanted to meet in Geneva with Assad on March 8, but Assad said that he could not make that date and instead opted for March 26. Barak wanted to show up with Clinton in Geneva, but Ross had to explain to him that it would be better if he waited to see how things went between Clinton and Assad before he made any travel plans. In the meantime, Barak forbade Secretary of State Madeleine Albright to meet with Assad and drop hints about the Israeli position before the summit. He also wanted Clinton to present the position as an American position.[18]

Barak had Greenberg poll the details of the Israeli summit offer with the Israeli public. Because only a minority (34 percent) supported a 100-meter-wide strip along the Kinneret, Barak widened the strip to 400 meters, which almost had a majority. Barak also had Greenberg test out various slogans for the referendum campaign, and a full budget for the campaign and tasking was prepared by the Prime Minister's Office.[19]

On March 26 the Syrian delegation arrived at the International Hotel in Geneva to finalize the terms of the peace treaty with Israel and discuss an improvement in relations with the United States. Their meeting with the U.S. delegation began at 10:30 the next morning in the hotel conference room. Barak had insisted that Clinton read word for word from a prepared memo so that there would be no mistakes. Clinton thought this was patronizing but agreed to it nevertheless. Clinton began, "The Israelis are agreed to withdraw fully to a *commonly agreed border."* Assad immediately became suspicious, because it did not have his formulation of the June 4, 1967, border—even though this border was really more of a concept than an actual line.

Ross then pulled out the map with the Israeli line marked. "The Israelis don't want peace; there is no point in continuing," muttered Assad. Clinton wanted to continue reading the script, but Assad tuned him out. Only six minutes had passed. It was clear that Assad was expecting an Israeli surrender to his conception of the border—one that would allow him to bathe in the lake—and not a bargaining session. When Clinton mentioned that Foreign Minister Shara had already conceded Israeli sovereignty over the lake, Assad looked at Shara and said, "Shara said that?" The foreign minister looked "like his life was passing before his eyes," reported several of the Americans. The session quickly broke up after a polite 45 minutes and the Syrian track was closed down, forcing Barak to turn to the Palestinian track, which had become blocked by the delay. Three months later Hafiz al-Assad was dead.[20]

Martin Indyk, Dennis Ross, and former Israeli ambassador to Washington Itamar Rabinovich all blamed the internal Syrian succession for Assad's behavior. By then he was dying and wanted to quickly wrap up the succession of his son, Bashar, and he wanted the meeting to conclude the peace treaty and improve his country's relations with the only superpower. If he could not do this, he wanted to be able to blame Israel. Rabinovich and Ross both believe that a peace treaty would have been possible if circumstances had been better. But Assad consistently refused any type of atmospherics that would have helped to sway Israeli public opinion, as Sadat did by coming to Jerusalem, and he had stalled for years before suddenly deciding that he was in a hurry to conclude a deal.[21]

Barak was crippled by a combination of the Israeli electoral system and his own weak coalition (which mostly comprised parties that had been in

Netanyahu's government before him and would just as quickly leave again), to say nothing of Netanyahu's evasiveness about the terms on offer from Israel to Syria during his tenure. American Jewish businessman Ron Lauder had acted as Netanyahu's special envoy to Damascus in 1998. He had worked out most of the terms of a peace treaty, but this was on the basis of a return to the June 4, 1967, line (concept), which Netanyahu refused to admit to publicly. So Barak was working off an initial ten-point memo that Netanyahu was willing to admit to, instead of off the final terms that had been agreed to when the secret-shuttle diplomacy ended. This misinformation might have cost several months' delay in Barak's coming to terms with the Syrian demands.[22]

Indyk also claims that Assad was suffering from dementia during his final months, which affected his memory. This allegation is based partly on one meeting that Indyk had with Assad in which he could not remember having attended a previous meeting with Indyk only seven months before. It may also have been the diagnosis of a CIA (or other American intelligence agency) doctor who specialized in creating medical profiles of foreign leaders based on observations by third parties and other limited input. Assad was apparently suffering from a weak heart, diabetes, and cancer. Ross wrote that when in Geneva he had met Assad and squeezed his upper arm and felt only bone—no muscle or fat, a sign of wasting away due to cancer. President Mubarak of Egypt met Assad in January and told Washington that Assad was not long for this world.[23] Assad's memories of bathing in the Kinneret may have been from the Mandate period before Israel was a state, when the borders were relatively open. Patients suffering from dementia often experience selective memory, with older memories being stronger than more recent memories.

Israeli *mizrakhan* (Orientalist) Barry Rubin wrote that this was proof that Assad did not really want peace with Israel but only an opening to Washington. But Rubin pretends that Barak had offered Assad a return of all of the territory lost, rather than a territorial swap.[24] For someone who prides himself on being a man of honor in a society where the concept of honor—even if badly warped by Western standards—is highly prized, this difference could be critical. Rubin also fails to take account of the timing of the offer, with the succession and Assad's failing mental and physical capacities being factors.

Secretary of State Madeleine Albright, in her own memoirs, listed five reasons for Barak's caution in dealing with Syria. First, a generation of Israelis had grown up believing that possession of the Golan was essential to defending Israel. Second, there were about 17,000 Israeli settlers on the Golan who might react violently to attempts to remove them. Third, there were a million

Soviet immigrants who did not want to give up any territory. Fourth, Sharon had accused Barak of "total surrender" on the Golan issue. Fifth, Israelis were put off by Assad's unwillingness to make any gesture to reassure them.[25]

Barak's coalition problems with Shas quickly abated, albeit only temporarily, following the collapse of the Syrian track. Natan Sharansky, the former Soviet refusenik and leader of the Russian Israel B'Aliya party, praised Barak for his courage. (In the Middle East, weak leaders are praised for being weak.) But Israeli negotiator General Amnon Lipkin-Shahak later privately blamed the failure on Barak for not being flexible enough at Shepherdstown: "The dialogue failed because I think that Barak understood that the Israelis are not yet ready to give up to Syria a presence on the Lake of Galilee."[26]

In the United States the various administration officials split over who was at fault in Geneva. Robert Malley, a French-born Jew turned naturalized American lawyer, later quoted Clinton at Camp David II as blaming Barak: "I went to Shepherdstown and was told nothing by you for four days. I went to Geneva and felt like a wooden Indian doing your bidding! I will not let it happen here." Albright blamed Assad for not dealing with a reasonable Israeli offer. Quandt, who was an Arabist specializing in Algerian and Palestinian politics, blamed Clinton for not saying no to Barak before Geneva. Assistant Secretary of State for Near East Affairs Ned Walker, who had traded places with Indyk when Indyk became ambassador to Israel for a second time, blamed Ross for supporting Barak on the land swap instead of telling him flat out that Assad would never go for it.[27]

Former Syrian ambassador Walid Moallem blamed Ross for not being objective and honest enough with the Israelis to tell Barak that the land swap would not work. He also blamed Indyk for not conveying Barak's timidity to Albright and Clinton, as well as Barak for not having prepared the Israeli public for concessions.[28] Note that Israelis feel free to blame their own leaders, but Syrians do not. Lipkin-Shahak, as a former chief of staff and former head of the Center Party, probably considered himself Barak's peer, whereas Moallem would have been dependent on Assad's son Bashar, the new Syrian dictator, for his status in Syria. The Syrians also felt intimidated by the tight American-Israeli cooperation that was on display throughout the process. At Shepherdstown the American delegates socialized with the Israelis, but not with the Syrians. At a Shabbat-evening dinner the Americans ate with the Israelis, and then afterward the Israelis sang Hebrew songs about the Golan. The Syrians paced furiously outside the dining room.[29]

• • •

Even while pursuing a Syria-first strategy, Barak still had to deal with the Palestinians. After Barak's first meeting with Yasir Arafat at the Erez

Crossing to Gaza on July 27, 1999, Arafat complained bitterly to head negotiator Saeb Erekat, "This man will do nothing ... he will not implement anything.... He will just blame us for the failure of everything." Barak wanted to skip implementing the third withdrawal promised to the Palestinians under Oslo II and go directly to final status talks—once he finished with the Syrian track. Clinton tried to convince Arafat to trust Barak, but he did not get very far. After the three years of wasted time under Netanyahu, Arafat was suspicious of his Israeli interlocutors.[30]

A summit was staged at Sharm al-Sheikh on September 4, 1999, co-sponsored by Egypt and Jordan. Barak, Arafat, Secretary of State Albright, President Mubarak and King Abdullah got together to see what they could thrash out regarding the Palestinian track. The result was the Sharm al-Sheikh memorandum, which reaffirmed what the Palestinians had been promised by Netanyahu the previous year at Wye River, while also stating that the land transfer did not have to take place until negotiations on the final status had advanced further. So Barak also got what he wanted. He was given five months to work out the transfer.[31]

In early January 2000 Arafat requested that Barak include three villages that were on the border of East Jerusalem in the land transfer that was to take place the following month in accordance with the Sharm al-Sheikh memorandum. Then Barak publicly announced that he would not turn over any of the villages to Arafat, thus humiliating the Palestinian leader. Arafat announced that he would not accept any part of the transfer without the three villages. Barak turned to Dennis Ross to resolve the crisis, and Ross used this as leverage to extract a promise to turn over the three villages: two on April 23 and the third exactly one month later. So instead of looking decisive to his domestic critics, Barak appeared weak.[32]

Public negotiations between Israel and the Palestinians began in November 1999 in the Washington, D.C., area. They were more exploratory than anything else because Barak was too fixated on the Syrian track to also make decisions on the Palestinian track. A secret channel opened up between Israeli team leader Oded Eran and Mahmoud Abbas. The talks started in the Jerusalem area, but then Abbas used his connections with the Swedish government to move them to a prime minister's vacation home outside Stockholm at Harpsund in May.

The Palestinians were represented by Ahmed Qurei (a.k.a. Abu Ala'a), a competitor with Abbas for Arafat's favor and co-architect of the original Oslo talks in 1993, and Hassan Asfour, one of the original participants in the Oslo talks and an enemy of Abbas. Barak sent Interior Minister Shlomo Ben-Ami, his aide Gilead Sher, and Secretary Gidi Grinstein, along with a security minder from the Shabak. Barak monitored the talks closely for progress via phone calls to his team. He would provide innovative technical solutions to problems such as tunnels and bridges for dealing with contradictions between Israeli security needs and Palestinian needs for continuity, but the Palestinians hated his ideas because they emphasized the artificial nature of the entity that was being created.[33]

Much progress was made in fleshing out the basic ideas from the Oslo II agreement. When questioned by Qurei, Ben-Ami volunteered that Israel would be satisfied with annexing 8 percent of the West Bank so that the settlement blocs could be incorporated into Israel proper. Unfortunately, one day a story by the Associated Press appeared in the international media citing Palestinian sources in stating that secret talks were taking place in a European capital. Even though the particular capital was never named, Ala'a felt exposed and feared that he would now be criticized for making concessions. The leak could have come from a jealous Palestinian rival such as Abbas getting back at his enemies in the Palestinian Authority. Or it could have come from an Israeli source opposed to the Oslo process and disguised by the AP as a Palestinian source. This exposure, plus the feeling by Barak that the secret channel had gone about as far as it could, meant that it was over.[34]

That same month Barak had the Israeli army pull out of Lebanon without any agreement with Hezbollah. This had the effect of discrediting the Palestinian Authority's negotiating strategy and making the PA and Arafat appear weak. Barak had made a campaign promise to get out of Lebanon within a year. He had originally intended to do so within the context of an agreement with Syria. Even without the agreement, he went ahead in order to fulfill his campaign pledge, without taking into account what effect this would have on negotiations with the Palestinians. And he allowed himself to appear to be retreating before Hezbollah, which controlled the timing by marching on South Lebanese Army and IDF positions in Lebanon. The SLA collapsed, and the IDF retreated across the border.[35]

Barak then began a campaign of needling Washington to pressure Arafat into a high-stakes summit similar to the Camp David I summit that had provided the crucial breakthrough in the Egyptian-Israeli peace process of the late 1970s. Barak felt vulnerable because there were security reports about increasing Palestinian dissatisfaction with their overall situation, and there were fears that a new intifada like the one from 1987 might break out. IDF intelligence had been predicting an uprising since the end of 1999, and IDF intelligence had correctly predicted the Palestinian red lines for Camp David II: no settlement without a right of return, without a Palestinian capital in East Jerusalem, without Palestinian sovereignty on the Temple Mount, and without the June 4, 1967, border.³⁶ During the campaign against Netanyahu in 1999, Barak had promised to make peace with either the Palestinians or Syria within a year of coming into power. His year would be up on July 3. With no real domestic agenda, Barak had to deliver on the peace issue, or he would be perceived as a failure and would be vulnerable to a collapse of his government. He had also promised the Palestinians and the United States an agreement by September 13, 2000—one year from the Sharm al-Sheikh summit.³⁷ The looming threat could take the form of a challenge from within the Labor Party—perhaps from former Prime Minister Shimon Peres, who had been ignored by Barak in the distribution of the main ministries, and even prevented from advising on how to deal with the peace agenda. Or it could take the form of either Sharon or Netanyahu threatening to lure away parties from Barak's coalition, as Peres had attempted with Shamir in early 1990. Weakness tends to attract enemies and Barak appeared weak in mid-2000.

Arafat was completely opposed to a summit because he claimed that things were not yet ready for such a meeting. In reality, this meant that Arafat did not feel politically able to make any major compromises, and so he wanted to avoid at all costs being placed in a situation in which he would have to make such compromises.³⁸

Arafat felt politically weak for several reasons. First, the economy had not improved—the combination of terrorist bombings, retaliatory closures of the territories, and Israeli road blocks and checkpoints had reduced the Palestinian economy rather than causing it to expand. In short, there was no peace dividend, or at least there would not be one until there was actual peace. Second, Hamas's terrorist "resistance" campaign had combined with the widespread corruption in the Palestinian Authority to increase the popularity of Hamas and decrease the popularity of Fatah. Third, Palestinians were beginning to perceive the "rais," or president/chairman, as being more a puppet of Israel than an autonomous actor. Because Arafat behaved like the only type of Arab ruler that he was familiar with from his time living in Kuwait, Egypt, Lebanon and Tunisia, and his travels to the other Arab states, he was being treated by his subjects as such. Fourth, Israel's Syria-first strategy had made Arafat appear weak to his constituency and his rivals. Arafat could regain his popularity and popular legitimacy only by standing up to the Israelis. But he was too dependent on them to be able to do that.

For Clinton, the clock was running out as well, and he wanted one last foreign policy success before he left office to add to his legacy. He had Northern Ireland, but that could still go bad, as only a temporary fix had allowed Prime Minister David Trimble to remain in office in May 2000, and, in any case, that was mainly Tony Blair's achievement. Clinton had avoided war in

North Korea in 1994, but most considered that to be through bribery of an horrendous dictator. He had restored Prime Minister Aristide to power in Haiti, but Haiti was still a mess. In March and April 1994 he had kept the United States out of Rwanda, and as a result genocide had occurred on his watch. He had ended the war in Bosnia in the Dayton peace talks in December 1995, but only after 200,000 had already died. He had also seen Slobodan Milosevic forced out of Kosovo in July 1999 without a single American life being lost. If Clinton was to be remembered as a great president, and not one who was just lucky enough to preside during a prosperous economic cycle, not to mention one who had also been impeached due to sexual misconduct and lying, he needed another major foreign policy success.

Clinton would have a full schedule starting in August. That was when the Democratic Convention was being held to nominate Vice President Al Gore as the Democratic nominee. Clinton did not want to steal Gore's thunder by holding a high-profile summit at the same time. In September and October he would have to free up as much time as possible to campaign for Gore and other Democratic candidates, including his wife Hillary, who would be running for the Senate in New York. Then, after the November election, he would be a lame duck with little coercive power to force a deal. So the summit had to be in June or July. He would need June to convince Arafat to show up and as much time as possible for his team to prepare their agenda. On June 15, Arafat met with Clinton in Washington. Clinton told him, "I promise you that under no circumstances will I place the blame for failure on you." On July 5, 2000, Clinton phoned both Arafat and Barak and issued invitations for a summit at Camp David that would start six days later.[39]

There have been many accounts about the Camp David II summit in July 2000 written both by participants and by those who were not present but relied on interviews with many of those in attendance. The longest account of the former type is probably that of Dennis Ross, who was most familiar with the issues involved. The longest account of the latter type is that by Clayton Swisher. The two accounts are almost directly opposite in assigning blame for failure. Ross, who identified with Israel to such an extent that the Palestinians he worked with referred to him as "Israel's lawyer," blamed Arafat for the failure of the summit. Most of the other Americans, with the exception of Robert Malley, agreed with him.[40] It is hard to be able to judge the truth of these accounts because, unlike President Jimmy Carter at Camp David I, Clinton did not keep a separate log with the proposals of the two sides and the American bridging proposals. The American strategy was not to figure out what were the bottom lines of both sides, necessary for each group in order to live with an agreement and survive politically, and then go after these goals by throwing their weight to one side or the other. Rather, it was simply to act as Israel's partner in persuasion and try to coerce the Palestinians into accepting Israel's offers.

Barak's strategy at Camp David was to lay out a series of positions and see if the Palestinians would bite. Barak broke many long-existing Israeli positions that had taken on lives of their own in Israeli politics. The greatest of these gambles was without a doubt his decision to accept the division of Jerusalem into Israeli and Palestinian spheres that would serve as the capitals of their respective states. Both teams accepted the principle that what was Jewish would remain Israeli, and what was Arab would remain Palestinian, when drawing up a division of the city. Barak had four red lines going into the summit: no return to the armistice lines; no foreign armies west of the Jordan River; no right of return for Palestinian refugees; and no division of Jerusalem.[41]

But the division and the summit floundered on the issue of the Temple Mount. Barak wanted Israeli sovereignty over the Temple Mount because it was the historic location of Judaism's most sacred site; the Palestinians wanted

Clinton, Arafat and Barak at Camp David, July 11, 2000. Photograph by White House photographer.

sovereignty over the site because the two mosques, Dome of the Rock and Al-Aksa, were located there and Arabs had always exercised control over the site since long before the British Mandate.[42] The Americans tried several compromise solutions, such as no sovereignty, divided sovereignty (with Israel having sovereignty below ground and Palestine above ground), or God exercising sovereignty, but all were rejected in turn by Arafat. Arafat even claimed at one point that the Jewish temple had never even been in Jerusalem, but rather in Nablus! This caused Clinton and even the American Arabic interpreter, an Egyptian Copt, to become very annoyed with him.[43]

But Arafat's strategy was to simply survive the summit by not agreeing to any compromises for which he could later be condemned by his Arab opponents. Because Jerusalem (Al-Quds) was an issue that united the entire Muslim world, whereas the Palestinian right of return is an issue that at best only has the backing of the Arabs (and at worst only that of the Palestinians and the rejectionists), Arafat opted to make his stand on Jerusalem rather than on the refugees. Because his goal was simply to get through Camp David in order to appease Clinton rather than to reach an agreement, Arafat had not prepared red lines, fall-back positions and counter-proposals, and he refused to engage in bargaining. This merely served to make him appear intransigent in both American and Israeli eyes. But steadfastness was (and is) a virtue in Palestinian culture.[44]

Defense correspondent Hirsh Goodman, who worked for the *Jerusalem Post* and then the *Jerusalem Report* for over three decades, in his memoirs faulted Barak for failing to realize before the Camp David summit that Arafat was incapable of reaching a final settlement. Hirsh claims that Barak should have gone for an interim settlement that would have salvaged something rather than achieve complete failure.[45] But given Barak's fear of Arafat's "salami tactics" of continually demanding new concessions from Israel, this does not seem likely. Barak was not going to grant independence to a Palestinian leader whom he did not trust at all. But it was certainly true that Barak refused to take advice from others and alienated those around him through his conduct. In this way he was much like Dayan—except that, unlike Dayan, he was in the top office instead of serving as a minister to the boss. He never established a basic legitimacy for his government with the people and did not prepare the Israeli public for the bold sacrifices that he himself was ready to make during negotiations for the sake of peace.[46]

Because the parties had decided that it was "all or nothing"—no partial agreements but only a final overall agreement would be binding—the summit was a failure. Instead of trying to mediate between Israel and the Palestinians after the summit, Clinton became involved in other activities (such as campaigning). The conflict only became a priority again once the Al-Aksa Intifada broke out at the start of October. Then the emphasis was on limiting the breakdown between the two sides. Clinton did not become involved again in mediation of a solution until near Christmas, when he released his Clinton Parameters as guidelines for negotiating a solution during his final weeks in office. Barak and the Israeli government accepted the parameters with a few clarifications requested, but the Palestinians had so many objections that their response amounted to a rejection. In a meeting with Clinton, Arafat refused to say that he accepted the parameters. The Clinton Parameters then lost effect once Clinton left office on January 20, 2001.[47]

Chapter Thirteen

Barak on Defense

Contact between Israeli and Palestinian negotiators continued on a regular basis in Jerusalem and Ramallah after Camp David, while Egypt mediated between the two sides on the Temple Mount issue. But on the Palestinian side only Arafat was empowered to make decisions. From Israel, Deputy Director of Shabak Israel Hasson and Foreign Minister Shlomo Ben-Ami met with American envoy Dennis Ross at the end of September. Hasson told Ross that the two sides were on the verge of a confrontation and begged Ross to introduce an American plan to bridge the gaps between them. Ben-Ami seconded this call for an American plan. But both Ross and Secretary of State Madeleine Albright thought that the gaps between the two sides were simply too wide to be bridged at that point. Instead, Ross offered discreet suggestions on specific issues. Afterward, Hasson took Palestinian negotiator Saeb Erakat on a tour of the Armenian Quarter to demonstrate that it would be impossible to partition it.[1]

At the start of that month Arafat and Barak had both attended the millennium Summit at the United Nations in New York. Barak met with over thirty heads of state from both Europe and the Third World in an attempt to get them to pressure Arafat into negotiating. Old friends of Arafat in turn urged him not to just reject Israeli offers. Barak was almost desperate to meet with Arafat, but the reverse was not true. At the UN they had a chance encounter, and Barak chased Arafat as the latter fled into an elevator. The two shook hands and Barak spun that to the press as "a short meeting."

President Clinton also met with Arafat during the summit, although Arafat had earlier rejected the idea of a three-way meeting with both Clinton and Barak. Clinton offered him several different solutions to the Temple Mount problem, but Arafat was not in the mood for creativity. He claimed that his hands were tied by the *fatwas*, or Islamic theological opinions, which Arafat had solicited as a means of protecting himself from Hamas claims of softness on the issue, offered by legal scholars regarding the Noble Sanctuary. This meeting was the last serious attempt to bridge the gap before the outbreak of the Al-Aksa Intifada.[2]

Three days before Sharon's visit to the Temple Mount, Arafat visited Barak at his home. The meeting did not really change anything, but Ben-Ami later pronounced it the most successful that the two leaders ever had. But this is a very low bar, as this was the first real meeting since Camp David, and the two did not really meet and negotiate before or during Camp David. This is supposedly when Arafat gave his permission (or his warning) about Sharon's visit to the Temple Mount. They agreed upon a new round of talks in Washington; Barak called Clinton and both pledged over the phone to be the other's partner for peace. Five days later Barak and Arafat were at each other's throats.[3]

Barak himself had long been predicting that a violent confrontation would occur if there was no resolution of the political crisis. He said this in a speech in May 1998—a year before his election as prime minister. In May 2000 Barak met with Yosef Efrati, the right-hand advisor of Rabbi Shalom Elishiv. He was trying to convince Efrati of the importance of turning over the three villages near Jerusalem that Barak had promised to Arafat the pre-

Barak converses with Arafat at Barak's home, September 25, 2000, three days before Al-Aksa Intifada. Photograph by Amos Ben-Gershom, Israeli Government Press Office.

vious month. "We must do all we can to reach a settlement with the Palestinians," said Barak. "We can very possibly be facing a new intifada. I can already imagine 10,000 Palestinians on the Palestinian parliament building that is now under construction under the cameras of CNN. Why do we need this?" Barak spoke of 3,000 dead before the two sides returned to the peace table—a pretty accurate prediction of at least the Palestinian losses between 2000 and 2005.[4]

On the same day that Barak returned home from Camp David, there appeared in the Israeli daily newspaper *Yediot Ahranot* the headline "Barak to IDF: Prepare for Confrontation." Journalist Hemi Shalev wrote, "In a region such as ours, I wouldn't get up and take the place of unsuccessful negotiators—certainly we are headed for a serious confrontation." From the end of 1999 the IDF's intelligence branch, Aman, had been predicting to Barak that the Palestinians would seek confrontation in the event of deadlock. Aman head Brigadier General Amos Gilad correctly predicted before Camp David that Arafat would not accept an agreement without the following: (1) a right of return for refugees; (2) East Jerusalem as Palestine's capital; (3) Palestinian sovereignty on the Temple Mount; and (4) the 1967 borders. Barak just ignored his warning. Gilad went on to predict that in the last quarter of 2000 Arafat would open up a new process of violence that would express itself in an attempt to create a war on the cameras of CNN in the absence of a political solution.[5]

For Barak's final five months in office, he had a schizophrenic nature. He reacted to what he perceived to be serious terrorist threats with very stiff military responses, while with polite suggestions he attempted to accelerate talks to reach a peace agreement. As the violence deteriorated, Barak became ever more desperate to reach a political solution as the only way to preserve his electoral viability and reputation.

Early on in the Intifada there was a situation in which two Israeli soldiers ended up in the wrong place by mistake and were arrested by the Palestinian police and detained for their own safety. A mob gathered outside the police station in Ramallah and demanded that the two soldiers be turned over to them. Eventually the police complied and the two were lynched. The wife of one of the soldiers called the station, and the phone was answered by a man who said in Arab-accented Hebrew, "I have just killed your husband," before he abruptly hung up.[6]

Barak ordered Chief of Staff Shaul Mofaz to retaliate for the attack. However, Mofaz was not inclined to do so, as he thought that it would not help the situation. The retaliation strike was the first time that the Israeli Air Force had been used against multiple targets on the West Bank since 1967. Barak did this without consulting the cabinet. But it did not help him politically. Dafna Goldberg found in a poll that 67 percent of Israelis thought that the response was too weak and only 28 percent thought it was about right. The Israeli public wanted reassurance and they could only gain that reassurance by brutally punishing the Palestinians.[7]

In another incident Barak wanted to use F-16 fighter bombers to retaliate for the bombing of an Israeli school bus near the settlement of Kfar Darom in Gaza. The military-political cabinet objected, and so Barak changed the plan to have attack helicopters rather than jets deliver the strike. Mofaz said there was no point in using attack helicopters. Beilin likewise opposed the strike and Peres and Lipkin-Shahak abstained. The bombardment caused widespread damage and wounded 80 Palestinians, while electricity and phone service were knocked out in most areas of Gaza. As a result, Egypt withdrew its ambassador, Muhammad Bassioni—this was the first time this had occurred since the Lebanon War in 1982. Before he left Bassioni met with Arafat, Abbas, and Erekat, and each one promised to pressure Mubarak to send him back. But Arafat had no intention of doing this and had, in fact, pressured Mubarak to withdraw Bassioni in the first place.[8]

In November 2000 Yuval Diskin, the number two man in the Shabak, submitted to Barak a report that he had written titled "The Myth of Arafat's Control." The premise of the report was that the Al-Aksa Intifada was a spontaneous outbreak of violence due to Palestinian frustrations over the political and economic situation—deadlock and recession. In many ways it was a rerun of the December 1987 Intifada, with Arafat attempting to assert control after the fact. But the Israeli public came to believe that the Intifada was a preplanned attempt to destroy Israel.[9] This was for a number of reasons. First, people like to personalize politics and to believe in heroes and villains, and Arafat was very suitable for the villain role. Second, this belief allowed the Israeli right to argue that Barak and Labor were foolish to have negotiated with Arafat and that they had thereby endangered the security of the state. Third, this allowed Barak to believe that Arafat could still end the violence and a deal could be negotiated. Fourth, this idea also fed into Israel's very dark outlook on the world, a result of the Holocaust and decades of Arab rejectionism and terrorism.[10] This popular belief, along with Barak's own errors, was responsible for his massive defeat in the following election.

The press referred to Barak's aggressive policy as a "policy of restraint," using a Hebrew term from the Arab Revolt of the 1930s. During a Knesset debate Barak announced, "There are no negotiations. All meetings are aimed only at ending the violence. We are in a struggle with terror." On January 1, 2001, Barak told visiting American Senator Arlen Specter and Ambassador

Martin Indyk that the peace process was over and he was declaring war on the Palestinian Authority. Barak's peace cabinet, known colloquially as "the dove coot," was responsible for supervising the negotiations with the Palestinians and decided to resist Barak. Beilin, Peres, and Lipkin-Shahak all expressed reservations about his course of action.[11]

In 2004 Ben-Ami revealed in the Hebrew version of his memoirs that the IDF had followed its own plan for dealing with the Intifada rather than the directives received from the government. Lipkin-Shahak repeatedly complained to Ben-Ami that colonels were implementing their own policies and using roadblocks to harass or punish the local population. The IDF's chief of staff at the time (since 1998) was Shaul Mofaz, who later became defense minister in the Sharon government after he finished his military career. Mofaz was intent upon restoring the IDF's deterrent capability, which he thought was damaged by its failure to retaliate sufficiently during the Oslo peace process. In November 2000 the IDF officially designated the Al-Aksa Intifada an armed conflict, complete with new procedures so that civilian deaths were no longer automatically investigated. This contributed to the escalation of the conflict. Colonel Shaul Arieli, Barak's military aide, later said, "The army had a quasi-autonomous policy, under the direction of Mofaz, for whom force was the only solution against the Intifada. In his view he had responsibility for the security of the Israeli people, which he would assume in his own way, whatever the decisions of the government."[12]

Barak and Ben-Ami decided to prove to Meretz that there was no point in negotiating with the Palestinians by sending a team off to Taba in late January to do just that. Ben-Ami was sent as the head of the delegation, along with Beilin, Gilad Sher, and Lipkin-Shahak of the Center Party. Ben-Ami mentions that the Palestinians rejected the idea of equal land swaps to accommodate the Israeli wish to incorporate the settlement blocs within Israel. This was because the Palestinians rejected the notion of settlement blocs and wanted the settlements left isolated and vulnerable. A secret channel was also developed (with Barak's permission) with Abu Ala'a, but nothing came of it. Barak finally ended the talks after two weeks because of the approaching election. The Taba talks eventually became the source of much mythology among the Israeli left.[13]

Barak went down to crushing defeat in the election against Sharon—a defeat greater than that administered two years earlier to Netanyahu by Barak. After the Labor Party objected to Barak serving as defense minister in the government of national unity established by Sharon in February 2001, Barak decided to leave politics and go into business to make some money. This was the same strategy pursued by Ezer Weizman when he quit as defense minister in March 1980 and by Netanyahu after his loss to Barak. Weizman stayed out of politics for four years before coming back with his Yahad list and negotiating his way into the Labor Party in late 1986. Netanyahu stayed out of politics for three years before returning as first foreign minister and then finance minister under Sharon. Barak stayed out for four years, working for Electronic Data Systems, based in Plano, Texas, and founded by Texas entrepreneur H. Ross Perot.[14] Barak was probably hired in order to help EDS attract Israeli clients and headhunt for Israeli talent for the company. He was thus gone during the Geneva Initiative and during the 2003 election, in which Amnon Mitzna ran as the Labor Party candidate for prime minister.

Barak returned to Israel in 2005 to contend for leadership of the Labor Party. But after polls showed him faring poorly, he dropped out of the contest. Amir Peretz, a flower grower from the frontier town of Sderot near Gaza, beat veteran leader Shimon Peres in an unexpected victory on November 9, 2005, which contributed to Peres's surprise defection to Kadima later that month. Peretz had immigrated to Israel as a child and served as a junior officer in the IDF during the Yom Kippur War before being badly injured in an accident in the Mitla Pass the following year. Peretz was backed by mizrakhim, peace advocates, and those who wanted to make social issues dominant in the party. The following year Sharon's breakaway Kadima Party formed a coalition government with Labor as its chief partner, along with Meretz. The Labor Party was offered the defense ministry and Peretz took it, the first non-technocrat civilian to hold this post since Menahem Begin in 1981.[15]

Three months later, while Peretz was still learning his job, the Second Lebanon War broke out when Hezbollah captured some IDF soldiers along the northern border in sympathy with Hamas, which was fighting Israel in the south. What followed was a war that lasted for 34 days between Hezbollah and Israel, with civilians on both sides being the main casualties. Israel used the IAF to strike at suspected Hezbollah facilities and rocket launch sites in southern Lebanon, while Hezbollah retaliated by firing rockets against Israeli cities and towns. Only in the final days of the war did Israeli ground forces cross into Lebanon and attack Hezbollah areas. The war resulted in the deaths of 1,200–1,300 Lebanese and 165 Israelis. About two-thirds of the Lebanese dead and nearly all the Israeli dead were civilians. About a million Lebanese and 300,000–500,000 Israeli civilians fled their homes during the fighting.[16]

The conduct of the war was heavily criticized in Israel and Prime Minister Ehud Olmert was reduced to a virtual lame duck overnight. Within the Labor Party there were demands for a new leadership election to replace Peretz. The two challengers were the former head of the Israeli navy and of

Shabak, Ami Ayalon, and Barak. The three-way contest quickly became a two-way contest between Barak and Ayalon. In the first round of voting Barak won only 39 percent of the total. So a second round of voting was required. On June 12, 2007, Barak narrowly defeated Ayalon in the second round, 51.3 to 47.7 percent, with most of Peretz's supporters voting for Ayalon. Six days later Barak was sworn in as defense minister. He would remain in this position until February 2013—a period of nearly six years.[17] This was longer than Rabin's tenure as defense minister in the 1980s, but not as long as Dayan had served for in the 1967–1974 period.

The Kadima government attempted to negotiate a final settlement with President Mahmoud Abbas of the Palestinian Authority in 2008. American Secretary of State Condoleeza Rice had decided to concentrate on three items during her final two years in office: an agreement with North Korea that would return that country to compliance with the Non-Proliferation Treaty of 1968, an agreement with Iran that would prevent it from acquiring nuclear weapons, and peace between Israel and the Palestinians, as well as stabilizing Afghanistan and Iraq. Rice launched the Annapolis process in November 2007 at a summit at the U.S. Naval Academy in Maryland. Prime Minister Ehud Olmert met with Abbas on a number of occasions, but the process ended in late 2008 with no Palestinian response to Olmert's last offer. Because of a corruption investigation against Olmert, he had resigned his position as leader of the Kadima Party on July 30, 2008, and Foreign Minister Tzipi Livni became party leader after defeating Shaul Mofaz in the leadership contest. Abbas may have been tempted to reach an agreement with Livni after she became prime minister, something that never occurred.[18]

Barak met with Rice in August 2007 in Israel and cautioned her that she could not control Palestinian internal politics and the struggle between Fatah and Hamas for supremacy. He annoyed Rice with his negativity about the chances for peace. He also warned Rice that Israel might have to invade Gaza in 2007 or 2008 in response to Palestinian rocket attacks. In January 2008 President Bush met with Prime Minister Olmert, Foreign Minister Livni and Defense Minister Barak in Jerusalem. Barak presented Bush with a list of eight Israeli security demands for the Palestinians. He again warned that Israel might invade Gaza in the near future. The total number of rocket and mortar incidents in southern Israel had risen dramatically from 165 in November to 213 in December and 377 in January. In February it would hit a high of 485 incidents. On February 27, Hamas launched 40 Qassam rockets into Israel. Israel responded by attacking the Interior Ministry and a police station in Gaza City. Barak told U.S. envoy Elliott Abrams the following month that he did not understand the thinking of the Palestinian leadership even after negotiating with them for so many years. "The closer we get [to agreement], the more they withdraw," Barak told Abrams.[19]

Barak is mainly noted for two things in his tenure as defense minister from 2007 to 2013. First, working with the United States, he developed the Iron Dome missile defense system, which was designed to destroy incoming tactical ballistic missiles and rockets by intercepting them during their descent stage. The new system was used in the November 2012 Operation Pillar of Cloud and proved quite satisfactory. The system was developed with Israeli technology and American funding.[20]

Second, during his tenure Israel conducted two campaigns against Hamas in Gaza: Operation Cast Lead from December 27, 2008, to January 18, 2009, and Operation Pillar of Cloud in November 2012. These two operations and the earlier fighting in Gaza in June 2006 seem to have established a pattern in which Israel will every few years conduct an intense bombing campaign and/or ground invasion of Gaza in order to destroy Hamas infrastructure, such as tunnels used for smuggling weapons in from Egypt. The purpose of Operation Cast Lead was to end rocket fire into southern Israel from Gaza, which had been going on since Sharon's disengagement from Gaza in August 2005. The goal of the rocket fire was to make life intolerable in Sderot and other towns near Gaza by forcing the residents to continually seek shelter.

Operation Cast Lead began with six days of air strikes by the IAF against Hamas infrastructure. Within the first two days the IAF had hit 240 different targets. When the rocket fire continued, the IAF targeted police stations in Gaza, as the police in Gaza are a Hamas paramilitary force. On January 3, Israeli troops entered the Strip and began calling in precise fire from artillery units, Israeli gunboats and the IAF. During the final week of the offensive the main emphasis was on destroying the main rocket units and hitting targets that had only been damaged earlier. The war resulted in between 1,166 and 1,417 Palestinian deaths and thousands more wounded, and 13 Israeli deaths (four from friendly fire). Some 15 percent of homes in the areas that the IDF was operating in were damaged or destroyed. Due to the high number of Palestinian deaths and the very extensive property damage caused to Palestinian public infrastructure and houses, Israel was heavily criticized by the United Nations for its conduct. The UN Human Rights Committee, with its usual suspects of Arab dictatorships and other Third World non-democratic regimes making up the bulk of its membership, appointed South African judge Richard Goldstone to conduct an inquiry. Goldstone had been both a critic of apartheid and a Zionist.[21]

The Israeli operation was planned so as to occur during the twilight period at the end of the Bush administration and the inauguration of Barack Obama as president so that Obama would confront a fait accompli. With Israel facing new elections on February 10, 2009, and the coalition parties performing quite poorly in the polls, there may have been a feeling that the conflict would make the parties appear tough and help them in the upcoming election the following month. It did not work out that way. Kadima ended up with one seat less than before, but this was only through cannibalizing Meretz and Labor of voters to replace those who had returned to the Likud, their natural home. Labor was reduced to only 13 seats and Meretz to a pitiable three seats—the same size as the Citizen's Rights Movement before Meretz was created in 1992. Tzipi Livni took Kadima into opposition, but Barak led Labor into the government.[22]

Barak and Prime Minister Benjamin Netanyahu had a unique and unusual relationship. Netanyahu's older brother Yonaton had been Barak's closest friend in Sayeret Matkal. He became Barak's successor as commander of the Unit in 1975, a year before he was killed at Entebbe. It was Barak who had informed Benjamin Netanyahu of his brother's death. Barak had also been Benjamin Netanyahu's commanding officer both before Barak became commander of the Unit and afterward. In October 1973 they were on the same flight back to Israel at the start of the Yom Kippur War and spent at least part of the flight in conversation. In the mid–1990s the two emerged as competitors in politics. Netanyahu became head of the Likud in 1993 and Barak a minister in Rabin's government in 1995 after his release from the army. Reporter Ilan Kfir predicted that the two would eventually face each other in a contest for the premiership back in 1986, when Netanyahu was virtually unknown in Israel.[23]

When they met in the election campaign, Netanyahu was at a low point after having accomplished little in his first term except for the Wye River agreement, which had cost him his job. Two years later Barak was in that same position, having accomplished only a retreat under fire from Lebanon. During Netanyahu's second term they had a close relationship largely because they had similar views about defense and differed mainly in their approaches to a final settlement with the Palestinians, which did not appear imminent. It was similar to the relationship between Rabin and Shamir when Rabin was defense minister. The difference was that Rabin and Shamir had never worked together before, whereas Barak and Netanyahu had.

Netanyahu and Barak tried to implement a policy of pushing the Palestinian population to overthrow Hamas rule in Gaza by maintaining a tight blockade that only let through the bare necessities of life. Like the Union blockade of the Confederacy during the American Civil War and the British blockade of Germany during the First World War, this was intended to erode civilian morale and the will to resist. The blockade fit into a grey area in international law somewhere between collective punishment, which is illegal, and economic warfare, which is allowed. Washington supported Israel's right to implement a blockade, under the condition that minimum health and nutritional needs of the population were met.

In May 2010 a flotilla of passenger and supply ships organized by activists in 37 countries set sail from Istanbul to Gaza to attempt to break the blockade by either bluffing their way through or forcing an incident that would put pressure on Israel to end the blockade. On May 30, while the flotilla was still in international waters, the Israeli navy broadcast a message calling on it to follow the gunboats into an Israeli port to be searched. The flotilla ignored the message, and on May 31 at 2 a.m. Israeli commandos began boarding the flagship of the flotilla, the *Mavi Marmara*. The passengers on the ship violently resisted the boarding, and in the process nine were killed and several dozen were injured. The IDF later claimed that ten of the commandos were injured, one seriously. It took the soldiers six hours to establish control of the ship. This incident led to a breaking of diplomatic relations between Israel and Turkey. The Turkish government was faulted for not knowing that there would be violent resistance even though the organization that had purchased the ship and organized the flotilla was recognized as a Specially Designated Terrorist Group by the U.S. government. Relations with Turkey were finally reestablished in 2013 through the mediation of the U.S. government.[24]

In January 2011 there was speculation about a vote by the Labor Party caucus to leave the government for the opposition. Barak decided to beat them to it by resigning from the party, along with his supporters, and forming a new party that would remain in the government. He recruited four other Labor Knesset members, including former general Matan Vilnai, and formed the Atzmaut, or Independence Party. This allowed him to gain support as an independent faction under the law because it was a third of the strength of the former party. This in turn allowed Barak to continue on as defense minister for another two years.[25] When Dayan had left the party in 1977 to become foreign minister, he took only his seat with him; by contrast, Barak split the party when it was at a low point in its existence, leaving it with only eight seats—fewer than Meretz had in the 1990s. Dayan also acted as he did in order to pursue peace with Egypt—which he achieved. Barak used his splitting of the party to finish the Iron Dome project and conduct Operation Pillar of Cloud—hardly of the same magnitude.

Operation Pillar of Cloud lasted from November 14 to November 21, 2012. It began with the death of the Hamas military head in Gaza, Ahmed

Jabari, killed as a target of opportunity rather than in order to cause a war. Hamas replied by firing rockets into Israel, and Israel responded with air strikes but no ground invasion (despite threatening one). The operation resulted in 133 deaths, of which 79 were of Hamas's military wing (or about two-thirds).[26] On the Israeli side, six were killed and 240 wounded.[27]

At the time of the election in January 2013, Barak was nearly 71 years old. This was older than Dayan had been when he died and older than Rabin when he was elected prime minister for the second time, but younger than Sharon when he finally became prime minister in 2001. Barak spoke as if he expected to become prime minister again. This is understandable—it is very difficult for a politician to think that his one chance in the highest office was a failure and he will not get another chance. But the Labor Party will never give him another opportunity. With Sheli Yakhimovich, a former journalist, as its new leader, Labor won 15 seats in 2013, two more than under Barak in 2009. This may lead to a civilianization in the party.

This means that Barak's only chance is with the Likud (or another party).[28] Although Barak got along with Netanyahu, he was not popular within the Likud as a whole, and he has no support base in that party. His position in 2013 was like that of Sharon in 1977 or Weizman in 1985. It took Sharon another two decades to reach the top, and Weizman had to settle for being elected president—a largely ceremonial post in Israel—in May 1993.

Conclusion

Here, as a summary, I should like to compare our four subjects in four different categories: character, attitudes toward party, military skills and attitudes toward negotiating with the Arabs. I will then draw policy conclusions.

By far the worst character of the four was Sharon, who was the most narcissitic of them all: unable to control his appetites for food or power, quarrelsome, dishonest and entirely selfish. His one redeeming character trait was his patriotism. Israeli psychoanalyst Avner Falk has remotely diagnosed Sharon as narcissistic and a "borderline personality," using Sharon's own memoirs and the biographies of Uri Benziman and the Miller-Zetouni team as sources. Falk writes that, as a child, Sharon was estranged from his parents: his mother was a distant woman who was emotionally withdrawn, and his father beat Sharon in an attempt to force him to fit his perfectionist demands and to release his own frustrations. Sharon never separated psychologically from his mother and developed his own personality. As a result, Sharon externalized his failures by blaming others and engaged in projection, denial and externalization as unconscious defenses. His military failures fit a pattern of incompetence for psychological reasons first revealed by British psychologist Norman Dixon in studies of British generals. Sharon's obesity served as an unconscious defense against feelings of anxiety, emptiness and a "lack of a clear sense of self."[1] Clearly, Sharon had major psychological problems, although whether one accepts Falk's diagnosis depends largely on one's confidence in the ability of psychoanalysis today to explain personal psychological problems.

By far the best of the four was Rabin, who was able to control his drive for power, was not particularly quarrelsome (except with Shimon Peres), and was impeccably honest and patriotic. In between are Dayan and Barak. Dayan revealed his narcissism through his need for sexual conquest and his inability to deal with more than a handful of people as equals. He admired Ben-

Gurion, tolerated Meir and Begin, and seems to have had genuine friendship with only a handful of colleagues from the Rafi Party, such as Shimon Peres and Gad Ya'acobi. Falk has pronounced both Sharon and Dayan to be narcissists.[2] Whereas Sharon would react to criticism with rage and feelings of shame and humiliation, Dayan would react to it with cool indifference—both of which are traits of narcissism. In addition, there would seem to be evidence for a similar diagnosis for Barak. Barak was contemptuous of politicians, as was Dayan.[3] Barak was also incapable of taking the advice of others on a regular basis (excepting his pollsters). Barak divorced the mother of his children after decades of marriage and married a childhood friend during his period out of power. And Barak tore apart the very party that had given him a second chance merely so that he could prolong his period as defense minister.[4] Supporting the diagnosis of narcissism for Barak, many of his critics have commented on his aloofness and his feeling that he was so much smarter than everyone else.

Falk "diagnoses" the source of Dayan's narcissism to be the same as Sharon's—a distant mother who was herself narcissistic. Falk used Shabtai Teveth's biography of Dayan, with its long description of his childhood, to make his "diagnosis" rather than Dayan's own memoirs, which skip rather briefly over his childhood and present an idealized, sanitized image. Falk argues that Dayan, like Sharon, spent his career fighting his own personal demons and looking for love and inner peace that he never experienced.[5]

Another trait that Dayan, Sharon and Barak shared was charisma. Dayan exhibited many of the facets of charisma, as mentioned by an expert on the subject: the charisma of imperfection (having only one eye); the charisma of the calling (his status as the first child of the first kibbutz and growing up in the first moshav); the charisma of the fighting stance (his bravery in Operation Dani and his willingness to take on Egypt in 1955–1956); the charisma of sexual mystique (his many well-publicized sexual conquests); the charisma of hoax (his ability to fool the Arabs in 1956 and in 1967); and the charisma of innovative lifestyle (his rich bourgeois lifestyle in his final years).[6]

Falk claimed that Dayan was "perhaps Israel's most charismatic politician." This claim was made in 1984. Then Dayan's only rival for the title was Menahem Begin. But Sharon was later a serious rival and arguably maintained his charisma for a longer period than did Dayan. Dayan was charismatic from the start of his period as chief of staff until the Yom Kippur War, when he suddenly lost his aura. Begin was charismatic within the "fighting family" of Herut from 1949 onward, but he only gained general charisma starting in late 1973, after Dayan had lost his. Begin maintained his general charisma for a decade, until the end of the First Lebanon War and the death of his wife.

Sharon had limited political charisma among his followers on the right in 1974. But he had largely lost it by the time of the 1977 election. He then regained it among the settlers during his term as agricultural minister and maintained it until the announcement of his intention to withdraw from Gaza in 2004. This is charisma that was maintained over a period of about 26 years—longer than for either Begin or Dayan.

Even the best of the four, Rabin, now regarded as the Israeli Lincoln, was willing to tear his party apart over the competition with Peres—as was Peres. Rabin was unable to stand Peres for two reasons. First, Peres was seen as responsible for his delay in reaching the top job in the army. Rabin probably blamed Ben-Gurion for this just as much as (if not more than) Peres, but Peres was a much safer target. Second, Peres was seen as having undermined him repeatedly throughout his political career: as defense minister in the first Rabin government, by ending the government of national unity with the Likud in 1990, and by capturing and holding the party leadership throughout the 1980s. Ezer Weizman seems to have displayed this exact same attitude toward Rabin and for the same reason—his military ambition. As I am not a trained psychologist, this is all I will say about character.

Judging from these four, one would have to conclude that loyalty to one's party is a relatively weak trait among military politicians. Dayan left Mapai/Labor twice in his career: once under the direction of his mentor David Ben-Gurion to join Rafi in 1965, and then under his own volition in 1977 to negotiate peace with Egypt. He later ran his own list in 1981 after Peres had organized his reentry into Labor. Sharon left the Likud twice: once in 1976 to form Shlomzion, and again three decades later to form Kadima. Barak left Labor only once. But it was Sharon's second defection and Barak's defection that were the most devastating to their respective parties. It took the Likud three years to recover from Sharon's Kadima split, and two years for Labor to recover from Barak's Atzmaut split.[7]

But party loyalty is relatively weak in Israel to begin with because of its multi-party franchise system and low entry barrier. Loyalty is weakest in the religious and Arab sectors, where MKs regularly switch parties. It is somewhat stronger among the secular Zionist parties, but still weak overall. Ezer Weizman had three political homes in his twenty-year career: Herut/Likud, Yahad, and Labor. Raful Eitan likewise had three homes in a career that lasted fifteen years: Tehiya, Tzomet, and the Likud. In Israel military politicians behave in much the same fashion as top professional athletes in major-league sports in America. Their first loyalty is to their own career and performance. They are thus willing to switch teams in order to further their careers. And like professional athletes and ordinary politicians, they are prone to sex scandals.[8]

As warriors, how can we rank these men? I would rate Barak as the highest overall. Although Dayan and Sharon demonstrated comparable bravery, and Rabin and Dayan had comparable planning skills, Barak combines both of these virtues. He had better knowledge of armored operations than Dayan and Rabin, but lacked the opportunities that the other three had to conduct conventional military operations on a large scale. The closest he came to Rabin's direction of the Six-Day War, to Dayan's direction of the Yom Kippur War, and to Sharon's direction of the First Lebanon War was in the two invasions of Gaza in 2008 and 2012. But he had very little opposition in both operations, so his control was never really put to the test. The best that can be said is that Barak's demonstrated planning ability in special operations indicates that he probably could have been as capable as Rabin in 1967 or Dayan in 1956 and 1973. By far the worst of the four was Sharon, who demonstrated a reckless disregard for potential casualties in his quest for glory in both the Sinai War in 1956 and Lebanon in 1982. Sharon was also the least militarily disciplined. The other three men demonstrated the ability to follow orders on a regular basis and understood the concept of civilian control of the military. Sharon simply did not.

Among these four military politicians, there was a clear preference for deals with Arab states over deals with the Palestinians. The only exception was when Rabin decided to negotiate with Arafat rather than Hafiz al-Assad in 1993, and that was largely the doing of Assad rather than Arafat. Had Assad been ready to negotiate seriously then, as Sadat had been in the winter of 1974 and the summer of 1975, Rabin probably would have negotiated with him. On the Palestinian issue, both Sharon and Dayan were unable to reconcile themselves to negotiating with the PLO. Dayan, had he lived for another ten or fifteen years, might well have made the same journey that Rabin did. But then again, he might not have. Barak went the furthest of all by not only negotiating with the PLO but also recognizing publicly that there would be a Palestinian state, something that Rabin did only privately. Barak made far-reaching concessions from the Israeli national consensus in 2000 at Camp David, but he later sounded like Sharon in denouncing Arafat and the Palestinians as not being ready for peace. That leaves an awfully frail basis for making peace with the Palestinians in the future, especially when one considers that since early 2001 the Israeli center-left has been too weak to form a coalition except from 2006 to 2009, when Kadima was interested. However, Kadima, for all practical purposes, no longer exists.[9]

Thus there is a good argument for favoring the Syrian track over the Palestinian track in future negotiations. However, the current Syrian civil war has rendered this track very problematic. If Assad remains in power, he will probably be too weak after the rebellion to afford to make a deal with Israel. If he loses, the possibility of a deal with Israel will depend upon the ideology of the winning Sunni majority coalition. Even if the rebels win and they are theoretically open to making peace with Israel, they might be so constrained by problems of legitimacy that their room to maneuver will be even more limited than that of Assad. It may be that future Israeli historians will look back at the years from 1999 to 2010 as a period of wasted opportunities as far as Syria was concerned.

How does one grade the relative negotiating skill of these four military politicians? First, Sharon did not engage in negotiations, leaving only three to compare. However, comparison is difficult, because Dayan was dealing mostly with Sadat's Egypt at a time when Sadat was eager for agreements with Israel. The Sinai as a piece of real estate was much less politically sensitive in Israel for military, religious and historical reasons than were the other territories that Israel conquered in 1967. Yet Dayan was also able to deal successfully with the sensitive Golan in 1974 in a way that Barak was not able to imitate in 1999–2000. Dayan was successful because he combined creativity and originality with an appreciation for the political needs of the other side, and he also understood when to be tough and when not to. Barak lacked this quality in his experiences with both the Syrians and the Palestinians.

Because of his emotional aloofness, Barak was not able to convince his cabinet colleagues of the desirability of the Syria-first strategy. Dayan was also aloof and emotionally reserved, but he could rely on Meir to convince the cabinet once he had convinced her. The same was true of Begin in 1978–1979. Barak, however, had to do the convincing himself and failed to do so. He just expected his cabinet ministers to follow orders, as did his subordinates in the army. Rabin, who was also shy and reserved, overcame his personality to use analytical arguments to convince his colleagues, unlike Barak. Rabin's analytical reputation helped him greatly with this task.

But when one looks at the political numbers of Barak's coalition compared with those for Meir in 1974, Rabin in 1975 and in 1992–1995, and Begin in 1978–1979, it may be simply that Barak was attempting the impossible. This seems to have been the case with the Palestinians, as Barak lacked a majority to negotiate a deal on terms acceptable to the Palestinians and Arafat had no expectation (and possibly no desire) of striking a deal. With the Syrians, it is difficult to decide if a deal was possible and just missed because of the narrow bargaining ground, or if one was impossible given the political needs of Barak and Assad. But this illustrates why no final settlement has yet been reached with the Syrians or the Palestinians. Rabin had a clear mandate to pursue an agreement with Egypt in 1975. Barak lacked this mandate in 1999.

Future historians may look back at the entire peace process era from 1974 to 2000 as a fleeting "moment" in history poised between the rejectionism of the Arabs from 1948 to 1973 and the growing territorial expansionism of the Israelis from 1967 to the present. Or possibly as two moments: one from 1974 to 1979, involving Sadat's Egypt, and another from 1992 to 2000, involving the PLO and Assad's Syria. The unequivocal victory of the Likud over Labor in 2001 ended this second moment on the Israeli side, and the Arab Spring of 2010 ended it on the Arab side.

In 1977 Israeli general turned academic Yehoshaphat Harkabi wrote a book titled *Arab Strategies and Israel's Response*. In it he analyzed the PLO's "phases" strategy and then looked at three different Israeli approaches towards the Arab question: the doves, the hawks, and the hawk-doves (or pragmatic hawks).[10] The first category was typified by those in the Shelli Party and in Mapam and the Citizen's Rights Movement—later in Meretz—who felt sorry for the Arabs and guilty over Israel having dispossessed the Palestinians in 1948. The second group consisted of those in the Likud and in Labor who simply equated the Arabs with European anti–Semites and did not empathize with the Arabs at all. These included Ben-Gurion, Meir, Begin, Shamir, Sharon and Netanyahu, among others. The third group, based primarily at the time on three individuals (Moshe Dayan, Yigal Allon, and Yitzhak Rabin) but representative of quite a few more in both the Labor Party and the Democratic Movement for Change of Yigael Yadin, consisted of those who understood the Arab mistrust of Israel, but did not feel guilty about Israel's victory in 1948 and were willing to make peace with select (and trustworthy) Arab leaders, such as King Hussein or Sadat. Barak also falls within this group, but Sharon did not. The real contest in Israeli politics has been between the pragmatic hawks and the ideological hawks. The doves have had to settle for backing the pragmatic hawks against the ideological hawks.

Avi Shlaim writes that Barak had a combination of hawkish and dovish tendencies, and thus effectively was a centrist.[11] The same could be said about Dayan and Rabin. All three men, before they began their respective periods of pragmatic negotiations with the Arabs, were considered hawks by the doves in Labor and its satellite parties.

In 2012 journalist Patrick Tyler published his book on Israeli history titled *Fortress Israel: The Inside Story of Israel's Military Elite and Why They Cannot Make Peace*.[12] There are two basic flaws with the book. First, Tyler treats all military politicians in Israel as if they were ideologically similar. In the one Knesset election that this author witnessed personally, in 1977, there were military politicians running in at least five different parties with very different platforms, ranging from Shelli on the left to the Likud on the right.[13]

The second flaw is that Tyler fails to accept that civilian politicians may be responsible for the parameters within which the military politicians function. It was Ben-Gurion who decided upon war with Egypt and collusion with Britain and France in 1956. It was Meir who shot down the idea of an interim agreement with Egypt in 1971. It was Begin who decided that autonomy would just be a fig leaf for de facto annexation of the West Bank by Israel in 1977–1980. And it was Shamir who shot down the idea of the international peace conference in 1987. Tyler makes a good case that Israel suffers from too much militarism. However, he makes no case that this is the fault of the military politicians—he merely assumes it.

With the Arabs, according to Harkabi, divided between those who want to wage a continual war of attrition against Israel and those who want to cut her down to her "natural dimensions" within the 1949 armistic lines, the question of peace must be negotiated between the second Arab school and the pragmatic hawks.[14] But this can occur only when these two groups are powerful within their respective countries. Among the two nations, there are four possible lineups of groups:

Arabs	Israel
rejectionists	ideological hawks
rejectionists	pragmatic hawks
moderates	ideological hawks
moderates	pragmatic hawks

Only with the last lineup is it possible to produce peace on the Palestinian track. This is the lineup that existed in the mid to late 1970s between Egypt and Israel, possibly in the 1990s between the PLO and Israel, and definitely in the period 2006–2009 between the PLO and Israel. The first period resulted in peace because both the Egyptian and the Israeli governments were strong enough to make compromises and wanted peace. It failed in the second instance because the PLO proved to be too weak, as did the Israeli governments. And in 2008 it failed because both the PLO/PA and the Israeli government were too weak. On the Syrian track it may be possible to produce peace with a combination of ideological hawks and moderates, depending upon the individuals involved.

But even without a peace process, military politicians will continue to play a major role in the Israeli party system. Because of the importance of security as an issue within Israeli politics, politicians will want to demonstrate to the electorate a mastery of this issue. The best way to demonstrate this is to have been a successful general in the IDF, preferably as a chief of staff (or, if one cannot be chief of staff, then at least as a successful commander of one of Israel's three geographical commands or as head of the IAF or Israeli navy). Unlike Tennessee in the early 1840s, the United States in the 1890s, and South Africa in the 1940s, there is little danger that mortality will quickly cut short the pool of candidates for an institutionalized position for military politicians. This is because, unlike the United States in the nineteenth century and South Africa in the early twentieth century, Israel does not experience a major war on average every twenty-five to thirty years, but rather every seven or eight years.[15] And Israel has a much larger standing army in the twenty-first century than America in the late nineteenth century or South Africa in the early twentieth century. The four politicians studied in this book will continue to serve as role models for future Israeli military politicians. Rabin was a model for Barak. Barak, despite his unsuccessful end, may prove to be a model for future Labor Party military politicians. And both Rabin and Sharon will probably serve as role models for future Likud military politicians

Because two of the four military politicians featured here went almost straight to the top within Israeli politics, and had a steep learning curve, it would behoove the system to train future military politicians in the nature of the Israeli political system and the issues involved in negotiations on both political tracks before they arrive in government. This would be an ideal opportunity for the Israel Democracy Institute to develop a seminar course that all departing IDF officers above a certain rank who have any interest in a political career would be encouraged to attend. If this became institutionalized, possibly through agreements among the IDF, the main political parties, and the IDI, then the chances would be much better that a future opportunity for peace will not be wasted because of the inexperience of the new "man on a white horse" (or tank). The first item for the course would be to stress to new military politicians the differences between the military environment that they are leaving and the political environment that they are entering. Rabin, to a certain extent, learned those rules as an ambassador in Washington, whereas Barak had no such intermediate career and so failed badly. (Weizman had a similar experience when he challenged Begin for the Herut Party leadership in 1972.)

Appendix: Military Politicians in the United States and South Africa

The extent of the military politician phenomenon—a class of elected officials who are former senior military officers—in Israel is unprecedented, but the existence of the general-turned-statesman class is not. Two other Western countries, the United States and South Africa (under white minority rule), saw the rise of similar classes in their earlier history. In this appendix I will review these two cases and explain my methodology for finding precedent in earlier settler societies.[1]

The United States had a class of military politicians for the first century of the presidency, starting with the 1780s and ending in 1893.[2] President Dwight D. Eisenhower in the 1950s and Generals Alexander Haig and Wesley Clark in the late twentieth and early twenty-first centuries do not constitute a revival of this class, but rather are individuals. I chose to define a "case" of military politicians as consisting of at least four prominent individuals who based their electoral careers—at least initially—on the fame they won on the battlefield or the senior rank they held in the military, and who entered politics in at least two separate periods or waves. Only the United States and South Africa, in addition to Israel, meet this low bar.

The American case consists of three separate waves: the Revolutionary War heroes; the Indian-fighter politicians and Mexican War heroes of the antebellum period from 1824 to 1860; and the Civil War presidents. The first wave stretched from the early 1780s until George Washington's retirement from the presidency in 1797. One individual, John Sevier, however, had a political career that extended almost to the outbreak of the War of 1812. James Monroe, who was an aide to General Washington during the Revolution, served as president in the early 1820s.

Later, two more Indian-fighter presidents, Andrew Jackson and Zachary

Taylor, would be elected president after fighting the British and the Mexicans, respectively. But Jackson won a commission in the U.S. Army after fighting as a major general in the Tennessee militia during the Creek War in 1813–1814, and Taylor fought Indians from the War of 1812 through the Second Seminole War in the late 1830s before his victory over Santa Anna at Buena Vista in 1847. The only Indian-fighter president elected president because of his battles with Indians was William Henry Harrison, who campaigned with the slogan "Tippecanoe and Tyler too!" to recall his victory over The Prophet in the Battle of Tippecanoe in 1811. Likewise, many Israeli Arab fighters would gain fame fighting regular Arab armies in 1948, 1956, 1967, 1973 and 1982 after earlier gaining rank by fighting Palestinian Arabs in the first part of the Israeli War of Independence in early 1948 or in the reprisal raids of the mid-1950s or in the War of Attrition of 1967–1968.[3] The United States, South Africa and Israel all had subsets of military politicians who were also native-fighter politicians.

In North America the various European powers fought a series of wars from 1688 until 1815, in which the American Indians were allies of one or both sides. First, from 1688 until 1763, the wars were between Britain and France. Then, from 1775 to 1815, they were between Britain and the United States. In the Franco-British wars the Indians tended to side with the French against the British colonists, and then, in the Anglo-American wars, with the British against the American settlers.

The British Empire outlawed slavery in 1834 and required those seeking compensation for their slaves to collect it in London. As a result, many future Afrikaners—the farmers of Dutch, German and French Huguenot ancestry known as Boers (for the Dutch and German word for "farmer")—left the Eastern Cape for the African interior. Between 1838 and 1848, some 10,000 Boers moved to northern Natal, the Orange River area, and the Transvaal in the Great Trek. There they battled the existing African ethnic groups, primarily the Zulus, Ndebeles and South Sothos, for control of the territory. Eventually they established two independent republics: the Orange Free State and the South African Republic (in the Transvaal).

Although there was a century (1779–1878) of fighting between Xhosa tribes in the Eastern Cape and white settlers and British troops, a class of African-fighter politicians did not emerge out of this conflict. This is for two main reasons. First, the Cape Colony did not have responsible government until 1873, twenty years after the end of the previous war, known as the Eighth Frontier War (or Eighth Xhosa War), in 1853. Second, the British lacked a tradition of elected military politicians and in the Cape, as in Britain, most members of parliament were either businessmen or professionals (usually lawyers).

Both republics had presidential systems copied from the United States. The Orange Free State elected lawyers and Protestant ministers as presidents. The South African Republic elected former military leaders from the Great Trek. South Africa's military politician period can be divided up into roughly four periods: from 1859 to 1877, from 1881 to 1902, from 1904 to 1948, and from 1980 to 1999. During the first period there was no real government administration—just a popular assembly (Volksraad) and a president, a few small towns, no political parties and no standing army. In the second period there was a one-and-a-half party system, some government administration, and a paramilitary police force as opposed to a standing army. In the third period, the Union of South Africa, there was a modern state with a standing army and a three- or four-party system, but a franchise restricted to whites (except in the Cape Province, where some Africans and mixed-race South Africans had the vote until the mid-1930s).

South Africa's final period of military politicians began in 1980, when Pieter Willem Botha, or P.W., decided to give up the defense ministry, which he had held since 1966, after he became prime minister in 1978. He decided that the chief of the South African Defence Force (SADF), General Magnus Malan, would become the next defense minister. Malan became head of the army in 1973 and head of the SADF in 1976. He was in charge of South Africa's 1975–1976 involvement in the Angolan civil war, when about 3,000 troops invaded southern Angola to shore up FNLA and UNITA guerrillas against the eventually victorious MPLA guerrillas, who were backed by Cuban troops. Malan was chosen by Botha to be a representative of the SADF in the government. He remained as defense minister for the next decade. A scandal involving secret funding for the Zulu Inkatha Freedom Party eventually forced him to resign as defense minister, and he briefly served as the water affairs and forestry minister before resigning from politics.[4]

In May 1993 former South African army commander General Constand Viljoen formed a party of former generals known as the Afrikaner Volksfront (or Afrikaner People's Front) after the existing right-wing Conservative Party had collapsed due to splits following the death of longtime leader Andreas Treurnicht in 1992. The party won about 1.7 percent of the vote and held a number of seats in the South African parliament until 1999.[5] The AVF is comparable to Israeli generals' parties like the Democratic Movement for Change of the 1970s or Ariel Sharon's Shlomzion in 1976–1977 or the Third Way in the 1990s. But because it existed mostly after white minority rule when whites were no longer the strongest force in national politics, the AVF demonstrates what may occur if in the future there is a one-state solution, with Palestinians and Israelis having democratic rights in a single state with a Palestinian majority.[6]

The combined American and South African experiences leave us with six cases to compare with that of Israel. Ideally, we are looking for a modern polity with a standing army, several political parties, and a moderate to severe external threat to the country. Let's list our six cases and see how many meet this minimal criterion:

- America's post–Revolutionary War period (1783–1799)
- America's antebellum period (1824–1857)
- America's postbellum period (1868–1893)
- Kruger's republic (1882–1900)
- The Union of South Africa (1910–1948)
- The Republic of South Africa (1980–1999)

We can start by eliminating the post–Revolutionary War period and Kruger's republic because they lacked a multiparty system. America's postbellum period had a three-party system, but the Greenback Party of the 1870s really cannot be compared to any Israeli parties, and so this period should probably be eliminated as well. And the Republic of South Africa simply did not have enough military politicians while the Afrikaners were still in charge to count. This leaves us with the American antebellum period and the Union of South Africa to compare with Israel—but for both of these cases there were weak three- or four-party systems as compared with Israel's much more numerous parties.[7] And the Union of South Africa lacked a severe external threat.

But before making these comparisons, it should be noted that the African and South African cases are much closer to each other than either is to the Israeli case. This can be noted in at least three particulars. First, in Israel the military politicians have distinct military and political careers that are separate and sequential. In both the United States in the nineteenth century and South Africa in the late nineteenth and early twentieth centuries, the military politicians have had overlapping military and political careers. Only Zachary Taylor, Ulysses S. Grant and Magnus Malan fit the Israeli profile of sequential careers.

Second, Israeli officers have an excellent professional education after their initial enlistment. South Africa lacked any formal training for its commandoes before the Union Defence Force, and many of the American Indian-fighter politicians also lacked any formal military training. Of the American military politicians, only Jefferson Davis and Grant were West Point graduates—and this at a time when the academy was primarily concerned with providing an engineering background for officers.

Third, both the United States in the nineteenth century and South Africa in the twentieth century had a mercenary tradition. One historian of the filibustering period claims that between 1849 and 1860 some five thousand Americans either took part in filibustering expeditions to Cuba, Mexico, and Central America or had committed themselves to expeditions that never got off the ground.[8] A proportionate number of South African men served as mercenaries in the Republic of the Congo in the 1960s, in Rhodesia in the 1970s, and in Angola and Sierra Leone in the 1990s following the end of apartheid.[9] Very few Israelis, however, have served as mercenaries abroad.

• • •

Not content to make comparisons relevant to the future of Israel's military politician class from only two other cases, about a decade ago I did secondary research in the history of all of Britain's settler colonies and the European colonial powers that were either democratic when they had their colonies or shortly afterward (such as Germany). Based on the American, South African and Israeli cases, I knew that three conditions were necessary for this phenomenon to occur. First, the country needed to be a democracy that was either independent or autonomous.[10] Second, it had to be in a prolonged serious conflict with its native population and/or its neighbors. Third, its military had to be a conscript force in order to create the proper link between the voters and war heroes. If any of these conditions was absent, the phenomenon would not appear. I found no cases of native-fighter politician classes in any of the British settler colonies, mainly because the British army was responsible for the defense of the country or because there was no serious prolonged conflict with the natives.

My research did turn up three borderline cases in Europe in the twentieth century: in Spain, France and Germany. Spain fought a colonial war in Spanish Morocco from 1912 to 1925, and several veterans of the fighting went on to serve in the regime of General Francisco Franco following the Spanish Civil War. But because these individuals served in an authoritarian dictatorship and came to power through military force, they cannot really be compared with the Israeli military politicians.[11] France had three former generals from the two world wars in office from 1934 to 1969: Marshal Henri Philippe Pétain, General Charles de Gaulle and General Joseph Marie Koenig. Pétain began his political career in 1934 and finished it a decade later when Vichy France was abolished due to the Allied liberation. De Gaulle began his political career in 1940 and ended it in 1969; it spanned from the very end of the Third Republic, including stretches at the start and end of the Fourth Republic, to the first decade of the Fifth Republic. Koenig served briefly as defense minister during the Fourth Republic in the mid–1950s.[12]

Weimar Germany had at least three military politicians from 1925 to 1934. During World War I, Paul von Hindenburg, the hero of the Battle of

Tannenburg, and Erich Ludendorff served as virtual co-dictators during the last two years of the war. When President Frederick Ebert died in 1925, Hindenburg was easily elected as his replacement. His National Socialist opponent was Ludendorff, who had marched with Hitler in the Munich putsch attempt in November 1923. Ludendorff later fell out with Hitler and formed his own nationalist party and was elected to the Reichstag. There was also a general, Kurt von Schleicher, serving as defense minister shortly before Hitler came to power. Hitler had him murdered two years later during the Night of the Long Knives.[13] But because the period is so short and Germany was so unstable, it does not compare well with Israel.

• • •

There are three historical instances of elected military politicians having institutionalized positions of power outside of Israel. The first was in Tennessee from 1820 to 1843 in the governor's mansion. All of the governors in the 1820s and most in the 1830s were veterans of the War of 1812—mostly of the Creek War and the Battle of New Orleans. The streak ran out both because of mortality and because, due to Indian removal in the late 1830s, there was no longer an Indian threat in Tennessee or anywhere else in the South (except Florida and Texas).[14]

The second instance was the Republican presidential nomination from 1868 to 1888, which was reserved for former Union generals from the Civil War, with the exception of the nomination of James Blaine of Maine in 1884.[15] With the exception of Ulysses S. Grant in 1868 and 1872 (and nearly in 1880), these men were professional politicians who served briefly as political generals during the Civil War. The politicians were nominated for their symbolic value rather than for their military competence (again, with the exception of Grant). This streak ended due to mortality—a lack of new Civil War generals. But in 1896 the Republicans nominated William McKinley, who had served as a major in the Union army. His vice-presidential running mate in 1900 was Theodore Roosevelt, who was a war hero from the Spanish-American War and a former assistant secretary of the navy. McKinley and Roosevelt were extensions of the Civil War trend that ended in 1893 when Benjamin Harrison concluded his one presidential term.[16]

The third instance was the prime ministers of the Union of South Africa from 1910 to 1948, all three of whom were former Boer War generals. But all were superb professional politicians first and temporary generals second.[17]

In both the United States and South Africa the streak of military politicians ended once the wars moved overseas. Both world wars were a controversial subject in Afrikaner politics, much as in Irish nationalist politics and for similar reasons. In South Africa the phenomenon started again in 1980 when the chief of staff, Magnus Malan, was appointed defense minister. He served for more than a decade as first defense minister (1980–1991) and then water minister. This was when South Africa was involved in a war in neighboring Namibia, which was the equivalent of the Sinai, the Golan, or the West Bank for Israel.[18]

It is safe to say that military politicians will remain a prominent feature of Israeli politics as long as the Arab-Israeli conflict (particularly between Israelis and Palestinians) continues. The only circumstance associated with the ending of the Indian-fighter phenomenon in America that repeated itself in the Middle East was the temporary loss by the Palestinians of a great power patron, but this was soon ended when Iran replaced the Soviet Union.[19] The same can also be said about the institutional control of the defense ministry by former generals and defense technocrats.

Chapter Notes

Chapter One

1. The details on the political careers of the generals mentioned below are from their Wikipedia entries, accessed in June 2013.

2. On Yadin see Asher Silberman, *A Prophet From Amongst You: The Life of Yigael Yadin* (New York: Addison-Wesley, 1994). On Weizman see Ezer Weizman, *On Eagle's Wings* (New York: Macmillan, 1977) and *The Battle for Peace* (New York: Bantam, 1981). The former is on his military career and the latter on his early political career and period as defense minister.

3. Raful Eitan, *A Soldier's Story* (Sure Sellers, Inc., 1991).

4. On both Eitan and Ze'evi see Ami Pedahzur, *The Triumph of Israel's Radical Right* (New York: Oxford University Press, 2012) pp.101, 103, 120, 76–77, 161–63.

5. Idem, p. 233.

6. Idem, pp. 162–63, 179, 183, 191; Yoram Peri, *Generals in the Cabinet Room* (Washington: USIP Press, 2006) pp. 137–40, 152–53.

7. Former Major General Mordechai Tzippori served as a minister in Begin's second government in the early 1980s.

8. Ya'alon is a prime example of someone who before 2000 probably would have joined Labor.

9. See Yoram Peri, *Between Battles and Ballots* (New York: Cambridge University Press, 1983) and *Generals in the Cabinet Room* (Washington: USIP Press, 2006) for a thorough study of civil-military relations in Israel.

Chapter Two

1. Moshe Dayan, *Story of My Life* (New York: Da Capo Press, 1992) pp. 21–25, 27.

2. Idem, pp. 30–31, 262–64; Robert Slater, *Warrior, Statesman: The Life of Moshe Dayan* (New York: St. Martin's Press, 1991) p. 69; Yael Dayan, *My Father, His Daughter* (New York: Farrar, Straus and Giroux, 1985) p. 27. An interest in sex is found in nearly all men and archaeology was a national obsession in Israel from the 1930s to the 1970s.

3. Dayan, op. cit. pp. 28–29.

4. Idem, p. 29; Y. Dayan, op. cit. p. 26; Mordechai Bar-On, *Moshe Dayan: Israel's Controversial Hero* (New Haven: Yale University Press, 2012) p. 5.

5. Dayan's daughter Yael would later serve in the Knesset for both Labor and Meretz. The Dayan family is the only real political family dynasty in labor Zionism. All three got elected largely on their own efforts because of their contribution to the party (Shmuel) or the nation (Moshe, Yael).

6. Avner Falk, "Moshe Dayan: Narcissism in Politics, *The Jerusalem Quarterly* 30,1984 pp. 113–24.

7. Dayan, op. cit. pp. 37–38.

8. Idem, pp. 38, 63–64; Y. Dayan, op. cit. p. 27; Ruth Dayan, *And Perhaps: The Story of Ruth Dayan* (New York: Harcourt, Brace, Jovanovich, 1973) .

9. Bar-On, op. cit. p. 18.

10. Idem; Dayan, op.cit. pp. 45–47.

11. The photo can be seen in Yigal Allon, *Shield of David: The Story of Israel's Armed Forces* (Littlehampton Book Services, 1970).

12. Dayan, op. cit. pp. 49–53, 55, 61.

13. Slater, *Rabin of Israel* (New York: St. Martin's Press, 1993) pp. 45–46.

14. Dayan, op. cit. pp. 66–71; Bar¬-On, op. cit. p. 24.

15. Dayan, op. cit. pp. 74–77; Bar-On, op. cit. pp. 26, 29.

16. Dayan, op. cit. pp. 77–78; Amos Perlmutter, *Israel: The Partitioned State* (New York:

Charles Scribner's Sons, 1985) pp. 99–100.; Falk, op. cit.
17. Dayan, op. cit. pp. 88–92; Bar-On, op. cit. p. 31; Martin Van Creveld, *Moshe Dayan* (London: Weidenfeld & Nicolson, 2004) p. 58.
18. Dayan, op. cit. pp. 93–96; Bar-On, op. cit. pp. 31–32; Ted Schwarz, *Walking with the Damned* (New York: Paragon House, 1992) pp. 291–92.
19. Dayan, op. cit. pp. 98–111; Bar-On, op. cit. pp. 33, 35; Van Creveld, op. cit. pp. 65–66; Slater, *Warrior, Statesman*, pp. 102–03.
20. Bar-On, op. cit. p. 34; Van Creveld, p. 66.
21. Dayan, op. cit. pp. 112–20.
22. All those from the ground forces in order to be eligible for the top two positions in the IDF must serve in at least one of the geographical commands and many serve in two or three.
23. Dayan, op. cit. pp. 126–27; Bar-On, op. cit. p. 37; Slater, *Warrior, Statesman*, p. 117
24. Slater, *Warrior, Statesman*, p. 118.
25. Most of the Mapai Old Guard and Ahdut Ha'Avoda had this attitude towards Arabs as did Begin. Dayan never studied Arabic formally but in his youth learned to speak some of the common phrases of the Arab fellahin or peasants.
26. Dayan, op. cit. pp. 96–98.
27. Idem, pp. 138–44; Slater, *Warrior, Statesman*, pp. 124–26.
28. Falk, op. cit.
29. On the origins of military politicians in Israel see Yoram Peri, *Between Battles and Ballots: Israeli Military in Politics* (New York: Cambridge University Press, 1985) pp.
30. Yitzhak Rabin, *The Rabin Memoirs* (Berkeley: University of California Press, 1996) p. 46; Anita Shapira and Evelyn Abel, *Yigal Allon, Native Son: A Biography* (University of Pennsylvania Press, 2007) for more information on the reasons for his leaving the army. See also Perlmutter, op. cit. p. 168.
31. Zorik was Dayan's mother's favorite son and Dayan was jealous of their relationship. Israeli psychiatrist Avner Falk argues that Dayan's famous order that units could not retreat before experiencing 50 percent casualties was a subconscious attempt to mirror what happened in his own family and possibly an attempt to compensate for unconscious guilt over his brother's death—Falk, op. cit.
32. Bar-On, op. cit. p. 47.
33. Idem, pp. 40, 49.
34. Idem, p. 50.
35. Slater, *Warrior, Statesman*, pp. 154- 55; Bar-On, op. cit. p. 54.
36. Avi Shlaim, *The Iron Wall* (New York: W W Norton, 2001) pp. 88–94, 98–123; Perlmutter, op. cit. p. 178; Slater, *Warrior, Statesman*, pp. 162–65.
37. Dayan, op. cit. pp. 177–78; Slater, *Warrior, Statesman*, p. 163; for an explanation of the whole affair from 1954–65 see Dan Kurzman, *Ben Gurion: Prophet of Fire* (New York: Simon and Schuster, 1983).
38. Shlaim, op. cit. pp. 124–29;
39. Bar-On, op. cit. p. 62.
40. Idem, pp. 64–65; Shlaim, op. cit. pp. 160–62.
41. Bar-On, op. cit. pp. 65–67; Ariel Sharon, *Warrior* (New York: Simon & Schuster, 2001) pp. 123–27; Shlaim, op. cit. p. 149.
42. Bar-On, op. cit. p. 68; Shlaim, op. cit. p. 155; Shimon Peres, *Battling for Peace* (New York: Random House, 1995) p. 104.
43. Bar-On, op. cit. pp. 71, 73–74.
44. Shlaim, op. cit. pp. 161–65.
45. Dayan, op. cit. pp. 211–34.
46. Idem, pp. 235–59; Bar-On, op. cit. p. 96.
47. Bar-On, op. cit. pp. 96–97; Slater, *Warrior, Statesman*, pp. 202–05.
48. Van Creveld, op. cit. p. 97.
49. Falk, op. cit.
50. Bar-On, op. cit. pp. 102–03.
51. Idem, p. 100; Slater, *Warrior, Statesman*, op. cit. pp. 208–09.
52. Bar-On, op. cit. pp. 104, 111–13.
53. Abba Eban, *An Autobiography* (New York: Random House, 1977) pp. 271, 275; Slater, *Warrior, Statesman*, p. 223; Bar-On, op. cit. p. 115.
54. Bar-On, op. cit. pp. 116, 119.
55. Slater, *Warrior, Statesman*, p. 225.
56. Bar-On, op. cit. pp. 120–22; Peres, op. cit. pp. 86–87.
57. Slater, *Warrior, Statesman*, pp. 234–37. The other two were *Story of My Life* in 1976 and *Breakthrough* in 1981 on the Egyptian-Israeli peace negotiations of 1977–79.
58. Bar-On, op. cit. pp. 123–24; Slater, *Warrior Statesman*, op. cit. pp. 238–43; Y. Dayan, op. cit. p. 168.

Chapter Three

1. Tom Segev, *1967* (New York: Metropolitan, 2007) p. 210; Slater, *Warrier, Statesman*, p. 245; Slater, *Rabin*, pp. 118–19.
2. Segev, op. cit. pp. 150–51.
3. Slater, *Warrior, Statesman*, p. 246.
4. Mordechai Bar-On, *Moshe Dayan: Israel's Controversial Hero* (New Haven: Yale University Press, 2012) pp. 125–26; Slater, *Warrior Statesman*, pp. 248–49.
5. Slater, *Warrior, Statesman*, pp. 250–51.
6. Idem, p. 251; Slater, *Rabin*, p. 135.
7. Slater, *Warrior, Statesman*, pp. 253–57.
8. Idem, pp. 257–58; Bar-On, op. cit. p. 127.

9. Bar-On, op. cit. pp. 128–29.
10. Bar-On, op. cit. pp. 131, 133, 138–40.
11. Idem, p. 141.
12. There is a famous photograph of the three entering the Old City together that is reproduced in Slater, *Warrior, Statesman*, and in Moshe Dayan, *Story of My Life* (New York: Da Capo Press, 1992). On Shemer, see Segev, op. cit. p. 381. On the effect of visiting holy places and touring the West Bank see Segev, pp. 424–31.
13. On the Allon Plan see Amos Perlmutter, *Israel: The Partitioned State* (New York: Charles Scribner's Sons, 1985) pp. 205, 286; Slater, *Warrior Statesman*, pp. 328–31.
14. Bar-On, op. cit. p. 144; Michael Bar-Zohar, *Shimon Peres: The Biography* (New York: Random House, 2007) pp. 307–11.
15. Bar-On, op. cit. p. 146.
16. Avi Shlaim, *Lion of Jordan: The Life of King Hussein in War and Peace* (New York: Alfred Knopf, 2008) pp. 281–314.
17. Bar-On, op. cit. pp. 147–48.
18. Idem, p. 150; Martin Van Creveld, (London: Weidenfeld & Nicolson, 2004) pp. 142–43.
19. The author lived on two kibbutzim in the mid-1970s and observed all of these weapons carried by soldiers. Afterwards he was a student in Jerusalem and observed mostly M-16s and Galils used by the soldiers.
20. On the French embargo see Abraham Rabinovich, *The Boats of Cherbourg* (Annapolis, MD: Naval Institute Press, 1997).
21. Bar-On, op. cit. p. 217; Perlmutter, op. cit. pp. 203–04.
22. Bar-On, op. cit. p. 153; Dayan, op. cit. pp. 449–50.
23. Dayan, op. cit. pp. 414–18; Van Creveld, op.cit. p. 143.
24. Dayan, op. cit. pp. 451–52; Slater, *Warrior Statesman*, pp. 313–14; William B. Quandt, *Peace Process, Revised Edition* (Berkeley: University of California Press, 2001) pp. 67–75.
25. Shlaim, op. cit. pp. 315–41; see Jack O'Connell and Vernon Loeb, *King's Counsel: A Memoir of War, Espionage, and Diplomacy in the Middle East* (New York: W W Norton, 2011) chapter entitled *September 1970* for the details about the intelligence deception that kept Iraq out of the war.
26. Avi Shlaim, *The Iron Wall* (New York: W W Norton, 2001) p. 299; on the "conseptzia" and other reasons for the Israeli surprise at the Arab attack see Chaim Hertzog, *The War of Atonement* (Boston: Little, Brown, 1975); Perlmutter, op. cit. pp. 227–29.
27. Bar-On, op. cit. p. 166.
28. Idem, p. 167; Dayan, op. cit. pp. 460–61; Amir Oren, "Moshe Dayan opposed pre-Yom Kippur War call-up due to fears of U.S. response," *Ha'Aretz* April 2, 2013.
29. Slater, *Warrior, Statesman*, p. 354; Bar-On, op. cit. pp. 169–71; Van Creveld, op. cit. pp. 162–65; Y. Dayan, op. cit. pp. 211–14.
30. Bar-On, op. cit. pp. 173–74, 177.
31. Ariel Sharon, *Warrior* (New York: Simon & Schuster, 2001) p. 305; Y. Dayan, op. cit. p. 215.
32. Sharon, op. cit. pp. 310–33.
33. Sharon, op. cit. p. 310.
34. Henry A. Kissinger, *Years of Upheaval* (Boston: Little, Brown, 1982) pp. 568–71.
35. Idem, pp. 792–98.
36. Dayan, op. cit p. 599; Sharon, op. cit. p. 338; Bar-On, op. cit. p. 183. Dayan claims that Labor lost seven seats, but other sources list five.
37. Dayan, op. cit. pp. 565–70.
38. Bar-On, op. cit. pp. 185–86.
39. Dayan, op. cit. pp. 591–92, 606–07; Bar-On, op. cit. p. 186.
40. Slater, *Warrior, Statesman*, pp. 378–79, 383; Slater, *Rabin*, pp. 205–19.
41. Bar-On, op. cit. p. 188.

Chapter Four

1. See Henry A. Kissinger, *Years of Upheaval* (Boston: Little, Brown, 1982) pp. 614–66, 799–804 and Kissinger, *Years of Renewal* (New York: Simon & Schuster, 1999) pp. 347–459, 925–84 for details; see also William B. Quandt, *Peace Process: Revised Edition* (Berkeley: University of California Press, 2001) pp. 130–73.
2. Richard Valeriani, *Travels with Henry* (Boston: Houghton Mifflin, 1979) as an example of the leading "tell-all" account.
3. Quandt, op. cit. pp. 148–53.
4. Jeffrey Z. Rubin, ed. *Dynamics of Third Party Intervention: Kissinger in the Middle East* (New York: Praeger, 1981) for a theoretical treatment of Kissinger's mediation technique in the Middle East. See particularly Edward Sheehan, "How Kissinger Did It," in Rubin, op. cit. pp. 44–91.
5. Rubin, op. cit. listed only one work that existed before Kissinger became national security advisor in 1969 and Kissinger famously wrote in the introduction to his first volume of memoirs, *White House Years* (Boston: Little, Brown, 1979) that a senior official only has the intellectual capital to use that he has acquired going into a position as he is far too busy reacting to events to learn from history or theory as he goes along.
6. Used particularly in the March and August 1975 shuttles for the Sinai II agreement.
7. Kissinger, *Years of Upheaval*, pp. 747–98.

8. Quandt, op. cit. pp. 132–34.
9. Kissinger, *Years of Upheaval*, p. 939; Henry A. Kissinger, *Years of Renewal* (New York: Simon & Schuster, 1999) p. 375; Rabin, pp. 247–49.
10. Quandt, op. cit. p. 143; Sheehan, op. cit. p. 65.
11. Kissinger, *Upheaval*, pp. 959, 1046–47.
12. Quandt, op. cit. p. 148.
13. Idem, pp. 148–52. See also Moshe Dayan, *The Story of My Life* (New York: Da Capo Press, 1992) pp. 576–80; Kissinger, *Upheaval*, pp. 1032–1110; Abba Eban, *An Autobiography* (New York: Random House, 1977) pp. 573–77 for first person accounts of the Syrian-Israeli disengagement negotiations.
14. Dayan, op. cit. pp. 581–89.
15. Yael Dayan, *My Father, His Daughter* (New York: Farrar, Straus & Giroux, 1985) pp. 222–23.
16. Mordechai Bar-On, *Moshe Dayan: Israel's Controversial Hero* (New Haven: Yale University Press, 2012) p 190.
17. Y. Dayan, op. cit. pp. 220–21.
18. Idem, p. 225; Bar-On, op. cit. p. 192; Michael Bar-Zohar, *Shimon Peres: The Biography* (New York: Random House, 2007) p. 327; Rabin, op. cit. p. 285.
19. Slater, *Warrior, Statesman*, p. 386; on Nitze see Nicholas Thompson, *The Hawk and the Dove: Paul Nitze, George Kennan and the History of the Cold War* (New York: Picador, 2010).
20. Y. Dayan, op. cit. p. 226 for the date. Either she is mistaken about the date or this is the date of their first phone conversation as the election was on May 17. Bar-On, op. cit. p. 193. Slater, op. cit. p. 391 lists May 21 as the date as does Dayan.
21. Moshe Dayan, *Breakthrough* (New York: Alfred Knopf, 1981) pp. 1–2, 4, 7.
22. Dayan was not noted for his work ethic, but for his brilliance and intuitive grasp of a situation. He had few real friends and if something did not interest him he did not work on it.
23. Dayan, Breathrough, pp. 38–54; Rabin, op. cit. pp. 320–21.
24. Dayan, Breakthrough, pp. 55–74; Bar-On, op. cit. p. 196.
25. Dayan, Breakthrough, pp. 75–76.
26. Idem, pp. 77, 82–83.
27. Idem, pp. 91–97, 109.
28. Idem, pp. 102–05; Slater, op. cit. p. 407.
29. Dayan, Breakthrough, pp. 110–14.
30. Idem, pp. 138–46; Slater, op. cit. p. 409.
31. Quandt, op. cit. p. 197.
32. Idem, pp. 197–203.
33. Breakthrough, pp. 182, 194.
34. Idem, pp. 272–78; Quandt, op. cit. pp. 228–34; Bar-On, op. cit. p. 206.
35. Dayan, Breakthrough, pp. 285–302; Y. Dayan, op. cit. pp. 237–38.
36. Dayan, Breakthrough, pp. 312–14, 315; Bar-On, op. cit. p. 209
37. Bar-On, op. cit. pp. 210–14.
38. Y. Dayan, op. cit. pp. 272–81, 283–84.
39. Slater, op. cit. pp. 442–43.

Chapter Five

1. Linda Benedikt, *Yitzhak Rabin: The Battle for Peace* (London: Haus Books, 2005) pp. 1, 5–8, 14.
2. Idem, pp. 17, 19–20; Slater, *Rabin*, pp. 40, 44–47, 49.
3. Leah Rabin, *Rabin: Our Life, His Legacy* (New York: G. P. Putnam's Sons, 1997) p. 65; Slater, op. cit. pp. 51–52; Dan Kurzman, *Soldier of Peace: The Life of Yitzhak Rabin, 1922-1995* (New York: HarperCollins, 1998) pp. 91–92.
4. Amos Perlmutter, *Israel: The Partitioned State* (New York: Charles Scribner's Sons, 1985) p. 103; Slater, op. cit. p. 58; Kurzman, op. cit. p. 95.
5. Slater, op. cit. pp. 55–57; Kurzman, op. cit. pp. 95–98.
6. Slater, op. cit. pp. 59– 61.
7. Idem, p. 64.
8. Kurzman, op. cit. p. 112.
9. Slater, op. cit. pp. 66–68.
10. Idem, pp. 69–70.
11. Idem, p. 72.
12. Idem, pp. 73–74; Kurzman, op. cit. pp. 123–27.
13. Kurzman, op. cit. pp. 131–33.
14. Slater, op. cit. pp. 70–71; Kurzman, op. cit. p. 128.
15. Slater, op. cit. p. 71.
16. Ted Schwarz, *Walking with the Damned* (New York: Paragon House, 1992) pp. 287–88, 292.
17. Idem, p. 293; Kurzman, op. cit. p. 139.
18. Kurzman, op. cit. pp. 140–45; Slater, *Rabin*, pp. 312–13. Shipler's book was the first book to contain the deleted text. David Shipler, *Arab and Jew* (London: Penguin, 2001) the first edition was published in 1984.
19. Slater, op. cit. pp. 77–78.
20. The Etzel and Lehi were integrated into the IDF after independence was declared except in Jerusalem, where it occurred following the Bernadotte assassination in mid-September 1948. Most volunteers were Jews except in the air force where many pilots were Gentiles.
21. Slater, op. cit. pp. 78–79.
22. Idem, pp. 79–81.
23. Idem, pp. 81–85; Rabin, pp. 42–43.
24. Slater, *Rabin*, p. 87
25. Slater, op. cit. p. 79; Y. Rabin, op. cit. pp. 45–46; Perlmutter, op. cit. p. 168.

26. Y. Rabin, op. cit. pp. 47–48, 58, 74–75; Slater, op. cit. pp. 91- 92.
27. Slater, op. cit. pp. 93–94.
28. Idem, pp. 95–97.
29. Idem, pp. 99, 101; Y. Rabin, op. cit. pp. 51–52; Kurzman, op. cit. p. 181.
30. Slater, op. cit. pp. 103–04, 105; Y. Rabin, op. cit. pp. 59–61.
31. Slater, op. cit. pp. 104–05; Rabin, op. cit. pp. 55–57.
32. Rabin, op. cit. pp. 54, 59; Kurzman, op. cit. p. 182; Michael Bar-Zohar, *Shimon Peres: The Biography* (New York: Random House, 2007) pp. 72–73.
33. There is no evidence that he actually looked at all of these aircraft—they are examples.
34. Slater, op. cit. p. 110; Rabin, op. cit. pp. 64–66; Kurzman, op. cit. pp. 199–200.
35. Y. Rabin, op. cit. pp. 62–64; Kurzman, op. cit. pp. 197–99.
36. Slater, op. cit. pp. 126–27; Y. Rabin, op. cit. pp. 75–76, Rabin lists the date as May 22 for his meeting with BG.
37. Y. Rabin, op. cit. pp. 81–83; L. Rabin, op. cit. pp. 107–08; Kurzman, op. cit. pp. 214–15.
38. Y. Rabin, op. cit. pp. 96–97.
39. Peled became a dove after studying Arabic literature after his release from the IDF. He studied the Palestinian narrative and sympathized with the Palestinians. He founded Shelli in 1977 with the Black Panthers as a peace party that called for negotiations with the PLO. Weizman became a dove after his son was wounded by an Egyptian sniper while serving along the Suez Canal during the War of Attrition. When Sadat came to Jerusalem he became a champion of the peace negotiations as defense minister in the Likud before resigning in March 1980. In 1985 he moved into the Labor Party and in the late 1980s was one of the most dovish members of the Labor Party. Tom Segev, *1967* (New York: Metropolitan Books, 2007) pp. 292–96; Ariel Sharon, *Warrior* (New York: Simon & Schuster, 2001) pp. 183–84.
40. Slater, op. cit. pp. 136, 137–38, 140–41, 144–45; Y. Rabin, op. cit. pp. 104–05, 115–16.
41. Slater, op. cit. p. 145.
42. Kurzman, op. cit. pp. 158–59.
43. Y. Rabin, op. cit. pp. 119–21.
44. Idem, pp. 122–23; Kurzman, op. cit. pp. 234–35.
45. Slater, op. cit. pp. 157–58, 170–72.
46. Idem, pp. 167–69, 173, 177–78; Y. Rabin, op. cit. pp. 148, 164–65.
47. Slater, op. cit. pp. 178–81; Kurzman, op. cit. p. 259.
48. Y. Rabin, op. cit. pp. 186–89; Slater, op. cit. pp. 171, 181–83.
49. Slater, op. cit. pp. 184–85; Y. Rabin, op. cit. pp. 232–33; L. Rabin, op. cit. p. 135.
50. Slater, op. cit. pp. 188–89; Kurzman, op. cit. p. 277.
51. Slater, op. cit. pp. 191, 193; Kurzman, op. cit. pp. 273, 281–82.
52. Slater, op. cit. pp. 197–98; Kurzman, op. cit. pp. 285–86.

Chapter Six

1. Slater, *Rabin*, pp. 204–19; Rabin, pp. 237–41; Dan Kurzman, *Soldier of Peace: The Life of Yitzhak Rabin, 1922-1995* (New York: HarperCollins, 1998) pp. 288–95; Abba Eban, *An Autobiography* (New York: Random House, 1977) pp. 570–73, 578.
2. William B. Quandt, *Peace Process, Revised Ed.* (Berkeley: University of California Press, 2001) pp. 153–54.
3. Slater, op. cit. pp. 230–34; Y. Rabin, op. cit. pp 247–48; Kurzman, op. cit. pp. 304–06; Quandt, op. cit. p. 157.
4. Gerald Ford, *A Time to Heal* (New York: Harper & Row, 1979) pp. 29–30, 33; Andrew D. Cain, *The Ford Presidency: A History* (Jefferson, NC: McFarland, 2009) pp. 31–32, 40; Douglas Brinkley, *Gerald R. Ford* (New York: Times Books, 2007) pp. 62, 65.
5. Henry A. Kissinger, *Years of Renewal* (New York: Simon & Schuster, 1999) pp. 357–64, 368–70, 382–84.
6. Kissinger, op. cit. pp. 357–59; by contrast see most books on the conflict or Middle East political surveys written by Arabist professors.
7. Stephen J. Stedman, *Peacemaking in Civil War: International Mediation in Zimbabwe, 1974-80* (Boulder, CO: Lynne Rienner, 1991) pp. 89–90; Kissinger, op. cit. pp. 382–84; Dean G. Pruitt, "Kissinger as a Traditional Mediator with Power," pp. 139–40 in Jeffrey Z. Rubin, *Dynamics of Third Party Intervention: Kissinger in the Middle East* (New York: Praeger, 1981) and Jeffrey Z. Rubin, "Integration and Commentary," in Rubin, op. cit. pp. 279–81, 284.
8. Quandt, op. cit. p. 161.
9. Ford, op. cit. p. 246; Crain, op. cit. p. 133.
10. Crain, op. cit. p. 135.
11. Idem, pp. 161–63.
12. Slater, op. cit. pp. 243—4; Kurzman, op. cit. pp. 316–17; Kissinger, op. cit. pp. 422–25, 429–30; Quandt, op. cit. p. 165.
13. Quandt, op. cit. p. 166.
14. Idem; Y. Rabin, op. cit. pp. 265–67; Kissinger, op. cit. pp. 439–43, 446.
15. Y. Rabin, op. cit. pp. 267–68; Shimon Peres, *Battling for Peace* (New York: Random House, 1995) p. 142; Kissinger, op. cit. pp. 447–49.

16. Kissinger, op. cit. pp. 449, 452; Quandt, op. cit. p. 168.
17. Quandt, op. cit. p. 168.
18. Kissinger, op. cit. pp. 453–54.
19. Idem, pp. 452–53; Y. Rabin, op. cit. pp. 271–74; Quandt, op. cit. pp. 168–70.
20. Kissinger, op. cit. pp. 903–1016, 1020–38; Y. Rabin, op. cit. pp. 289–90.
21. Y. Rabin, op. cit. pp. 283–89; Peres, op. cit. pp. 152–69; Kurzman, op. cit. pp. 335, 338–39; Slater, op. cit. pp. 251–54; Michael Bar-Zohar, *Shimon Peres: The Biography* (New York: Random House, 2007) pp. 338–39.
22. Slater, *Rabin*, pp. 252–54; Rabin, op. cit. pp. 283–89; Benny Morris, *Righteous Victims* (New York: First Vintage, 2001), p. 384.
23. A good example is the London Agreement that he negotiated with Hussein in London in April 1987 behind the back of Shamir. Another is the start of the Oslo process in early 1993.
24. Matti Golan, *The Secret Conversations of Henry Kissinger* (New York: New York Times Book Co., 1976) pp. 5–31; Kurzman, op. cit. p. 320; Slater, op. cit. p. 266; Y. Rabin, op. cit. p. 308.
25. Slater, op. cit. pp. 264–65. The author was in Israel at the time as a student and still remembers the phrase.
26. Idem, pp. 269–70.
27. Idem, pp. 273–79; Rabin, op. cit. pp. 310–13; Leah Rabin, *Rabin: Our Life, His Legacy* (New York: G P Putnam's Sons, 1997) pp. 169–72.
28. Slater, op. cit. pp. 295–96; Y. Rabin, op. cit. p. 314; Kurzman, op. cit. pp. 343, 362.
29. Slater, op. cit. pp. 280–81.
30. L. Rabin, op. cit. pp. 174–75, 183; Kurzman, op. cit. p. 376.
31. Kurzman, op. cit. p. 390.
32. Bar-Zohar, op. cit. pp. 299–300, 346.
33. Idem, pp. 363–64; Ariel Sharon, *Warrior* (New York: Simon & Schuster, 1981) p. 530; Peres, op. cit. pp. 201–04.
34. Slater, op. cit. pp. 325–26; Avi Shlaim, *The Iron Wall* (New York: WW Norton, 2001) p. 427.
35. David Horovitz, ed. *Shalom, Friend: The Life and Legacy of Yitzhak Rabin* (New York: New Market Press, 1996) pp. 106–07; Kurzman, op. cit. p. 396.
36. Yitzhak Shamir, *Summing Up* (Boston: Little, Brown, 1994) pp. 172–73. This occurred in 1989.
37. Shlaim, op. cit. p. 437.
38. Shlaim, op. cit. p. 433.
39. Kurzman, op. cit. p. 395; Horovitz, op. cit. pp. 108–09.
40. Shlaim, op. cit. p. 434.
41. Idem, pp. 437–38.
42. Idem, pp. 438–39.
43. Slater, op. cit. pp. 327–29; Kurzman, op. cit. pp. 399–400.
44. Bar-Zohar, op. cit. pp. 402–12.
45. Michael Bar-Zohar, *Facing a Cruel Mirror* (New York: Charles Scribner's Sons, 1990) pp. 1–2; Shlaim, op. cit. pp. 450–52.
46. Slater, op. cit. pp. 331–34.
47. Idem, p. 334; Kurzman, op. cit. p. 407.
48. Slater, op. cit. pp. 334–39; Kurzman, op. cit. p. 409; Shlaim, op. cit. pp. 453–54.
49. Shlaim, op. cit. pp. 457–59.
50. Shamir, op. cit. pp. 183–86.

Chapter Seven

1. Slater, *Rabin*, pp. 347–48; Dan Kurzman, *Soldier of Peace: The Life of Yitzhak Rabin, 1922-1995* (New York: HarperCollins, 1998) pp. 414–15.
2. Slater, op. cit. pp. 348–49; Kurzman, op. cit. pp. 415–18; Colin Shindler, *The Land Beyond Promise: Israel, Likud and the Zionist Dream* (New York: I B Tauris, 2002) pp. 249–58; Yitzhak Shamir, *Summing Up* (Boston: Little, Brown, 1994) pp. 203–06; Nir Hefez and Gadi Bloom, *Ariel Sharon* (New York: Random House, 2006) pp. 281–83.
3. Slater, op. cit. pp. 354–55.
4. Idem, pp. 355–57; Kurzman, op. cit. pp. 421–22.
5. Avi Shlaim, *The Iron Wall: Israel and the Arab World* (New York: WW Norton, 2001) pp. 484–93.
6. Slater, op. cit. pp. 372–74.
7. Idem, pp. 375–80; Kurzman, op. cit. pp. 428–29; Shimon Peres, *Battling for Peace* (New York: Random House, 1995) pp. 271–72.
8. Slater, op. cit. pp. 380, 388–89, 400; Kurzman, op. cit. pp. 431–32; Leah Rabin, *Rabin: Our Life, His Legacy* (New York: G P Putnam's Sons, 1997) pp. 207–09.
9. Shindler, op. cit. p. 264 Figure 18.1; Shamir, op. cit. pp. 253–55.
10. Glenn Frankel, *Beyond the Promised Land* (New York: Touchstone, 1996) pp. 315–19.
11. Frankel, op. cit. p. 328; Shindler, op. cit. p. 279; Wikipedia, "Israeli legislative election 1992," accessed Apr 16, 2013 lists three parties of the Right that failed to make the cutoff: Tehiya 1.2 percent; Geulat Israel .5 percent, and Torah VeAretz, the list of Rabbi Levinger .1 percent for a total of 1.8 percent wasted vote among the Right and ultra-Orthodox. See also Ehud Sprinzak, *Brother Against Brother* (New York: The Free Press, 1999) p. 217.
12. Slater, op. cit. pp. 413–14.
13. Idem, pp. 417–18; Kurzman, op. cit. pp. 438–40; Efraim Inbar, *Rabin and Israel's*

National Security (Baltimore: Johns Hopkins University Press, 1999) pp. 137–47.
14. Slater, op. cit. pp. 446–47, 455–59; Samuel Segev, *Crossing the Jordan: Israel's Hard Road to Peace* (New York: St. Martin's Press, 1998) pp. 190–92.
15. Inbar, op. cit. pp. 145–49; Segev, op. cit. pp. 152–53; Slater, op. cit. pp. 431, 443, Kurzman, op. cit. pp. 444, 475; Frankel, op. cit. p. 323.
16. Robert Slater, *Rabin of Israel: Warrior for Peace, 1922-1995* (New York: St. Martin's Press, 1996). All further citations refer to this later edition. Kurzman, op. cit. pp. 444–47; Segev, op. cit. pp. 179–80, 182–83.
17. Slater, op. cit. pp. 575–80; Kurzman, op. cit. pp. 450–55.
18. Shlaim, op. cit. p. 514.
19. Slater, op. cit. pp. 577–79.
20. Idem, pp. 580–81; Segev, op. cit. pp. 212–14.
21. Slater, op. cit. pp. 584–85; Kurzman, op. cit. pp. 463–64.
22. Slater, op. cit. pp. 590–91; Kurzman, op. cit. p. 469; Sprinzak, op. cit. pp. 1–4, 239–43.
23. Slater, op. cit. pp. 591–93; Kurzman, op. cit. pp. 472–73.
24. Shlaim, op. cit. pp. 541–42, 544; Segev, op. cit. pp. 307–08.
25. Slater, op. cit. p. 589; Kurzman, op. cit. pp. 476–77; Michael Bar-Zohar, *Shimon Peres: The Biography* (New York: Random House, 2007) p. 462; L. Rabin, op. cit. pp. 248, 253.
26. Slater, op. cit. pp. 601–02; Bar-Zohar, op. cit. p. 451; David Horovitz, ed. *Shalom, Friend: The Life &Legacy of Yitzhak Rabin* (New York: Newmarkert, 1996) pp. 267–70.
27. Hefez and Bloom, pp. 301–02.
28. Peter Beinart, *The Crisis of Zionism* (New York: Times Books, 2012) pp. 105–07, 115–16; Hefez and Bloom, p. 296. Netanyahu's ties to the Boston Group were made known by reporters during the 2012 presidential campaign.
29. Slater, op. cit. p. 599; Horovitz, op. cit. p. 251. At his funeral he made a very unpresidential address talking about the food and drink they had shared together rather than about his accomplishments.
30. Horovitz, op. cit. pp. 216–17; L. Rabin, op. cit. pp. 273–74; Shlaim, op. cit. p. 527.
31. For an explanation of the concepts see Sprinzak, op. cit. pp. 5, 279–80; Horovitz, op. cit. p. 225.
32. Horovitz, op. cit. pp. 218–21; Sprinzak, op. cit. pp. 276–85.
33. Uri Savir, *The Process* (New York: Random House, 1998) pp. 223–40.
34. Shlaim, op. cit. p. 528; Kurzman, op. cit. p. 498; Horovitz, op. cit. p. 222.

35. Horovitz, op. cit. pp. 226–27.
36. Slater, op. cit. pp. 603–05; Kurzman, op. cit. pp. 506–09.
37. Sprinzak, op. cit. pp. 284–85; Horovitz, op. cit. pp. 229–31, 242–43.
38. A religious Zionist who responds frequently to various liberal Zionist blogs, who goes by the name of Ya'akov Ben-David made this claim of Rabin closing down the Oslo process in a response to the author. Horovitz, op. cit. pp. 266–71,
39. Uri Milstein, *The Rabin File: An Unauthorized Expose* (Tel Aviv: Gefen, 1999); see Kurzman, op. cit. p. 498 on Milstein.
40. Shaul Webber, *Yitzhak Rabin: The Growth of a Leader* (Samuel Wachtman's Sons, 2013).
41. Efraim Inbar, *Rabin and Israel's National Security* (Baltimore: Johns Hopkins University Press, 1999).
42. Sharon's coma also caused a flurry of books, but due to the failure of the disengagement from Gaza to end terrorist attacks his reputation will suffer a major downturn in the near future. There is not even a single biography of Yitzhak Shamir in either English or Hebrew other than his own memoirs. The single third-person biography is in French and concentrates on his careers as an underground operative in the Lehi and Mossad rather than his career as a politician. The last new biography of Golda Meir was published in 2009 and she attracts attention mainly in America because of her youth spent there. Few biographies of Levy Eshkol exist, but Moshe Sharett has attracted attention in recent years because of his dovish positions.

Chapter Eight

1. Ariel Sharon, *Warrior* (New York: Simon & Schuster, 2001) pp. 12–13; Uzi Benziman, *Sharon: An Israeli Caesar* (New York: Adama, 1985) pp. 11–12; Anita Miller, Jordan Miller, & Sigalit Zetouni, *Sharon: Israel's Warrior Politician* (Chicago: Academy Chicago, 2002) p. 3.
2. Ted Schwarz, *Walking with the Damned* (New York: Paragon House, 1992) pp. 90–92.
3. Sharon, op. cit. pp. 15–16, 25, 35–36; Benziman, op. cit. pp. 21–22.
4. Hefez and Bloom, *Ariel Sharon*,pp. 31–32; Sharon, op. cit. pp. 15, 30–31, 34, 36.
5. Sharon, op. cit. pp. 36, 50.
6. Idem, pp. 52–61; Benziman, op. cit. pp. 26–31; Hefez and Bloom, p. 43.
7. Sharon, op. cit. pp. 65–67.
8. Sharon, op. cit. pp. 68–69.
9. Idem, pp. 72–76.
10. Idem, pp. 76–78, 80–81.

11. Idem, pp. 83–86; Benziman, op. cit. pp. 44–46.
12. Sharon, op. cit. pp. 88–91; Benziman, op. cit. pp. 52–55.
13. David Landau, *Arik: The Life of Ariel Sharon* (New York: Alfred Knopf, 2014) pp. 46, 49–50, 52.
14. Sharon, op. cit. pp. 95–96.
15. Idem, pp. 92–95, Benziman, op. cit. pp. 60–62; Hefez and Bloom, p. 62
16. Sharon, op. cit. pp. 119, 144–45. Gur was chief of staff from 1974–1978 before joining the Labor Party and serving as an MK for at least one term. Eitan was chief of staff from 1978 to 1983 and then joined the Tehiya party of Geula Cohen. After serving as an MK for Tehiya from 1984–88, he formed his own faction, Tzomet, which he headed in the Knesset from 1988 to 1996 when he joined the Likud as a faction.
17. Benziman, op. cit. pp. 77–79.
18. Idem, pp. 80–81.
19. Idem, pp. 82–85; Sharon, op. cit. pp. 151, 153.
20. Sharon, op. cit. pp. 156, 158–61; Benziman, op. cit. pp. 86–87.
21. Benziman, op. cit. pp. 88–89.
22. Idem, p. 90. .
23. Idem.
24. Sharon, op. cit. pp. 162–63; Benziman, op. cit. pp. 91–92.
25. Sharon, op. cit. p. 168; Uri Dan, *Ariel Sharon: An Intimate Portrait* (New York: Palgrave Macmillan, 2006) p. 30.
26. Sharon, op. cit. pp. 164–78; Benziman, op. cit. pp. 93–94.
27. Sharon, op. cit. pp. 165–67.
28. Idem, pp. 179–80; Benziman, op. cit. pp. 99–101.
29. Sharon, op. cit. pp. 181, 184–85; Benziman, op. cit. p. 103; Dan, op. cit. pp. 34–35.
30. Sharon, op. cit. pp. 190–94, see diagram p. 197 and map on p. 200 for more details; Benziman, op. cit. pp. 106–07.
31. Gilad Sharon, *Sharon: The Life of a Leader* (New York: HarperCollins, 2011) pp. 125–32 for a good short description of Sharon's role in the 1967 war. Numerous books and articles were written about the war. Air forces tended to study Israel's destruction of the Arab air forces on the first day of the war. The armies concentrated on Israel's conquest of the Sinai where Israeli forces faced modern Soviet equipment. The in-depth studies concentrated on the actions of Sharon's division and Tal's division.
32. Sharon, op. cit. p. 201; Miller et al. op. cit. pp. 74–75.
33. Sharon, op. cit. pp. 214–15.
34. Benziman, op. cit. pp. 108–09; Dan, op. cit. pp. 42–43.
35. Benziman, op. cit. pp. 111–12; Sharon, op. cit. p. 221.
36. Sharon, op. cit. pp. 222–27; Benziman, op. cit. pp. 112–13; Dan, op. cit. pp. 53–55; Hefez and Bloom, p. 120.
37. Sharon, op. cit. pp. 260–62; Benziman, op. cit. pp. 116–17.
38. Benziman, op. cit. pp. 117–18.
39. Sharon, op. cit. pp. 270–71; Hefez and Bloom, p. 133.
40. Sharon, op. cit. pp. 288–93.
41. Idem, pp. 301–05; Benziman, op. cit. pp. 143–47.
42. Sharon, op. cit. pp. 314–33 for Sharon's personal account; Benziman, op. cit. pp. 152–72 for a more objective account.
43. Sharon, op. cit. p. 338. The copyright for the English edition is 1975. I saw a Hebrew edition in the late 1970s while in Israel and assume that it was first published in 1974 and then translated into English, but they could have both been published in the same year. See Amos Perlmutter, *Military and Politics in Israel, 1948-67* (New York: Routledge, 1977) epilogue for the effect of the war on the fortunes of various generals.

Chapter Nine

1. Anita Miller, Jordan Miller & Sigalit Zetouni, *Sharon: Israel's Warrior Politician* (Chicago: Academy Chicago, 2002) p. 97.
2. Uzi Benziman, *Sharon: An Israeli Caeser* (New York: Adama, 1985) pp. 128–33; Ariel Sharon, *Warrior* (New York: Simon & Schuster, 2001) pp. 277–86; Ned Temko, *To Win or To Die* (New York: William Morrow, 1987) p. 185; Amos Perlmutter, *The Life and Times of Menachem Begin* (Garden City, NY: Doubleday, 1987) p. 308.
3. Miller et al. op. cit. pp. 101, 116.
4. Idem, pp. 121–22.
5. Sharon, op. cit. pp. 346–47; Hefez and Bloom, pp. 181–84; Benziman, op. cit. p. 186.
6. Benziman, op. cit. pp. 187–200; Hefez and Bloom, pp. 185–88.
7. These were: Pinchas Lavon, Levy Eshkol, and Dayan. Sharon, op. cit. p. 354; Benziman, op. cit. p. 202.
8. Miller et al. op. cit. pp. 136–38; Hefez and Bloom, pp. 192–93.
9. Benziman, op. cit. p. 212; Sharon, op. cit. pp. 400–01; Hefez and Bloom, pp. 199–200.
10. Benziman, op. cit. pp. 221, 224–25; Miller, op. cit. p. 150.
11. Sharon, op. cit. pp. 382–83; Perlmutter, op. cit. pp. 362–66.
12. Sharon, op. cit. pp. 432–35.
13. Miller et al. op. cit. p. 129; Howard M. Sachar, *A History of Israel from the Rise of Zion-*

ism to Our Time, 2nd Edition (New York: Alfred Knopf, 1996) pp. 902–03.
14. Hefez and Bloom, pp. 212–15; Benziman, op. cit. p. 231.
15. Sachar, op. cit. pp. 903–04.
16. Hefez and Bloom, pp. 216–18; Miller et al. op. cit. p. 162.
17. Miller et al, op. cit. p. 162.
18. Benziman, op. cit. pp. 242–44.
19. Sachar, op. cit. pp. 908–09.
20. Idem, pp. 909–11; Hefez and Bloom, p. 235; Gilad Sharon, *Sharon: The Life of a Leader* (New York: HarperCollins, 2011) p. 275.
21. Sachar, op. cit. pp. 911, 913. The mercenary was Eli Hobeika who defected to the Syrians after the Sabra and Shatila massacre.
22. Sachar, op. cit. p. 914.
23. Idem, pp. 914–15. The author was active in Peace Now when it was first formed until he left the country in August 1980.
24. Sachar, op. cit. p. 915; Sharon, op. cit. p. 509.
25. Idem, pp. 916–18.
26. Hefez and Bloom, pp. 246–51; Sharon, op. cit. p. 522; Avner Falk, *Fratricide in the Holy Land* (Madison: University of Wisconsin Press, 2004) pp. 65–66.
27. Temko, op. cit. pp. 288–92.
28. Benziman, op. cit. pp. 256–57, 260–61; Sachar, op. cit. p. 912; Miller et al. op. cit. pp. 165–66; Arthur Hertzberg, *Jewish Polemics* (New York: Columbia University Press, 1992) pp. 128–31. Examples of movies are *Lebanon* (2009) and *Waltzing with Bashir* (2008).
29. Sharon, op. cit. p. 530; Hefez and Bloom, pp. 258–59.
30. Uri Dan, *Ariel Sharon: An Intimate Portrait* (New York: Palgrave Macmillan, 2006) pp. 124–25.Miller et al. op. cit. pp. 174–77.
31. Colin Shindler, *The Land Beyond Promise: Israel, Likud and the Zionist Dream* (New York: I.B. Tauris, 2001) p. 208; Hefez and Bloom, pp. 262–63.
32. Moshe Maoz, *Asad: The Sphinx of Damascus* (New York: Grove Weidenfeld, 1988) p. 168.
33. Hefez and Bloom, pp. 263, 275.
34. Idem. pp. 264, 267
35. Idem; Dan, op. cit. p. 77.
36. Hefez and Bloom, pp. 278–79.
37. Hefez and Bloom, pp. 290–91; G Sharon, op. cit. p. 303.
38. Hefez and Bloom, pp. 301–02.
39. Idem, pp. 304–06, 309; Dan, op. cit. pp. 135–37.
40. Hefez and Bloom, pp. 317–18.
41. G Sharon, op. cit. pp. 310–11.
42. Hefez and Bloom, pp. 324–27.

Chapter Ten

1. Freddy Eytan, *Ariel Sharon* (Paris: Studio 9, 2006) pp. 98–100; Hefez and Bloom, p. 327.
2. Anita Miller, Jordan Miller & Sigalit Zetouni, *Sharon: Israel's Warrior-Politician* (Chicago: Academy Chicago, 2002) pp. 241–44, 247–49.
3. Idem, pp. 257–58.
4. Hefez and Bloom, pp. 332–33.
5. Gilad Sharon, *Sharon: The Life of a Leader* (New York: HarperCollins, 2011) pp. 340–43.
6. Hefez and Bloom, p. 341.
7. Ahron Bregman, *Elusive Peace: How the Holy Land Defeated America* (New York: Penguin, 2005) pp. 123–24, 125.
8. Bernard Wasserstein, *Divided Jerusalem* (London: Profile Books, 2002) p. 318.
9. Charles Enderlin, *Shattered Dreams: The Failure of the Peace Process in the Middle East, 1995–2002* (New York: Other Press, 2003) p. 303.
10. Hefez and Bloom, pp. 344–46; Miller et al. op. cit. pp. 300–02; G Sharon, op. cit. p. 346; Dennis Ross, *The Missing Peace* (New York: Farrar, Straus and Giroux, 2004) p. 728.
11. Hefez and Bloom, pp. 348–49.
12. Idem, pp. 350–55.
13. Miller et al. op. cit. pp. 357, 363–64; Hefez and Bloom, p. 358.
14. Mark Matthews, *Lost Years: Bush, Sharon and Failure in the Middle East* (New York: Nation Books, 2007) pp. 11–14, 18–23, 24–25; Hefez and Bloom, op. cit. pp. 360–61.
15. Eytan, op. cit. pp. 112–14; Hefez and Bloom, pp. 366–69.
16. Hefez and Bloom, p. 371.
17. Uri Dan, *Ariel Sharon: An Intimate Portrait* (New York: Palgrave Macmillan, 2006) pp. 209–11.
18. Eytan, op. cit. p. 115; Hefez and Bloom, pp. 374–77; Dan, op. cit. pp. 203–04; G. Sharon, op. cit. p. 474.
19. Hefez and Bloom, pp. 392–4.
20. Idem, pp. 413–15.
21. Colin Shindler, *A History of Modern Israel* (New York: Cambridge University Press, 2008) pp. 326–32; Bernard Reich, *A Brief History of Israel* (New York: Checkmark Books, 2005) pp. 235–37.
22. On the Road Map see Aaron D. Miller, *The Much Too Promised Land* (New York: Bantam, 2008) pp. 73–74, 350–53; William B. Quandt, *Peace Process, Third Edition* (Washington: The Brookings Institution, 2005) Chapter 13, pp. 385–414; Hefez and Bloom, pp. 351–58; Eytan, op. cit. pp. 135–43; G. Sharon, op. cit. p. 563.

23. Dan, op. cit. pp. 206-08, 246-47.
24. The author saw so many parallels between the two leaders that he wrote a double biography of the two leaders. He later decided not to get it published, but there was enough material for the biography. Sharon founded three political parties; Jackson was the main founder of the Democratic Party in the late 1820s along with Martin Van Buren. Jackson fought Indians around Nashville as a young attorney and militia member in the late 1780s. He later fought them in a second round during the Creek War of 1813-14, within the War of 1812. The third round was the First Seminole War of 1818. The fourth and final round was the Indian removal of the 1830s, which led to the Black Hawk War of 1832 when he was president and the Second Seminole War of 1835-42. Both started their military careers while teenagers.
25. Hefez and Bloom, pp. 425, 430.
26. The author wrote his doctoral dissertation partially on the Indaba.
27. Charles Enderlin, *The Lost Years: Radical Islam, Intifada, and Wars in the Middle East 2001-2006* (New York: Other Press, 2007) pp 152-53.
28. Dan, op. cit. p. 216.
29. For a summary of the various affairs see Hefez and Bloom, pp. 400-12; Eytan, op. cit. pp. 124-31.
30. G. Sharon, op. cit. pp. 542-43.
31. Hefez and Bloom, pp. 435, 438-40; Eytan, op. cit. p. 158.
32. Hefez and Bloom, pp. 441, 443; G. Sharon, op. cit. pp. 556-57.
33. G. Sharon, op. cit. p. 551.
34. Hefez and Bloom, pp. 446, 449-50.
35. Idem, pp. 451, 453.
36. Idem, pp. 457, 459-61.
37. Eating shellfish is against Jewish dietary law. Idem, pp. 461-62; Eytan, op. cit. p. 163.
38. Hefez and Bloom, p. 463; Sylvain Cypel, *Walled: Israeli Society at an Impasse* (New York: Other Press, 2005) pp. 450-53; Charles Enderlin, *The Lost Years: 2001-2006* (New York: Other Press, 2007) p. 266; Mark Matthews, *Lost Years: Bush, Sharon and Failure in the Middle East* (New York: Nation Books, 2007) p. 388.
39. Hefez and Bloom, pp. 463-64.
40. Idem, pp. 466-67; Enderlin, op. cit. pp. 263-65.
41. Enderlin, op. cit. p. 264.
42. Hefez and Bloom, p. 469. Ramon's reward was to be appointed minister of justice in the new Kadima government in April 2006.
43. Idem, pp. 471-72.
44. Idem, pp. 472-73; Dan, op. cit. pp. 275-76.
45. Hefez and Bloom, pp. 474, 476.
46. Idem, pp. 478, 481-82; Eytan, op. cit. pp. 218, 234-35. Sharon was 77—nearly 78, when he had the stroke. Only a handful of politicians in Israel have had political careers beyond age 80 among them Ben-Gurion and Peres. Sharon was probably severely cognitively impaired as a result of the stroke if not brain dead. Voters will not take a chance on a leader who had been in a coma for years before recovering. And now the party that he created barely exists anymore.
47. Hefez and Bloom, p. 485; Livni founded her own party, which won six seats.
48. Karl Vick, "Ariel Sharon: Israel's Soldier and Strongman, 1928-2014," *Time* Jan. 11, 2014.

Chapter Eleven

1. "Ehud Barak," and "Mishmar haSharon," *Wikipedia* accessed June 1, 2013; and "Yisrael Mendel Brog," *Geni* (www.geni.com) accessed June 1, 2013; Ben Kaspit and Ilan Kfir, *Ehud Barak: Soldier No. 1* (Israel: Alfa Communications, 1998) [Hebrew] pp. 14-15, 19-22, 25. The kibbutz is not listed in the index of Benny Morris's book *1948* and was in the area that was not conquered by the Arab invasion, but it would have been subject to Palestinian ambushes of vehicles moving along the roads to it during the first few months of the civil war phase of the war.
2. Kaspit and Kfir, op. cit. pp. 25-26; "Former Prime Minister Ehud Barak," *ynet news* accessed June 1, 2013.
3. Kaspit and Kfir, op. cit. pp. 33-34.
4. Idem, p. 39.
5. "Sayeret Matkal," *Wikipedia* accessed June 1, 2013; Glenn Frankel, *Beyond the Promised Land* (New York: Touchstone/Simon & Schuster, 1996) p. 335.
6. Ben Kaspit and Ilan Kfir, *Netanyahu: The Road to Power* (Secaucus, NJ: Carol, 1998) p. 65; Kaspit and Kfir, Barak, op. cit. p. 52.
7. Kaspit and Kfir, Barak, op. cit. p. 61.
8. Idem, pp. 72-74.
9. "Sabena Flight 571," and "Black September," *Wikipedia*, accessed June 1, 2013; Caspit and Kfir, *Netanyahu*, pp. 61-65.
10. The sources for my account are: Simon Reeves, *One Day in September* (New York: Arcade Publishing, 2000) pp. 179-82; Aaron J. Klein, *Striking Back* (New York: Random House, 2005) pp. 157-70; and Michael Bar-Zohar and Eitan Haber, *The Quest for the Red Prince* (New York: William Morrow, 1983) pp. 168-77.
11. Klein, op. cit. pp. 158-59; Bar-Zohar and Haber, op. cit. p. 170.
12. Klein, op. cit. pp. 160-61.

13. Bar-Zohar and Haber, op. cit. p. 168.
14. Reeves, op. cit. pp. 179–80; Klein, op. cit. p. 165; Bar-Zohar and Haber, op. cit. pp. 172–73.
15. Klein, op. cit. p. 166; Bar-Zohar and Haber, op. cit. p. 175.
16. Reeves, op. cit. p. 182; Klein, op. cit. p. 168; Bar-Zohar and Haber, op. cit. p. 177.
17. Klein, op. cit. p. 169; "Ehud Barak," and "George Jonas," *Wikipedia* accessed June 1, 2013. The scene of Barak in Beirut from the movie *Munich* was not in the book by Jonas or in *Sword of Gideon*. Apparently Spielberg inserted it either to make the film more up to date or in tribute to Barak or both.
18. Kaspit and Kfir, Netanyahu, pp. 68, 79.
19. Kaspit and Kfir, Barak, pp. 132–35.
20. Idem, pp. 136–43.
21. Idem, pp. 145–46.
22. The following account of the Entebbe rescue is based on Iddo Netanyahu, *Yoni's Last Battle* (New York: Gefen, 2002) pp. 24–119, 213–16.
23. Netanyahu, op. cit. pp. 27–31.
24. Idem, pp. 40, 44, 57, 87, 98, 100.
25. Idem, pp. 52, 71, 82–83. Mofaz was chief of staff when Barak was prime minister and Vilnai was one of the Labor MKs who followed Barak into his breakaway Atzmaut (Independence) Party.
26. Kaspit and Kfir, Barak, pp. 168–69.
27. Kaspit and Kfir, Barak, pp. 174–75.
28. Idem, p. 176.
29. Idem, pp. 191, 225.
30. Kaspit and Kfir, Barak, pp. 226–29.
31. Frankel, op. cit. pp. 334–35.
32. "Ehud Barak," *Jewish Virtual Library* at jewishvirtuallibrary.org/jsource/biography/barak/html accessed June 4, 2013 and "Ehud Barak," *Wikipedia* accessed June 4, 2013.
33. Kaspit and Kfir, Barak, p. 308.
34. Raviv Drucker, *Harakiri* (Tel Aviv: Yediot Ahranot Books, 2002) pp. 100–01; Yossi Beilin, *Touching Peace: From the Oslo Accord to a Final Agreement* (London: Weidenfeld and Nicolson, 1999) p. 124.
35. Kaspit and Kfir, Barak, pp 341, 349.
36. Idem, 342–47.
37. Idem, pp. 349–50.
38. Idem, pp. 351–53.
39. Idem, pp. 353–54.
40. Idem, pp. 355–56.
41. Idem, pp. 357, 359–60.
42. Idem, pp. 364–65.
43. Idem, pp. 368–69.
44. "Ehud Barak," *Jewish Virtual Library* accessed June, 4, 2013.
45. Kaspit and Kfir, Barak, pp. 371–75.
46. Dennis Ross, *The Missing Peace: The Inside Story of the Fight for Middle East Peace* (New York: Farrar, Straus and Giroux, 2004) pp. 491–93; "One Israel," *Wikipedia* accessed June 4, 2013. See also Stanely B. Greenberg, *Dispatches from the War Room: In the Trenches with Five Extraordinary Leaders* (New York: Thomas Dunne, 2009) pp. 269–347. The second time for Peres was in November 2005. He was reappointed party leader after Mitzna's defeat in the 2003 election.
47. Greenberg, op. cit. pp. 270–74, 464 note 2.
48. Avi Shlaim, *The Iron Wall: Israel and the Arab World* (New York: WW Norton, 2001) p. 606; Bernard Reich, *A Brief History of Israel* (New York: Checkmark, 2005) p. 193.
49. This is what happened in March 1990 when the Rabin-Shamir plan came into trouble in the Likud.
50. Greenberg, op. cit. pp. 292–93, 295, 298, 300, 306, 309; "Israeli general election, 1999," *Wikipedia* accessed June 5. 2013; Shlaim, op. cit. p. 607; Reich, op. cit. p. 193.
51. Kaspit and Kfir, Barak, p. 380.

Chapter Twelve

1. William B. Quandt, *Peace Process, Revised Edition* (Berkeley: University of California Press, 2001) p. 358; Itamar Rabinovich, *Waging Peace* (Princeton: Princeton University Press, 2004) pp. 125–26.
2. Rabinovich, op. cit. pp. 126–27; Shlomo Ben-Ami, *Scars of War, Wounds of Peace* (New York: Oxford University Press, 2006) p. 242.
3. Barry Rubin, *The Truth About Syria* (New York: Palgrave Macmillan, 2007) pp. 28, 31.
4. Saladin is a hero to many modern Arabs since the rise of Zionism in the mid-1930s, but few mention to foreigners that he was a Kurd and not an Arab. It is telling that Saladin like Assad was not a Sunni Arab.
5. Rubin, op. cit. pp. 87–96; Rabinovich, op. cit. pp. 20–21.
6. Netanyahu, p. 100.
7. Rabinovich, op. cit. pp. 60–61, 76–77.
8. Clayton E. Swisher, *The Truth About Camp David* (New York: Nation Books, 2004) pp. 67–68; Martin Indyk, *Innocent Abroad* (New York: Simon & Schuster, 2009) pp. 23, 25; Ahron Bregman, *Elusive Peace: How the Holy Land Defeated America* (New York: Penguin, 2005) p. 27; Quandt, op. cit. p. 359.
9. Bregman, op. cit. pp. 23–26.; Swisher, op. cit. pp. 82–84.
10. Rubin, pp. 6, 34; Swisher, op. cit. p. 62; Dennis Ross, The Missing Peace: *The Inside Story of the Fight for Middle East Peace* (New York: Farrar, Straus and Giroux, 2004) pp. 571, 573; Stanley B. Greenberg, *Dispatches from the*

War Room: In the Trenches with Five Extraordinary Leaders (New York: Thomas Dunne, 2009) p. 326.
  11. Raviv Drucker, *Harakiri* (Tel Aviv: Yediot Ahronot Books, 2002) [Hebrew] pp. 75–83.
  12. Swisher, op. cit. pp. 78–80.
  13. Bregman, op. cit. pp. 39, 48–49, 53, 116 photo #1; Drucker, op. cit. p. 89.
  14. Drucker, op. cit. pp. 84–85, 88, 90.
  15. Bregman, pp. 49, 54; Ross, op. cit. p. 566 footnote; Drucker, op. cit. p. 96 .
  16. Rabinovich, op. cit. p. 136.
  17. Bregman, op. cit. p. 54; Swisher, op. cit. pp. 91–92; Ross, op. cit. pp. 573–75.
  18. Ross, op. cit. pp. 579–81; Drucker, op. cit. p. 104.
  19. Drucker, op. cit. pp. 88, 104–05. The most popular slogan was "A secure future for the children of Israel." The most popular for a no campaign was "Vote No. We will never compromise on the security of Israel."
  20. Idem, pp. 583–87; Swisher, op. cit. pp. 98–101; Drucker, op. cit. p.106.
  21. Ross, op. cit. pp. 588–90; Rabinovich, op. cit. pp. 139–40; Indyk, op. cit. p. 278.
  22. Indyk, op. cit. pp. 246–47; Ross, op. cit. pp. 511–13.
  23. Indyk, op. cit. pp. 242, 250, 271; Ross, op. cit. p. 587.
  24. Rubin, op. cit. pp. 106–07, 117, 180. Rubin's failure to note that a land swap was involved is intellectually dishonest, although he might be right about Assad's cynical use of the peace process.
  25. Madeleine Albright, *Madame Secretary* (New York: Miramax, 2003) pp. 476–77.
  26. Swisher, op. cit. p. 127.
  27. Idem, pp. 111, 115, 122–23.
  28. Idem, pp. 128–29.
  29. Drucker, op. cit. p. 108.
  30. Bregman, op. cit. pp. 15–16; Ross, op. cit. pp. 503–05.
  31. Bregman, op. cit. pp. 16–17.
  32. Idem, p. 50.
  33. Idem, pp. 64–69.
  34. Idem, p. 69.
  35. Idem, pp. 76–77.
  36. Drucker, op. cit. p. 296.
  37. Idem, p. 17; Ross, op. cit. p. 508.
  38. Swisher, op. cit. pp. 234–35.
  39. Idem, p. 242; Bregman, op. cit. pp. 83–84; Ross, op. cit. pp. 628–31.
  40. Ross, op. cit. pp. 650–711; Swisher, op. cit. pp. 250–334 on the summit, pp. 357, 373–74, on the blame game.
  41. Stanley B. Greenberg, op. cit. p. 330.
  42. From the 7th century to the 20th century, Arab or Muslim control over al-Haram al-Sharif was only lacking during the 12th century when the Crusaders controled it. Then Saladin reconquered Jerusalem in 1187. Muslims gave control to the Crusaders of Jerusalem during part of the 12th century under a peace treaty.
  43. Ross, op. cit. pp. 694–66; Swisher, op. cit. pp. 305–06.
  44. Rabinovich, op. cit. pp. 152–53; Swisher, op. cit. p. 306; see Omar M. Dajani, "Surviving Opportunities: Palestinian Negotiating Patterns in Peace Talks with Israel," pp. 39–80 in Tamara C. Wittes, *How Israelis and Palestinians Negotiate* (Washington, D.C.: U.S. Institute of Peace, 2005) for details explaining Palestinian behavior at Camp David.
  45. Hirsh Goodman, *Let Me Create a Paradise, God Said to Himself* (New York: Public Affairs, 2005) p. 254.
  46. Idem, pp. 254–55; Ben-Ami, op. cit. pp. 281–82.
  47. Ross, op. cit. pp. 753–55; Bregman, op. cit. pp. 145–46.

Chapter Thirteen

  1. Raviv Drucker, *Harakiri* (Tel Aviv: Yediot Ahranot Books, 2002) [Hebrew] p. 302; Shlomo Ben-Ami, *Scars of War, Wounds of Peace* (New York: Oxford University Press, 2006) p. 270.
  2. Drucker, op. cit. pp. 304–05.
  3. Idem, p. 305.
  4. Ibid., p. 294.
  5. Idem, pp. 295–96.
  6. Ibid., p. 309.
  7. Idem, p. 310.
  8. Idem, pp. 310–11.
  9. Charles Enderlin, *The Lost Years: Radical Islam, Intifada, and Wars in the Middle East 2001–2006* (New York: Other Press, 2007) pp. 2–3, 5.
  10. For two works that support this view of Arafat as the initiator of the AAI see Yossef Bodansky, *The High Cost of Peace* (Roseville, CA: Prima, 2002) and Efraim Karsh, *Arafat's War* (New York: Grove Press, 2003). I used these two to write the section on the Al-Aksa Intifada in my previous book, *When Peace Fails" Lessons From Belfast for the Middle East* (Jefferson, NC: McFarland, 2010) but I'm no longer sure. I'm agnostic about Arafat's role in initiating the Intifada.
  11. Idem, pp. 307–08. The term is *medinut hahavlaga* and described the Hagana's policy of not using counter-terrorism against the Arabs as the Irgun Zvai Leumi did in 1937–39 and from 1947–48 along with the Lohemei Herut Israel.
  12. Enderlin, op. cit. pp. 7,9.
  13. Ben-Ami, op. cit. pp. 273–76; for the mythical version see Yossi Beilin, *The Path to*

Geneva: The Quest for a Permanent Agreement 1996-2004 (New York: RDV, 2004) pp. 227-30. American Ambassador Martin Indyk agreed with Ben-Ami's version. See Martin Indyk, *Innocent Abroad* (New York: Simon & Schuster, 2009) p. 372.

14. "Ehud Barak," and "Electronic Data Services," *Wikipedia* accessed May 30, 2013.

15. "Ehud Barak," and "Amir Peretz," *Wikipedia* accessed May 30, 2013. Shimon Peres and Moshe Arens of the Likud were the two technocrats who served in the office after 1967. All others were former generals.

16. "Gaza War," *Wikipedia* accessed May 30, 2013.

17. Ken Ellingwood, "Barak wins Labor contest, gets new chance at power," *Los Angeles Times* June 13, 2007.

18. Condoleeza Rice, *No Higher Honor* (New York: Crown, 2011) p. 656; "Ehud Olmert," *Wikipedia* accessed May 30, 2013.

19. Eilliott Abrams, *Tested By Zion* (New York: Cambridge University Press, 2013) pp. 244, 263, 266-67, 270.

20. "Iron Dome," *Wikipedia* accessed Sep. 7, 2013.

21. "Gaza War," *Wikipedia* accessed May 30, 2013; Hanan Greenburg, "240 targets attacked in IDF operation," *Y Net* Dec. 28, 2008 accessed Sep. 7, 2013; Ali Waked, "95 more bodies uncovered in Gaza," *Y Net* Jan. 18, 2009 accessed Sep. 7, 2013. Waked gives a figure of 1,300 Palestinian dead and 5400 injured.

22. This is based upon a reading of *Ha'Aretz* by the author at the time.

23. Ben Kaspit and Ilan Kfir, *Netanyahu: The Road to Power* (Secaucus, New Jersey: Carol, 1998) pp. 60-61, 74, 271.

24. "Mavi Marmara," *Wikipedia* accessed May 30, 2013; Jonathan Schanzer, "The Terror Finance Flotilla," *The Weekly Standard* May 31, 2010 2: 10 p.m.

25. Jonathan Lis, "Ehud Barak quits Labor to form 'centrist, Zionist and democratic' party," *Ha'Aretz* Jan. 17, 2011.

26. 69 percent.

27. Lis, op. cit.

28. Since Israeli independence prime ministers have come from only four parties: Mapai, the Labor Party, the Likud, and Kadima. Whoever heads the coalition becomes prime minister and Kadima is just about eliminated and Labor is too weak to organize a coalition probably for another decade, by which time Barak will be over 80.

Chapter Fourteen

1. Avner Falk, *Fratacide in the Holy Land: A Pyschoanalyst's View of the Arab-Israeli Conflict* (Madison: University of Wisconsin Press, 2004) pp. 36-72. See especially pp. 37-37, 40-41, 47-48, 59, 70-71,

2. He then refers readers to his book in Hebrew on Dayan: *Dayan haIsh ve ha'Aggadah* (Tel Aviv: Ma'ariv Library, 1985) [Hebrew] for his diagnosis of Dayan. See also Falk, "Moshe Dayan: Narcissism in Politics," *The Jerusalem Quarterly,* 30, 1984, pp. 113-24; and Falk, "Moshe Dayan: The infantile roots of political action," *The Journal of Psychohistory,* 11, 1983, pp. 271-88.

3. Falk, Fraticide, op. cit. p. 184. He refers to Barak and Arafat as "two narcissistic and stubborn leaders" as revealed by the pushing incident at Camp David. See Fraticide, pp. 73-86 for a full diagnosis of Arafat. No further diagnosis of Barak is provided in the book.

4. On Barak's divorce and remarriage see "Ehud Barak," *Wikipedia* accessed June 7, 2013.

5. Falk, "Narcissism in Politics," op. cit.

6. Falk, "Narcissism in Politics," op. cit. Here he quotes from Irvine Schiller, *Charisma* (Toronto: University of Toronto Press, 1984).

7. Peres also left his party twice. He joined Rafi at Ben-Gurion's urging in 1965 and then forty years later he left Labor to join Kadima at Sharon's urging. Peres's motivation is this latter case seems to have been a desire to be elected president after having lost to the Likud candidate in July 2000.

8. I'm thinking mainly of Dayan and Yitzhak Mordechai here.

9. In 2013 it was reduced to two seats in the Knesset.

10. Yehoshaphat Harkabi, *Arab Stratagies and Israel's Response* (London: Pan, 1999), this is probably a reissue of thefirst edition.

11. Avi Shlaim, *The Iron Wall: Israel and the Arab World* (New York: WW Norton, 2001) p. 608.

12. Patrick Tyler, *Fortress Israel: The Inside Story of the Military Elite Who Run the Country and Why They Cannot Make Peace* (New York: Farrar, Straus and Giroux, 2012). See the preface for his argument.

13. Shelli, the Labor Party, the Democratic Movement for Change, the Likud, and Shlomzion.

14. This discussion is based both upon the author's memory of the book, which he owned in the late 1970s and on a reader review on the Amazon page for the book.

15. There were 31 years between the end of the War of 1812 in January 1815 and the start of the Mexican War in 1846 and then thirteen years between the end of the Mexican War in February 1848 and the start of the Civil War in April 1861. But then 33 years between the end of the Civil War in May 1865 and the Spanish-

American War in April 1898. That is an average of 25.6 years between wars. For South Africa there were twelve years between the end of the Second Anglo-Boer War in May 1902 and the start of World War I in August 1914, and then twenty-one years between the end of World War I in November 1918 and the start of World War II in September 1939. This averages to one every fifteen years on average. Israel by contrast has experienced major wars in 1948, 1956, 1967, 1969–70, 1973, 1982, 1987–90, 2000–04. These are gaps of 8, 10.5, 2, 3, 9, 5, and 10 years. This comes out to about 7.5 years between major wars on average.

Appendix

1. For more on this subject and the basis for this chapter see Thomas G. Mitchell, *Indian Fighters Turned American Politicians* (Westwood, CT: Praeger, 2003).

2. It might be argued that William McKinley who rose to the rank of major in the Civil War and Theodore Roosevelt, who was a volunteer lieutenant colonel in the Spanish-American War were extensions of this trend, but I end it with the end of the class of general-officer politicians.

3. There are different dates given for the War of Attrition. The narrowest is from March 1969 until August 1970 and the most expansive is from the aftermath of June 1967 to August 1970. The anti-fedayeen portion was primarily in 1967–68.

4. For Malan's own story see Magnus Malan, *My Life in the SA Defence Force* (Pretoria: Protea Book House, 2006).

5. "Afrikaner Volksfront," *Wikipedia* accessed Dec. 1, 2013.

6. I want to make clear that I'm not advocating a one-state solution.

7. In antebellum America from 1828 to 1860 there were three parties, with the third party only being viable at the state and local levels for most of this period, and only in the North. In the Union of South Africa there were initially four parties that by 1920 had been reduced to three.

8. There were expeditions to Cuba in 1849 and 1850, with the latter resulting in the members all being killed or imprisoned at hard labor. William Walker undertook an expedition to northern Mexico from California in 1853, and then the following year invaded Nicaragua. Walker was fighting in Nicaragua from 1854 to 1856 before being driven out. He twice tried to return in 1858 and 1860. The last time he was captured and executed by a Honduran firing squad. See Robert E. May, *Manifest Destiny's Underworld: Filibustering in Antebellum America* (Raleigh: University of North Carolina Press, 2004).

9. South Africans were in Katanga in 1961 and in the eastern Congo from 1964 to 1967 under the command of Michael Hoare, Alistaire Wickes and Jeremy Puren in V Commando. Individual South Africans served in the Rhodesian military throughout the bush war of the 1970s. And a mercenary company contracted for the services of veterans of the Namibian border war for Angola and Sierra Leone in the 1990s.

10. South Africa under white rule excluded first most blacks and then all Africans from voting from 1910 until 1994, but it was democratic within the white polity in that the government had to answer to a white electorate in free elections—it has been classified as a *herren volk democracy* or master-race democracy.

11. Franco's younger brother Ramon was elected to the Spanish parliament and even served briefly as a minister of aviation in the Second Republic of 1931–36 but this was more due to his breaking a number of international aviation records than for his fame as a combat pilot in Morocco. He was killed in combat during the civil war fighting on the nationalist side.

12. Richard Griffiths, *Petain: A Biography of Marshal Philippe Petain* (Garden City, NY: Doubleday, 1972); Charles Williams, *The Last Great Frenchman: A Life of Charles de Gaulle* (New York: J. Wiley & Sons, 1993).

13. Ian Kershaw, *Hitler, 1889–1936: Hubris* (New York: W W Norton, 1999); Anthony Read, *The Devil's Disciples: Hitler's Inner Circle* (New York: WW Norton, 2003) pp. 94–100, 123, 256–58, 371.

14. The threat remained in Texas until 1875 and in southern Florida until 1858, but the threat in Florida was relatively minor.

15. For the military and political backgrounds of these individuals and an explanation of the phenomenon see James M. Perry, *Touched with Fire: Five Presidents and the Civil War Battles that Made Them* (New York: Public Affairs, 2003) and Charles W. Calhoun, *From Bloody Shirt to Full Dinner Pail: The Transformation of Politics and Governance in the Gilded Age* (New York: Hill and Wang, 2010).

16. The five so-called Civil War presidents were: Ulysses S. Grant, Rutherford B. Hayes, James Garrison, Chester A. Arthur, and Benjamin Harrison. Arthur was Garrison's vice president and replaced him following his assassination in 1881.

17. Two of the three, Jan Smuts and James Barry Munnik Hertzog, began their political careers as European-trained lawyers serving as attorneys general in the two Boer republics

shortly before the outbreak of the Second Anglo-Boer War in 1899. The third, Louis Botha, was a prominent rancher and cattle breeder.

18. For Malan's story see Magus Malan, *My Life in the SA Defence Force* (Pretoria: Protea, 2006).

19. For more details see Thomas G. Mitchell, *Indian Fighters Turned American Politicians* (Westport, CT: Praeger, 2003).

Bibliography

Abrams, Elliott. *Tested by Zion.* New York: Cambridge University Press, 2013.

Bar-On, Mordechai. *The Gates of Gaza.* New York: St. Martin's Press, 1994.

———. *Moshe Dayan: Israel's Controversial Hero.* New Haven: Yale University Press, 2012.

Bar-Zohar, Michael. *Facing a Cruel Mirror.* New York: Charles Scribner's Sons, 1990.

———. *Shimon Peres: The Biography.* New York: Random House, 2007.

Bar-Zohar, Michael, and Eitan Haber. *The Quest for the Red Prince.* New York: William Morrow, 1983.

Beinart, Peter. *The Crisis of Zionism.* New York: Times Books, 2012.

Ben-Ami, Shlomo. *Scars of War, Wounds of Peace.* New York: Oxford University Press, 2006.

Benedikt, Linda. *Yitzhak Rabin: The Battle for Peace.* London: Haus Books, 2005.

Benziman, Uzi. *Sharon: An Israeli Caesar.* New York: Adama Books, 1985.

Bregman, Ahron. *Elusive Peace: How the Holy Land Defeated America.* New York: Penguin, 2005.

Caspit, Ben, and Ilan Kfir. *Ehud Barak: No. 1 Soldier* [Hebrew]. Israel: Alpha Communications, 1998.

———, and ———. *Netanyahu: The Road to Power.* Secaucus, NJ: Carol, 1998.

Creveld, Martin van. *Moshe Dayan.* London: Weidenfeld & Nicolson, 2004.

Dan, Uri. *Ariel Sharon: An Intimate Portrait.* New York: Palgrave Macmillan, 2006.

Dayan, Moshe. *Breakthrough.* New York: Alfred Knopf, 1981.

———. *Story of My Life.* New York: Da Capo Press, 1992.

Dayan, Yael. *My Father, His Daughter.* New York: Farrar, Straus & Giroux, 1985.

Drucker, Raviv. *Harakiri* [Hebrew]. Tel Aviv: Yediot Aharanot Books, 2002.

Enderlin, Charles. *The Lost Years: Radical Islam, Intifada, and Wars in the Middle East 2001–2006.* New York: Other Press, 2006.

Eytan, Freddy. *Ariel Sharon: A life in times of turmoil.* Paris: Studio 9, 2006.

Falk, Avner. "Moshe Dayan: Narcissism in Politics," *The Jerusalem Quarterly 1984.*

———. *Fraticide in the Holy Land.* Madison: University of Wisconsin Press, 2004.

Frankel, Glenn. *Beyond the Promised Land.* New York: Touchstone, 1996.

Harkabi, Yehoshafat. *Arab Strategies and Israel's Response.* London: Pan, 1999.

Hefez, Nir, and Gadi Bloom. *Ariel Sharon: A Life.* New York: Random House, 2006.

Horovitz, David, ed. *Shalom, Friend: The Life and Legacy of Yitzhak Rabin.* New York: Newmarket Press, 1996.

Inbar, Efraim. *Rabin and Israel's National Security.* Baltimore: Johns Hopkins University Press, 1999.

Kimmerling, Baruch. *Politicide.* New York: Verso, 2006.

Kissinger, Henry. *Years of Renewal.* New York: Simon & Schuster, 1999.

———. *Years of Upheaval.* Boston: Little, Brown, 1982.

Klein, Aaron J. *Striking Back.* New York: Random House, 2005.

Kurzman, Dan. *Soldier of Peace: The Life of*

Yitzhak Rabin, 1922–1995. New York: HarperCollins, 1998.

Landau, David. *Arik: The Life of Ariel Sharon.* New York: Alfred Knopf, 2014.

Matthews, Mark. *Lost Years: Bush, Sharon and Failure in the Middle East.* New York: Nation Books, 2007.

Miller, Anita, Jordan Miller and Sigalit Zetouni. *Sharon: Israel's Warrior Politician.* Chicago: Academy Chicago, 2002.

Neff, Donald. *Warriors at Suez.* New York: Simon & Schuster, 1981.

Netanyahu, Iddo. *Yoni's Last Battle.* New York: Gefen, 2002.

Nichols, David A. *Eisenhower 1956.* New York: Simon & Schuster, 2011.

Peri, Yoram. *Between Battles and Ballots.* New York: Cambridge University Press, 1983.

_____. *Generals in the Cabinet Room.* Washington: U.S. Institute of Peace Press, 2006.

Perlmutter, Amos. *The Life and Times of Menachem Begin.* Garden City, NY: Doubleday & Co., 1987.

Rabin, Leah. *Rabin: Our Life, His Legacy.* New York: G. P. Putnam's Sons, 1997.

Rabin, Yitzhak. *The Rabin Memoirs.* Berkeley: University of California Press, 1996.

Rabinovich, Itamar. *Waging Peace.* Princeton: Princeton University Press, 2004.

Reeves, Simon. *One Day in September.* New York: Arcade Publishing, 2000.

Ross, Dennis. *The Missing Peace.* New York: Farrar, Straus & Giroux, 2004.

Schwarz, Ted. *Walking with the Damned.* New York: Paragon House, 1992.

Segev, Samuel. *Crossing the Jordan.* New York: St. Martin's Press, 1998.

Sharon, Ariel, and David Chanoff. *Warrior.* New York: Simon & Schuster, 2001.

Sharon, Gilad. *Sharon: The Life of a Leader.* New York: HarperCollins, 2011.

Shlaim, Avi. *The Iron Wall: Israel and the Arab World.* New York: W.W. Norton, 2001.

Shindler, Colin. *A History of Modern Israel.* New York: Cambridge University Press, 2008.

Slater, Robert. *Rabin of Israel: Warrior for Peace.* New York: Harper Paperbacks, 1996.

_____. *Warrior, Statesman: The Life of Moshe Dayan.* New York: St. Martin's Press, 1991.

Sprinzak, Ehud. *Brother Against Brother.* New York: The Free Press, 1999.

Swisher, Clayton E. *The Truth About Camp David.* New York: Nation Books, 2004.

Temko, Ned. *To Win or To Die.* New York: William Morrow, 1987.

Index

Abu Jihad 101, 176–77
Abu Nidal 141
Ahdut ha'Avoda party 2, 13, 16, 26, 32, 36, 39, 40, 76, 86
Al-Aksa Intifada 16, 157, 177, 200, 202, 204, 205, 239n10
Albright, Madelein 150, 190, 192–93, 194, 201
Allon, Yigal 2, 13, 26, 32, 36, 38, 40, 47, 55, 68, 69, 72, 76, 86, 115, 129, 217; and Dayan 2, 19, 20–21, 23, 25, 32, 35–36, 39, 57, 78; and Kissinger 83, 86, 87, 89, 90; and Rabin 1, 36, 67, 70–75, 79, 87, 89, 96, 98
Allon Plan 37, 38
Arafat, Yasser 87, 100, 101, 106, 110, 147, 151, 154, 158, 160, 162, 196, 197, 200, 216, 239n10, 240n3; and Barak 153, 177, 180, 186, 193–95, 199, 201, 202, 204, 215; and Netanyahu 155; and Rabin 87, 111, 112, 113, 115, 116, 118, 149, 215; and Sharon 142, 146, 148, 150, 155, 158, 159, 162, 215
Assad, Hafiz al- 84, 87, 90, 95, 107, 109, 140, 144, 147, 186, 191–92, 217, 238n4, 239n24; and Barak 186–90, 192–93, 216; and Kissinger 53; and Rabin 110, 187, 215

Barak, Aharon 62, 144
Barak, Ehud 1–3, 5, 14; Abu Jihad assassination 176–77; and Al-Aksa Intafada 203–5; and Arafat 193–94, 195, 198–99, 202; at Camp David 196–99; character of 213; as chief of staff 177–78; childhood 167–68; as defense minister 207–11; and Ehud Olmert 207–8; election campaign 1999 183–84; Entebbe 174–75; as foreign minister 179–81; as interior minister 179; as Labor Party leader 206–7; as negotiator 216; and Netanyahu, Benjamin 209; in 1973 war 173–74; in 1982 war 175; Operation Spring of Youth 170–72; Palestinian track 153, 193–200; and Rabin 179, 182; Sayeret Matkal career 168–72; Syrian negotiations 153, 185–93; as warrior 215
Begin, Menahem 4, 5, 14, 58, 59, 60, 61, 68, 72, 73, 98, 108, 111, 119, 121, 145, 147, 148, 151, 206, 216, 218, 219; and Dayan 22, 36, 40, 66, 213, 214; and Sharon 130, 136, 138, 140, 142, 144,
Ben-Gurion, David 21, 22, 23, 25, 27, 28, 29, 31, 32
Berger, Sandy 150
Botha, Louis 17, 242n17
Brzezinski, Zbigniew 58, 62

Camp David: 1978 summit 2, 19, 58, 61–63, 64, 138, 144, 150, 197; 2000 summit 3, 15, 153, 157, 188, 193, 195, 197–99, 201, 202, 203, 215
Carter, Jimmy 56, 58, 59, 61, 62, 64, 97–98, 197
Christopher, Warren 111, 180, 187
Civil War presidents 221, 241n16
Clinton, Bill 109, 111, 113, 150, 187, 190, 191, 193, 194, 196, 197, 198, 199–200, 201

Dayan, Moshe 5, 16, 22–23, 38; and Allon 19, 20, 25, 35; in Arab Revolt 19–20; and Begin 22, 36, 40, 56–57, 64, 66, 213, 214; character of 213; as chief of staff 27–32; childhood 18–19; as defense minister 36–48; and Hagana 20–21, 21–22; and Kissinger 46, 49; as negotiator 216; in

Index

1967 war 36–37; in 1969–70 war 39–40; in 1973 war 42–45; and Palmakh 21, 27; and Rabin 21, 25–26, 34–35, 36, 37, 41; and Sadat 61–62; and Sharon 26, 44; as warrior 215; and Weizman 19, 35, 56, 59, 60, 62
Dayan, Rahel 28–29, 31, 55, 63–65
Dayan, Ruth 19, 28, 29, 31, 33, 228n8
Dayan, Shmuel 18–19, 228n5
Democratic Movement for Change 14, 56, 98, 137, 140, 217, 223, 240n13
Disengagement (Gaza) 159–64, 208

Eban, Abba 32, 40, 46, 51, 80, 82–83, 229n53, 231n13
Egypt: in Camp David peace process 2, 4, 56–64, 138–39, 187, 195; in Kissinger shuttle diplomacy 3, 46, 52, 87–95, 111, 137, 216, 218; in 1948 war 22–24, 69, 74–75, 123; in 1956 war 28, 30–31, 126, 218; in 1967 war 34–35, 80–81, 129; in 1969–70 war 39–41, 83, 169; in 1973 war 42–45, 132–33, 173–74; in Rhodes negotiations 75–76
elections: 1973 14, 46, 136; 1977 14, 56, 97–98, 138; 1981 14, 65, 140; 1984 14, 99, 145; 1988 14, 103, 147; 1992 14, 107–8, 114; 1996 14, 149, 180–82; 1999 14, 151, 183–84; 2001 15, 154, 205; 2003 15, 157, 206; 2013 211
Entebbe rescue 96, 101, 174, 209, 238n22
Eshkol, Levi 32, 38, 39, 78, 80

Fatah 41, 42, 103, 131, 140, 141, 147, 156, 163, 169, 170, 176, 196, 207
Ford, Gerald 51, 87, 88, 91–92, 93, 96, 232n4

Gahal 13, 46, 130, 135–36, 148
Gaza Strip 5, 16, 26, 28, 31, 36, 61, 76, 100, 102–3, 105, 110, 111, 112, 115, 124, 125, 130–31, 138, 155, 157, 158, 159–64, 177, 194, 204, 206, 207, 208, 209, 210, 214, 215
Golan Heights 14, 36, 37, 39, 40, 43, 53, 65, 76, 81, 82, 94, 95, 109–10, 128, 169, 177, 178, 185–93, 216, 227
Grant, Ulysses 4, 17, 132, 224, 226, 241n16
Gush Emunim 38, 136

Hamas 103, 109, 111–12, 115, 156, 162, 163, 165, 196, 201, 206, 207, 208, 209, 210–11
Harrison, William H. 4, 222
Hussein, King of Jordan 2, 37, 38, 39, 49, 84, 87, 88, 89, 95, 100, 101–3, 112, 113, 150, 151, 217, 230n16
Hussein, Saddam 140, 147, 186

Intifada 15, 41, 100, 102–3, 106, 147, 148, 159, 175, 177, 195, 204
Iran 64, 103, 109, 140, 151, 155, 207
Iraq 42, 69, 74, 81, 103, 109, 123, 138, 140, 141, 158, 186, 207
Irgun Zvai Leumi 16, 21–22, 23, 68, 70, 72–73, 74, 114, 121, 135, 146, 231n20
Israel Labor Party 1–5, 13–17, 37–39, 46, 48, 54–56, 79, 86, 96–100, 103, 105–10, 113, 116, 118, 125, 131, 136–37, 140, 145–46, 148, 150–51, 154, 157, 159, 162, 164–65, 176, 178–79, 181–85, 196, 204–6, 209–11, 214, 217, 228n8, 230n36, 232n39, 238n25, 240n28

Jackson, Andrew 4, 17, 158, 221–22, 237n24
Jarring, Gunnar 41, 84
Jerusalem 16, 23–24, 26, 37, 46, 59, 69, 72, 78, 81–82, 106, 115, 117, 118, 138, 153, 184, 194, 195, 198–99, 202, 203, 231n20
Jordan: in Karameh Battle 41, 169; in negotiations, diplomacy 49, 51, 64, 87–89, 95, 100, 101, 103, 109, 112–13, 177, 194; in 1948 war 23–25, 69, 71, 122–23; in 1967 war 34, 36–37, 81, 82
Jordanian Option 37–38, 103, 140

Kissinger, Henry 2, 45, 49–53, 88, 89–90, 94, 230n4, 230n5; and Dayan 46, 53, 63; and Rabin 51, 83–84, 87, 90, 92, 93, 95, 97

Lebanon 19, 21, 42, 69, 95, 109, 171–72; first war (1982) 14, 31, 65, 100, 140–44, 145, 146–47, 158, 175, 186, 204, 213, 215, 236n8; second war (2006) 206; withdrawals from 99, 105, 195, 209
Lehi 16, 21, 22–23, 27, 68, 70, 73, 74, 116, 121, 146, 231n20, 234n42
Levy, David 99, 105, 114, 145–49, 151, 183–84, 188

Mapai 16, 25, 28, 32, 33, 36, 39, 79, 86, 121, 130, 214, 229n25
Meir, Golda 5, 38, 39, 41–42
Meretz 108–10, 118, 150, 151, 154, 157, 159, 163, 184, 185, 205, 206, 209, 210, 217, 228n5
Mossad 42, 57, 101, 139, 170, 172, 176, 177

National Religious Party 16, 36, 56, 64, 80, 87–88, 97, 108, 115, 140, 154, 155, 157
Nixon, Richard 45, 51, 55, 83, 84, 85, 87, 88

Palestine Liberation Organization (PLO) 65, 87, 88, 89, 100, 101, 103, 105–6, 109–13, 140–43, 146, 163, 170, 177, 185, 186, 215, 217, 218, 232n39
Peres, Shimon 14, 15, 29, 38, 88, 100, 102, 104, 109, 176, 184, 187, 237n46, 238n46, 240n7, 240n15; and Barak 174, 179, 180–82, 183, 204–5; and Dayan 29, 30, 33, 55, 79, 86, 213; and Rabin 48, 56, 78, 79, 83, 86–87, 92–93, 96–98, 99, 101, 106, 107, 108, 112–15 passim, 117, 212, 214; and Sharon 137, 145, 147, 148, 155, 156, 162, 164–65, 206

Rabin, Yitzhak 3, 13, 15, 38, 40, 47, 51, 55, 56, 65, 174, 179, 180, 181–88 passim, 207, 209, 211, 212, 215, 217, 219; and Allon 1, 13, 22, 72–75, 87, 98; and Altalena 72–73; as ambassador 82–85; and Arafat 111–13; assassination of 116–17; and Ben-Gurion 76, 78, 96; character of 212; as chief of staff 79–80; childhood 67; and Dayan 1, 21, 23, 25–26, 34–36, 37, 41, 55, 67, 77, 78; as defense minister 99–106; and Intifada (1987) 102–3; and Kissinger 51, 83, 84, 90–95; as labor minister 86; legacy of 117–18; in 1948 war 69–75; and 1967 crisis, war 80–82; and Oslo peace process 110–16; in Palmakh 67–69; in peacetime IDF 75–79; and Peres 48, 78, 86–87, 96–97, 99, 101, 106, 107, 108, 112, 113–14, 115, 117; as prime minister (1974–77) 87–98; as prime minister (1992–95) 108–18; and Rabin Plan 105–6; and Sharon 85, 124, 127–28, 136–37, 147, 149; as warrior 215; and Weizman 79, 80, 86, 115
Rafi 16, 33, 36, 39, 48, 65, 81, 86, 110, 135, 213, 214
Rogers, William 41, 83
Ross, Dennis 180, 187, 190–94, 197, 201

Sadat, Muhammad Anwar as- 42, 45, 50, 52, 57, 58, 59, 60, 61, 62, 88, 89, 90, 91–92, 95, 99, 109, 139, 144, 191
Shamir, Yitzhak 63, 99–102, 104–8, 114–16, 138–39, 143, 145–48, 176, 179, 184, 187, 196, 209, 217–18, 234n42, 238n49
Sharon, Ariel "Arik" 1, 2, 4, 16, 17, 59, 86, 99, 114, 115, 117; and Al-Aksa Intifada 155–58; and Begin 62, 130, 135, 136, 138, 139, 140–44; and Ben-Gurion 27, 29; character of 212–13; childhood 121–22; and Dayan 26, 30–31, 35, 44; as defense minister 140–44; and disengagement 159–64, 208; as foreign minister 149–51; formation of the Likud 131, 135–36; as Israeli Patton 134; and Kadima 164–65; and legal investigations 159–60; as lesser minister 144–49; made Likud leader 151; and Netanyahu 148–49, 151, 154, 155, 157, 160, 161, 164; in 1948 war 122–23; in 1956 war 30–31, 125–26; in 1967 war 127–29; in 1973 war 132–33; in 1982 war 141–44, 175; personal tragedies 127, 129–30, 147–48, 152–53; as prime minister 154–65; and Rabin 85, 86, 105, 128, 136–37, 148–49; and Road Map 158; Shlomzion 137–38; as Southern commander 130–31; Temple Mount visit 153–54, 202; Unit 101/paratroopers 26–27, 29, 30, 123–25, 168; as warrior 215
Smuts, Jan 17, 241n17
South Africa (compared) 1–4, 16, 17, 116, 155, 159, 219, 221, 222–25, 226–27
Syria 21, 29, 42, 67, 79–80, 83–84, 95, 103, 128, 138, 140, 143, 144, 172, 180; in 1948 war 22, 69, 74; in 1967 war 34, 36, 80, 81; in 1973 war 43, 44, 48; in 1982 war 14, 141, 142, 175; Syrian track 15, 25, 48, 49, 50, 51, 52–54, 57, 65, 87, 94, 109–10, 118, 153, 177, 178, 182, 185–93, 194, 195, 196, 215–16, 217, 218

Taylor, Zachary 4, 17, 222, 224

United States (compared) 1, 2, 16, 17, 219, 221–22, 224, 226–27

Vance, Cyrus 58–59, 60, 62

Weizman, Ezer 1, 2, 4, 13, 14, 16, 17, 19, 35, 36, 56, 59, 60, 62, 75, 79, 80, 81, 86, 100, 115, 128, 131, 135–36, 138, 139, 141, 147, 151, 176, 205–6, 211, 214, 219, 232n39

Zionism 2, 20, 37, 56, 228n5, 238n4

www.ingramcontent.com/pod-product-compliance
Ingram Content Group UK Ltd.
Pitfield, Milton Keynes, MK11 3LW, UK
UKHW041937140426
5217IPUK00014B/534